Second Workshop on Financial Technology and Natural Language Processing (FinNLP 2020)

Kyoto, Japan
5 January 2021

ISBN: 978-1-7138-2827-3

FinNLP 2020

The Second Workshop on Financial Technology and Natural Language Processing

in conjunction with IJCAI-PRICAI 2020

Proceedings of the Workshop

January 5, 2021

Kyoto, Japan

Sponsor

Preface

It is our great pleasure to welcome you to the Second Workshop on Financial Technology and Natural Language Processing (FinNLP).

The aim of FinNLP is to provide a forum for international participants to share knowledge on applying NLP to the FinTech domain. With the sharing of the researchers in this workshop, we hope that the challenging problems of blending FinTech and NLP will be identified, the future research directions will be shaped, and the scope of this interdisciplinary research area will be broadened.

Due to a great trial of all of us, the COVID-19 virus, the IJCAI-PRICAI conference is postponed to January 2021. In order to accelerate the development of this field, we decide to publish the proceedings in advance. This year, the participants of FinNLP still bring several novel ideas to this forum. We also cooperate with Fortia Financial Solutions to hold two shared tasks in FinNLP, including learning semantic representations (FinSim) and sentence boundary detection in PDF noisy text (FinSBD-2).

We have many people to thank. Dialekti Valsmou Stanislawski and Ismail El Maarouf lead their teams to hold the successful shared tasks and help review several submissions. All of program committee members work very hard to provide their insightful comments to the submissions, and help us select the suitable papers for FinNLP-2020. Many thanks to all participants for submitting their interesting works and sharing their ideas. Besides, we would like to express our gratitude to the MOST Joint Research Center of AI Technology and All Vista Healthcare for financial support.

Chung-Chi Chen, Hen-Hsen Huang, Hiroya Takamura, Hsin-Hsi Chen
FinNLP 2020 Organizers
July 2020

Organizations

Organizers

Chung-Chi Chen, National Taiwan University

Hen-Hsen Huang, National Chengchi University

Hiroya Takamura, National Institute of Advanced Industrial Science and Technology

Hsin-Hsi Chen, National Taiwan University

Shared Task Organizers

Willy Au

Abderrahim Ait Azzi

Bianca Chong

Ismail El Maarouf

Youness Mansar

Virginie Mouilleron

Dialekti Valsamou-Stanislawski

Program Committee

Paulo Alves, Universidade Católica Portuguesa

Alexandra Balahur, European Commission's Joint Research Centre

Paul Buitelaar, Insight Centre for Data Analytics at NUIG

Damir Cavar, Indiana University

Pablo Duboue, Textualization Software Ltd.

Jinhua Du, American International Group, Inc.

Ismail El Maarouf, Fortia Financial Solutions

Sira Ferradans, Independent Researcher

Kiyoshi Izumi, The University of Tokyo

Changliang Li, Kingsoft Corporation

Nedim Lipka, Adobe Inc.

Hiroki Sakaji, The University of Tokyo

Dialekti Valsamou-Stanislawski, Fortia Financial Solutions

Chuan-Ju Wang, Academia Sinica

Annie T.T. Ying, EquitySim

Wlodek Zadrozny, University of North Carolina in Charlotte

Table of Contents

Financial News Annotation by Weakly-Supervised Hierarchical Multi-label Learning

Hang Jiang[1] , Zhongchen Miao[1] , Yuefeng Lin[1] , Chenyu Wang[1] , Mengjun Ni[1] , Jian Gao[1] , Jidong Lu[1] , Guangwei Shi[1]

[1]Innovation Lab, Shanghai Financial Futures Information Technology Co., Ltd, Shanghai, China

{jianghang, miaozc, linyf, wangcy1, nimj, gaojian, lujd, shigw}@cffex.com.cn

Abstract

Financial news is an indispensable source for both investors and regulators to conduct research and investment decisions. To focus on specific areas of interest among the massive financial news, there is an urgent necessity of automatic financial news annotation, which faces two challenges: (1) supervised data scarcity for sub-divided financial fields; (2) the multifaceted nature of financial news. To address these challenges, we target the automatic financial news annotation problem as a weakly-supervised hierarchical multi-label classification. We propose a method that needs no manual labeled data, but a label hierarchy with one keyword for each leaf label as supervision. Our method consists of three components: word embedding with heterogeneous information, multi-label pseudo documents generation, and hierarchical multi-label classifier training. Experimental results on data from a well-known Chinese financial news website demonstrate the superiority of our proposed method over existing methods.

1 Introduction

To target information of concern among massive financial news quickly, there is a natural demand to search and analyze financial news based on topics. To cater for this, most financial news media adopt a manual annotation solution, which is too tedious to cope with rapidly growing financial news. Besides, manual annotation is not intelligent enough to meet the personalized needs of everyone. Therefore, to improve the searching efficiency and analysis accuracy of financial news, a critical step is automatic financial news annotation.

Indeed, the automatic financial news annotation is a classic problem of natural language processing (NLP), that is, text classification. Although related research keeps emerging, however, compared to those common scenarios of fully-supervised flat single-label text classification, our task faces two major challenges. First, supervised model training heavily relies on labeled data, while annotated corpus for each sub-divided financial field is cost expensive, considering the significant professional knowledge requirements for manual annotation. Second, a piece of financial news usually talks about multiple financial products and concepts from multiple levels and perspectives, but it is difficult to apply existing mature neural networks to multi-label and hierarchical text classification simultaneously.

In recognition of the challenges above, we propose a weakly-supervised hierarchical multi-label classification method for financial news. Our method is built upon deep neural networks, while it only requires a label hierarchy and one keyword for each leaf label as supervision, without any labeled data requirements. To leverage user-provided supervised keywords and semantic information in financial news, even though they are unlabeled, our method employs a two-step process of pre training and self training. During the pre-training process, we train a classifier with pseudo documents driven by user-provided keywords. Specifically, we model topic distribution for each category with user-provided keywords and generate multi-label pseudo documents from a bag-of-word model guided by the topic distribution. Self-training is a process of bootstrapping, using the predictions of unlabeled financial news as supervision to guide pre-training classifier fine-tuning iteratively. To ensure the effectiveness of self-training, a novel confidence enhancement mechanism is adopted. Besides, we include multi-modal signals of financial news into the word embedding process by heterogeneous information networks (HIN) [Sun and Han, 2012] encoding algorithm.

To summarize, we have the following contributions:

1. We propose a method of weakly-supervised hierarchical multi-label classification for financial news driven by user-provided keywords. With our proposed method, users do need to provide a label hierarchy with one keyword for each leaf label as the supervised source but not any manual labeled data.

2. To bridge the gap between low-cost weak supervision and expensive labeled data, we propose a multi-label pseudo documents generation module that almost reduces the annotation cost to zero.

3. In the hierarchical multi-label classification model training process, we transform the classification problem into a regression problem and introduce a novel confidence enhancement mechanism in the self-training process.

4. We demonstrate the superiority of our method over var-

Proceedings of the Second Workshop on Financial Technology and Natural Language Processing

ious baselines on a dataset from Cailianshe[1] (a well-known Chinese financial news website), conduct a thorough analysis of each component, and confirm the practical significance of hierarchical multi-label classification by an application.

2 Related Work

Financial text mining

As an important branch of fintech, financial text mining refers to obtaining valuable information from massive unstructured text data, which has attracted the attention of many researchers. The research object of text mining can be a company's financial report [Bai *et al.*, 2019], as well as self-media content such as Weibo (Chineses twitter) [Wang *et al.*, 2019]. The purpose of the research is also different, for example, studies [Sun *et al.*, 2016; Seong and Nam, 2019] analyze market prediction using financial news, and study [Kogan *et al.*, 2009] is dedicated to risk discovery. In our work, we take the financial news as the research object, and annotate each piece of news with multiple labels from a label hierarchy automatically.

Weakly-supervised text classification

Despite the maturity of adopting neural networks in supervised learning, the requirements for labeled data are extremely expensive and full of obstacles, so weakly-supervised learning emerges as the times require. Above all classic works, it can be roughly divided into two directions: extending the topic model in the semantic space by user-provided seed information [Chen *et al.*, 2015; Li *et al.*, 2016], and transforming weakly-supervised learning to full-supervised learning by generating pseudo documents [Zhang and He, 2013; Meng *et al.*, 2018].

Hierarchical text classification

Hierarchical classification is more complicated than flat one, considering the hierarchy of labels. A lot of research on applying SVM in hierarchical classification [Cai and Hofmann, 2004; Liu *et al.*, 2005] has been started from the first application of [Dumais and Chen, 2000]. Hierarchical dataless classification [Song and Roth, 2014] projects classes and documents into the same semantic space by retrieving Wikipedia concepts. [Meng *et al.*, 2019; Zhang *et al.*, 2019] is a continuation of the work in [Meng *et al.*, 2018], which solves the problem of hierarchical classification through a top-down integrated classification model. To our best knowledge, there is no hierarchical multi-label classification method based on weak supervision so far.

3 Problem Statement

We take the financial news annotation as a task of weakly-supervised hierarchical multi-label classification. Specifically, each piece of news can be assigned multiple labels, and each category can have more than one children categories but can only belong to at most one parent category.

To solve our task, we ask users to provide a tree-structured label hierarchy $\mathcal{T}$ and one keyword for each leaf label in

---

[1]The website of Cailianshe: https://cls.cn

$\mathcal{T}$. Then we propagate the user-provided keywords upwards from leaves to root in $\mathcal{T}$, that is, for each internal category, we aggregate keywords of its all descendant leaf classes as supervision.

Now we are ready to formulate the problem. Given a class hierarchy tree $\mathcal{T}$ with one keyword for each leaf class in $\mathcal{T}$, and news corpora $\mathcal{D} = \{D_1, D_2, ..., D_N\}$ as well. The weakly-supervised hierarchical multi-label classification task aims to assign the most likely labels set $C = \{C_{j_1}, C_{j_2}, ..., C_{j_n} | C_{j_i} \in \mathcal{T}\}$ to each $D_j \in \mathcal{D}$, where the number of assigned labels is arbitrary and C_{j_i} stays for classes at any level.

4 Methodology

The framework of our method is illustrated in Figure 1, which can be divided into three phases. Because the corpus we use is in Chinese, word segmentation is an essential step before classification. Considering the specificity of the financial corpus, we construct a financial segmentation vocabulary including financial entities, terminologies and English abbreviations by neologism discovery algorithm [Yao *et al.*, 2016].

4.1 Word embedding with heterogeneous information

Compared to plain textual data, financial news is a complex object composed of multi-modal signals, including news content, headline, medium, editor, and column. These signals are beneficial to topic classification, for example, editors are indicative because two pieces of news are more likely to share similar topic if they are supplied by the same editor as editors usually have stable specialty and viewpoints.

To learn d-dimensional vector representations for each word using such significant multi-modal signals in the corpus, we construct a HIN centered upon words [Zhang *et al.*, 2019]. Specifically, corresponds to heterogeneous information in financial news, we include seven types of nodes: news (N), columns (C), headlines (H), media (M), editors (E), words (W) and labels (L). In which, headlines (H) and words (W) are tokens segmented from title and content respectively. As a word-centric star schema is adopted, we add an edge between a word node and other nodes if they appear together, thus the weights of edges reflect their co-occurrence frequency.

Given a HIN following the above definition of nodes and edges, we can obtain word representations by learning nodes embeddings in this HIN. We use ESIM [Shang *et al.*, 2016], a typical HIN embedding algorithm, to learn nodes representations by restricting the random walk under the guidance of user-specified meta-paths. To guide the random walk, we need to specify meta-paths centered upon words and assign the weights by the importance of meta-path. In our method, we specify meta-paths as $W-N-W$, $W-H-W$, $W-M-W$, $W-E-W$, $W-C-W$ and $W-L-W$ with empirical weights, modeling the multi-types of second-order proximity [Tang *et al.*, 2015] between words. Furthermore, we perform normalization $v_w \leftarrow v_w/||v_w||$ on embedding vector v_w for each word w.

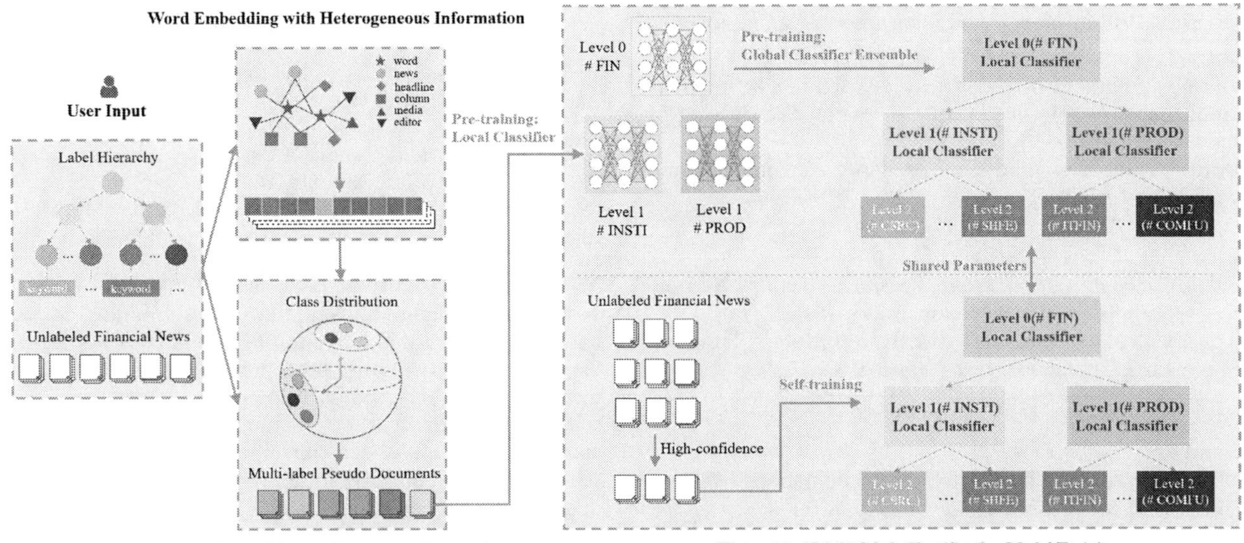

Figure 1: The framework of proposed method.

4.2 Multi-label pseudo documents generation

In this section, we first model class distribution in a semantic space with user-provided keywords, and then generate multi-label pseudo documents as supervised training data based on them.

Modeling class distribution

Assume that words and documents shared a uniform semantic space, so that we can leverage user-provided keywords to learn a class distribution [Meng *et al.*, 2018].

Specifically, we first take the inner product of two embedding vectors $\boldsymbol{v}_{w_1}^T \boldsymbol{v}_{w_2}$ as similarity measurement between two words w_1 and w_2 to retrieve top n nearest keywords set $K_j = \{w_{j0}, w_{j1}, ..., w_{jn}\}$ in semantic space for each class j based on user-provided keyword w_{j0}. Remind that we do not specify the parameter n above but terminate the keywords retrieving process when keyword sets of any two classes tend to intersect to ensure the absolute boundary between different classes. Then we fit the expanded keywords distribution $f(\boldsymbol{x}|C_j)$ to a mixture von Mises-Fisher (vMF) distributions [Banerjee *et al.*, 2005] to approximate class distribution for each class:

$$f(\boldsymbol{x}|C_j) = \sum_{h=1}^{m} \alpha_h f_h (\boldsymbol{x}|\boldsymbol{\mu}_h, \kappa_h) \qquad (1)$$

where $f_h (\boldsymbol{x}|\boldsymbol{\mu}_h, \kappa_h)$, as a component in the mixture with a weight α_h, is the distribution of the h-th child of category C_j, m is equal to the number of C_j's children in the label hierarchy. In $f_h (\boldsymbol{x}|\boldsymbol{\mu}_h, \kappa_h)$, μ_h is the mean direction vectors and κ_h is the concentration parameter of the vMF distribution, which can be derived by Expectation Maximization (EM) [Banerjee *et al.*, 2005].

Pseudo documents generation

Given distribution for each class, we use a bag-of-words based language model to generate multi-label pseudo documents. We first sample l document vectors d_i from various class distribution $f(x|C)$ (l is not specific), and then build a vocabulary V_{d_i} that contains the top γ words closest to d_i in semantic space for each d_i. Given a vocabulary set $\mathcal{V}_d = \{V_{d_1}, V_{d_2}, ..., V_{d_l}\}$, we choose a number of words to generate pseudo document with probablility $p(w|D)$. Formally,

$$p(w|D) = \begin{cases} \beta p_B(w) & w \notin \mathcal{V}_d \\ \beta p_B(w) + (1 - \beta)p_D(w) & w \in \mathcal{V}_d \end{cases} \qquad (2)$$

where β is a "noisy" parameter to prevent overfitting, $p_B(w)$ is the background words distribution (i.e., word distribution in the entire corpus), $p_D(w)$ is the document-specific distribution, that is,

$$p_D(w) = \frac{1}{l} \sum_{i=1}^{l} \frac{\exp\left(d_i^T \boldsymbol{v}_w\right)}{\sum_{w' \in V_{d_i}} \exp\left(d_i^T \boldsymbol{v}_{w'}\right)} \qquad (3)$$

where $\boldsymbol{v}_w$ is the embedding of word w. Meanwhile, pseudo labels need to be expressed. Suppose existing k document vectors d_i are generated from class j, then the label of class j of document D can be represented by,

$$label^*(D)_j = tanh(\sigma(\frac{k(1 - \beta)}{l} + \frac{\beta}{m})) \qquad (4)$$

where σ is a scale parameter to control the range of $label^*(D)_j$, and generally takes an empirical value.

Otherwise, if $\forall d_i$ is not generated from class j,

$$label^*(D)_j = \beta/m \qquad (5)$$

Algorithm 1 Multi-label Pseudo Documents Generation

Input: Class distribution set $\{f(x|C_j)|_{j=1}^m\}$.
Parameter: number of probability distribution β to generate multi-label pseudo documents for each class; number of pseudo documents γ.
Output: A set of γ multi-label pseudo documents D^* and corresponding labels set $\mathcal{L}^*$

1: Initialize $D^* \leftarrow \emptyset$, $\mathcal{L}^* \leftarrow \emptyset$, $p \leftarrow \emptyset$;.
2: **for** *class index j from 1 to m* **do**
3:     **for** *probability distribution index i from 1 to β* **do**
4:         Sample document vector d_i from $f(x; C_j)$;
5:         Calculate probability distribution $p(w|d_i)$ based on Eq 2 // parameter $l = 1$ in Eq 2;
6:         $p \leftarrow p \cup p(w|d_i)$
7:     **end for**
8: **end for**
9: Sample γ probability distribution combinations from p
10: **for** *combination index i from 1 to γ* **do**
11:     $D_i^* \leftarrow$ *empty string*
12:     Calculate probability distribution $p(w|D_i)$ based on Eq 2
13:     Sample $w_{ik} \sim p(w|D_i)$
14:     $D_i^* = D_i^* + w_{ik}$ //concatenate w_{ik} after D_i^*
15:     Calculate label $\mathcal{L}_i^*$ based on Eq 4 and Eq 5
16:     $D^* \leftarrow D^* \cup D_i^*$
17:     $\mathcal{L}^* \leftarrow \mathcal{L}^* \cup \mathcal{L}_i^*$
18: **end for**
19: **return** $D^*, \mathcal{L}^*$

---

where m is the number of children classes related to the local classifier.

Algorithm 1 shows the entire process for generating multi-label pseudo-documents.

4.3 Hierarchical multi-label classifier training

In this section, we pre-train CNN-based classifiers with pseudo documents and refine it with real unlabeled documents.

Pre-training with pseudo documents

Hierarchical classification model pre-training can be split into two parts: local classifier training for nodes and global classifier ensembling. We trained a neural classifier $M_L(\cdot)$ for each class with two or more children classes. $M_L(\cdot)$ has multi-scale convolutional kernels in the convolutional layer, ReLU activation in the hidden layer, and Sigmoid activation in the output layer. As the pseudo label is a new distribution instead of binarization vectors, we transform task from multi-label classification to regression and minimizing the mean squared error (MSE) loss from the network outputs to the pseudo labels.

After training a series of local classifiers, we need to build a global classifier G_k by integrating all local classifiers from the root node to level k from top to bottom. The multiplication between the output of the parent classifier and child classifier can be explained by conditional probability formula:

$$p(D_i \in C_c) = p(D_i \in C_c \cap D_i \in C_p)$$
$$= p(D_i \in C_c | D_i \in C_p)\, p(D_i \in C_p) \quad (6)$$

where, class C_c is the child of class C_p. When the formula is called recursively, the final prediction can be obtained by the product of all local classifier outputs on the path from the root node to the target node.

Self-training with unlabeled real documents

To take advantage of semantic information in the real documents, we utilize the prediction of real documents as supervision in the self-training procedure iteratively. However, if the predictions are used as the supervision for the next iter self-training directly, the self-training can hardly go on because the model has been convergent in pre-training. To obtain more high-confidence training data, we adopt a confidence enhancement mechanism. Specifically, we calculate the confidence of predictions by Eq 7 and only reserve data with high-confidence as training data.

$$conf(q) = -\frac{\log(\sum_{i=1}^m q_i + 1)}{\sum_{i=1}^m q_i \log q_i}. \quad (7)$$

where $m \geq 2$ is the number of children of C_j.

In addition, we notice the true label of a real document is either zero or one, thus, we conduct a normalization on G_k's predictions by the following formula:

$$label^{**}(D_i)_j = \frac{label^*(D_i)_j}{\max_{j'}(label^*(D_i)_{j'})} \quad (8)$$

When the change rate of G_k's outputs of real documents is lower than δ, the self-training will stop earlier.

5 Experiments

Three things will be demonstrated in this section. First, the performance of our method is superior to various baselines for the weakly-supervised hierarchical multi-label financial news classification task (Section 5.2). Second, we carefully evaluate and analyze the components in our method proposed in Section 4(Section 5.3). Third, we reveal the business significance in the task of hierarchical multi-label classification for financial news by an application(Section 5.4).

5.1 Experiments setup

Dataset

We collect a dataset from a well-known Chinese financial news website, Cailianshe, to evaluate the performance of our method.

The dataset statistics are provided in Table 1: the news corpus consists of 7510 pieces of financial news with 2 super-categories and 11 sub-categories, covering the major institutions and product categories in China mainland financial markets. The label hierarchy refers to Figure 2 for details, in which the colored italics are user-provided keywords for leaf labels.

Figure 2: The label hierarchy for Chinese financial market.

dataset	classes (level1+level2)	docs
FIN-NEWS-CN	2+11	7510

Table 1: Dataset Statistic

It should be noted that we maintained an unbalanced dataset to truly reflect the market size and shares of the Chinese financial market. For example, financial futures account for only 10% but stocks account for 53% in the dataset. This is because there is a mature stock market in China, while the beginning of financial futures in China is late and the initial stage comes into being until China Financial Futures Exchange (CFFEX) launches CSI 300 futures in 2010 to some extent.

Baselines

- **WeSHClass** [Meng *et al.*, 2019] provides a top-down global classifier for the hierarchical classification, which supports multiple weakly supervised sources.

- **HiGitClass** [Zhang *et al.*, 2019] utilizes HIN encoding to solve a hierarchical classification task of GitHub repositories, with user-provided keywords as weak seed information.

Note that WeSHClass and HiGitClass can only output at most a single-label at each level. To compare with our method, we adjust the activation and loss function of baselines to fit a multi-label classification task, but they are still unable to generate multi-label pseudo documents.

Evaluation Metrics

According to the common standards for evaluating classification, we use Micro-F1 and Macro-F1 scores as metrics for classification performances at level 1, level 2, and overall classes respectively.

5.2 Performance comparison with Baselines

Table 2 demonstrate the superiority of our proposed method over baselines on the financial news dataset. It can be observed from Table 2 that our method has a significant improvement over baselines, whether at level 1, level 2, or overall classes. This is because we borrow the self-training mechanism of WeSHClass and HIN encoding of HIGitClass at the same time, and propose a suitable multi-label pseudo documents generation module in addition. However, for fine-grained labels, our method is still far from excellent although the average F1 scores improvement approaches 20% at level 2 comparing to baselines, which reflects the difficulty of this task.

5.3 Components Performance Evaluation

To evaluate each components, we carefully analyze performance of models with or without different components in Figure 3 and Figure 4.

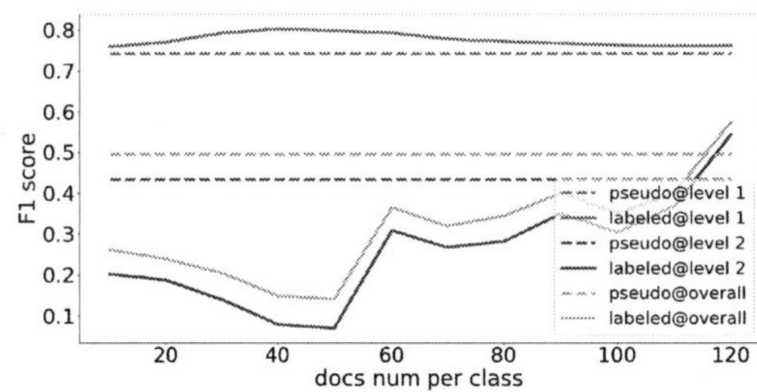

Figure 3: Performances Comparision of classificaton with pseudo documents and manual annotation documents

Qualitatively, the effectiveness of the multi-label pseudo document generation module has been demonstrated in previous training, and its quantitative value will be carefully analyzed by replacing the pseudo documents with manually labeled data. As we can observe in Figure 3, F1 score of

Method	Macro (level1)	Micro (level1)	Macro (level2)	Micro (level2)	Macro (overall)	Micro (overall)
WeSHClass	0.71373	0.80225	0.34627	0.48468	0.4085	0.60728
HiGitClass	0.68329	0.86769	0.24623	0.40716	0.31338	0.47073
Our method	**0.743**	**0.89723**	**0.44765**	**0.60173**	**0.50185**	**0.73977**

Table 2: Performance comparison for all method, using Micro-F1 and Macro-F1 scores as metrics at all levels.

pseudo documents training model is slightly lower than **labeled documents training model** at level 1, but for level2 and overall classes, the former stays lower than the latter until the number of labeled documents reaches 120 per class. To some extent, this component can save 1560 (120 $per\ class \times$ 13 $classes$) pieces of documents labeling cost.

To analyze the effect of heterogeneous information and self-training, we conduct model ablation experiments to compare performances of two variants (**No heterogeneous information** and **No self-training**) and our **Full method**. Here, the method of No heterogeneous information means heterogeneous information is not included in the word embedding process, and the method of No self-training means the self-training process is removed from the complete model. Overall F1 score in Figure 4 illustrates that both No heterogeneous information and No self-training perform are worse than the Full method. Therefore, embedding words with heterogeneous information and self-training with unlabeled real data play essential roles in financial news classification.

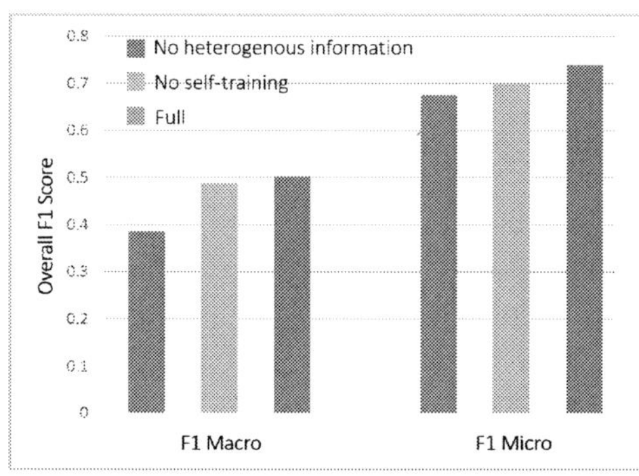

Figure 4: Comparison among No heterogeneous information, No self-training and Full method.

5.4 Application

A good classification can not only label each document appropriately but also can mine the hidden information behind the corpus. This section gives an example of a practical application, that is, discovering a correlation of business significance behind labels. In brief, we calculate the Pearson coefficients across all labels to draw a label correlation matrix in Figure 5, whose colors from shallow to deep represent the labels correlation is from weak to strong.

We only analyze the lower triangular matrix due to its symmetry, observing following two phenomena: (1) Correlations between different exchanges and products are different (e.g., CFFEX has a strong correlation with financial futures) and

correlations between different exchanges are different as well (e.g., there is a strong correlation between Shanghai Stock Exchange (SSE) and Shenzhen Stock Exchange (SZSE)). This phenomenon implies the main products of exchanges and their relationships. (2) Commodity futures are highly uncorrelated with stock exchanges or securities products such as stocks, while financial futures are not. This is because commodity futures (e.g., petroleum futures) take spot commodities as subject matter but financial futures (e.g., stock indexes futures) take securities products as subject matter. These phenomena are aligned with the reality of China's financial market, which demonstrates that targeting the financial news annotation task as hierarchical multi-label classification does have its practical application value, such as quickly understanding the relationship between different institutions, products, and concepts in complex financial markets.

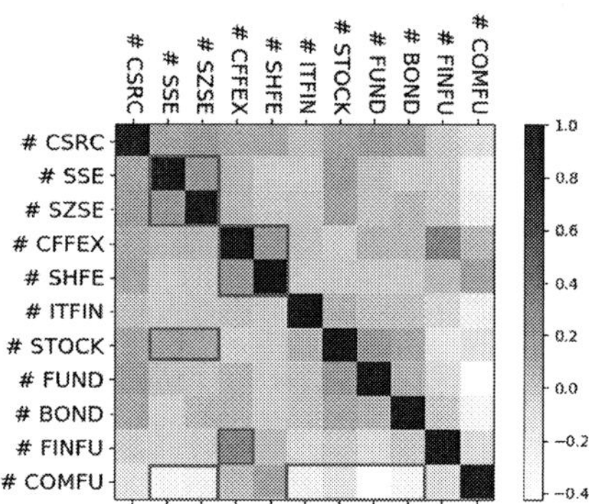

Figure 5: The labels correlation matrix, reflecting information about relationship between different financial concepts.

6   Conclusion

In this paper, we proposed a weakly-supervised hierarchical multi-label classification method with three modules for financial news, which enables us to effectively overcome challenges of supervision scarcity and the multifaceted nature of financial news. Experiments on a Chinese financial news dataset demonstrate the performance of our near-zero cost solution for hierarchical multi-label classification. Besides, we reveal the practical value and business significance of hierarchical multi-label classification in a real-world application. In the future, we would like to improve the quality of pseudo documents by label promotion methods such as the label propagation mechanism. With more accurate labels for pseudo documents, the performance of the model trained with pseudo documents will be further improved.

References

[Bai *et al.*, 2019] Haodong Bai, Frank Z Xing, Erik Cambria, and Win-Bin Huang. Business taxonomy construction using concept-level hierarchical clustering. *arXiv preprint arXiv:1906.09694*, 2019.

[Banerjee *et al.*, 2005] Arindam Banerjee, Inderjit S Dhillon, Joydeep Ghosh, and Suvrit Sra. Clustering on the unit hypersphere using von mises-fisher distributions. *Journal of Machine Learning Research*, 6(Sep):1345–1382, 2005.

[Cai and Hofmann, 2004] Lijuan Cai and Thomas Hofmann. Hierarchical document categorization with support vector machines. In *Proceedings of the thirteenth ACM international conference on Information and knowledge management*, pages 78–87, 2004.

[Chen *et al.*, 2015] Xingyuan Chen, Yunqing Xia, Peng Jin, and John Carroll. Dataless text classification with descriptive lda. In *Twenty-Ninth AAAI Conference on Artificial Intelligence*, 2015.

[Dumais and Chen, 2000] Susan Dumais and Hao Chen. Hierarchical classification of web content. In *Proceedings of the 23rd annual international ACM SIGIR conference on Research and development in information retrieval*, pages 256–263, 2000.

[Kogan *et al.*, 2009] Shimon Kogan, Dimitry Levin, Bryan R Routledge, Jacob S Sagi, and Noah A Smith. Predicting risk from financial reports with regression. In *Proceedings of Human Language Technologies: The 2009 Annual Conference of the North American Chapter of the Association for Computational Linguistics*, pages 272–280, 2009.

[Li *et al.*, 2016] Chenliang Li, Jian Xing, Aixin Sun, and Zongyang Ma. Effective document labeling with very few seed words: A topic model approach. In *Proceedings of the 25th ACM international on conference on information and knowledge management*, pages 85–94, 2016.

[Liu *et al.*, 2005] Tie-Yan Liu, Yiming Yang, Hao Wan, Hua-Jun Zeng, Zheng Chen, and Wei-Ying Ma. Support vector machines classification with a very large-scale taxonomy. *Acm Sigkdd Explorations Newsletter*, 7(1):36–43, 2005.

[Meng *et al.*, 2018] Yu Meng, Jiaming Shen, Chao Zhang, and Jiawei Han. Weakly-supervised neural text classification. In *Proceedings of the 27th ACM International Conference on Information and Knowledge Management*, pages 983–992, 2018.

[Meng *et al.*, 2019] Yu Meng, Jiaming Shen, Chao Zhang, and Jiawei Han. Weakly-supervised hierarchical text classification. In *Proceedings of the AAAI Conference on Artificial Intelligence*, volume 33, pages 6826–6833, 2019.

[Seong and Nam, 2019] NohYoon Seong and Kihwan Nam. Predicting stock movements based on financial news with systematic group identification. *Journal of Intelligence and Information Systems*, 25(3):1–17, 2019.

[Shang *et al.*, 2016] Jingbo Shang, Meng Qu, Jialu Liu, Lance M Kaplan, Jiawei Han, and Jian Peng. Meta-path guided embedding for similarity search in large-scale heterogeneous information networks. *arXiv preprint arXiv:1610.09769*, 2016.

[Song and Roth, 2014] Yangqiu Song and Dan Roth. On dataless hierarchical text classification. In *Twenty-Eighth AAAI Conference on Artificial Intelligence*, 2014.

[Sun and Han, 2012] Yizhou Sun and Jiawei Han. Mining heterogeneous information networks: principles and methodologies. *Synthesis Lectures on Data Mining and Knowledge Discovery*, 3(2):1–159, 2012.

[Sun *et al.*, 2016] Andrew Sun, Michael Lachanski, and Frank J Fabozzi. Trade the tweet: Social media text mining and sparse matrix factorization for stock market prediction. *International Review of Financial Analysis*, 48:272–281, 2016.

[Tang *et al.*, 2015] Jian Tang, Meng Qu, Mingzhe Wang, Ming Zhang, Jun Yan, and Qiaozhu Mei. Line: Large-scale information network embedding. In *Proceedings of the 24th international conference on world wide web*, pages 1067–1077, 2015.

[Wang *et al.*, 2019] Chenyu Wang, Zhongchen Miao, Yuefeng Lin, and Jian Gao. User and topic hybrid context embedding for finance-related text data mining. *2019 International Conference on Data Mining Workshops (ICDMW)*, pages 751–760, 2019.

[Wei and Zou, 2019] Jason Wei and Kai Zou. EDA: Easy data augmentation techniques for boosting performance on text classification tasks. In *Proceedings of the 2019 Conference on Empirical Methods in Natural Language Processing and the 9th International Joint Conference on Natural Language Processing (EMNLP-IJCNLP)*, pages 6382–6388, Hong Kong, China, November 2019. Association for Computational Linguistics.

[Yao *et al.*, 2016] Rongpeng Yao, Guoyan Xu, and Jian Song. Micro-blog new word discovery method based on improved mutual information and branch entropy. *Journal of Computer Applications*, pages 2772–2776, 2016.

[Zhang and He, 2013] Pu Zhang and Zhongshi He. A weakly supervised approach to chinese sentiment classification using partitioned self-training. *Journal of Information Science*, 39(6):815–831, 2013.

[Zhang *et al.*, 2019] Yanyong Zhang, Frank F. Xu, Sha Li, Yu Meng, Xuan Wang, Qi Li, and Jiawei Han. Higitclass: Keyword-driven hierarchical classification of github repositories. *2019 IEEE International Conference on Data Mining (ICDM)*, pages 876–885, 2019.

Variations in Word Usage for the Financial Domain

Syrielle Montariol[1,2,4*] , **Alexandre Allauzen**[3] , **Asanobu Kitamoto**[4]
[1] Université Paris-Saclay, CNRS, LIMSI, 91400, Orsay, France.
[2] Société Générale, Paris, France
[3] ESPCI, Université Paris Dauphine - PSL, Paris, France
[4] National Institute of Informatics, Tokyo, Japan
`syrielle.montariol@limsi.fr, alexandre.allauzen@espci.fr,`
`kitamoto@nii.ac.jp`

Abstract

Natural languages are dynamic systems; the way words are used vary depending on many factors, mirroring the divergences of various aspects of the society. Recent approaches to detect these variations through time rely on static word embedding. However the recent and fast emergence of contextualised models challenges the field and beyond. In this work, we propose to leverage the capacity of these new models to analyse financial texts along two axes of variation: the diachrony (temporal evolution), and synchrony (variation across sources and authors). Indeed, financial texts are characterised by many domain-specific terms and entities whose usage is subject to high variations, reflecting the disparity and evolution of the opinion and situation of financial actors. Starting from a corpus of annual company reports and central bank statements spanning 20 years, we explore in this paper the ability of the language model BERT to identify variations in word usage in the financial domain, and propose a method to interpret these variations.

1 Introduction

It is well know that all languages gradually evolve over decades and centuries, mirroring the evolution of the society. However, variation in word usage is not limited to long-term evolution. Many fine-grained variations can be found at a smaller scale. One the one hand, in the short term, the usage of a word can vary in response to sudden events that do not necessarily alter its meaning, but can momentarily change the way it is used. On the other hand, the usage of a word can vary depending on the person that uses it: several dimensions (geographical, cultural) can lead communities to use words in a different way depending on the local interests and concerns. These two kinds of variations are called *diachronic* (through time) and *synchronic* (across any other dimension than time).

In the financial domain, detecting the variations in word usage through time can lead to better understanding of the stakes and concerns of each time period [Purver *et al.*, 2018].

---

*Contact Author

In a synchronic way, many dimensions can be observed: how the words are used depending on the business line, the country of origin, the company or organisation that produces the document... This way, the opinions, behaviour and preoccupations of the writer can transpire through its specific usage of words. This information can be useful to financial analysts to better understand the variations of concerns and viewpoints of financial actors (for example, by analysing text from the regulatory authorities), identify the impact of an event on different actors through time (using high temporal granularity data sources), or analyse the evolution of a crisis.

In other words, we look for *weak signals* through the scope of word usage change. A weak signal is an element observed from data that has ambiguous interpretation and implication, but may be of importance in the understanding and prediction of events (present or future). In the financial domain, any change in strategy, emerging concern or unusual event linked to a financial actor can be a weak signal; identifying relevant weak signals and interpreting them is an extremely challenging task.

In this paper, we study word usage change as a potential signal of evolution in the situation and opinion of a financial actor. When an analyst reads a set of financial documents, the diachronic and synchronic variations in word usage are not immediately visible. But they might reveal valuable information, if they can be detected and interpreted. For example, it can be shown that the connotation of the vocabulary used by central banks in their reports and statements is strongly influenced by the economic situation [Buechel *et al.*, 2019], despite the sensitivity of their position.

As a growing amount of historical textual data is digitised and made publicly available, automated methods of Natural Language Processing (NLP) emerge to tackle the diachronic aspect of this task. The models usually rely on static word embeddings such as Word2Vec [Mikolov *et al.*, 2013] which summarise all senses and uses of a word into one vector at one point in time. This prevents the model from detecting more fine-grained variations of word usage (polysemy) according to its various contexts of occurrences. To tackle this problem, a new set of methods called contextualised embeddings has appeared recently. They allow to represent words at the token level by relying on their context. Several pre-trained language models (BERT [Devlin *et al.*, 2019], ELMO [Peters *et al.*, 2018]...) have appeared for this purpose in the past

Proceedings of the Second Workshop on Financial Technology and Natural Language Processing

two years. We rely on the model BERT, as Wiedemann *et al.*[2019] show its superiority in disambiguating word senses compared to other contextualised embeddings models.

In this paper, we use BERT to determine in a fine-grained way the different kinds of use of a word and the distribution of these uses in a financial corpus. Our goal is to analyse financial texts in a diachronic and synchronic way, as a preliminary investigation to address the following questions:

In a synchronic way, what do word usages reveal about the opinion and behaviour of different financial actors? In a diachronic way, what does it says about their evolution? Can it allow to better understand past and ongoing events through the scope of word usage change?

The key points of this paper are:

1) Studying word use variations across any dimension in the financial domain (e.g. time, business line, financial actor).

2) Proposing a method to measure and interpret the variations of a word usage across a dimension.

The model and the pipeline are described in section 3. The experiments in section 4 are made on a corpus of annual company reports and a corpus of central bank statements, both spanning two decades, described in section 4.1.

2   Related Work

Before the generalisation of word embeddings, measuring diachronic semantic change used to rely on detecting changes in word co-occurrences, and on approaches based on distributional similarity [Gulordava and Baroni, 2011].

A more recent set of methods rely on word embeddings [Mikolov *et al.*, 2013] and their temporal equivalent, diachronic word embeddings models. They rely on the assumption that a change in the context of a word mirrors a change in its meaning or usage. These models have undergone a surge in interest these last two years with the publication of several literature review articles [Tahmasebi *et al.*, 2018].

These models usually consist in dividing a temporal corpus into several time slices. The two most broadly used methods are *incremental updating* [Kim *et al.*, 2014] and *vector space alignment* [Hamilton *et al.*, 2016]. In the first one, an embedding matrix is trained on the first time slice of the corpus and updated at each successive time slice using the previous matrix as initialisation. For the second method, an embedding matrix is trained on each time slice independently. Due to the stochastic aspect of word embeddings, the vector space for each time slice is different: an alignment has to be performed by optimising a geometric transformation.The alignment method was proved to be superior to the incremental updating method, on a set of synthetic semantic drifts [Shoemark *et al.*, 2019]. It has been extensively used in the literature. However, these methods do not take into account the polysemy of words, summarising all the possibles senses into one vector at each time step. An exception is the system from Frermann and Lapata [2016] which analyses the evolution of sets of senses using a Bayesian model.

In parallel, the analysis of synchronic variations is mostly done through domain-specific word sense disambiguation (WSD). Some research use similarity measures between static word embeddings to analyse the variations in a vocabulary among several communities [Tredici and Fernández, 2017]. More recently, Schlechtweg *et al.* [2019] analyse both diachronic and synchronic drifts using static word embeddings with vector space alignment.

The recent rise of contextualised embeddings (for example BERT [Devlin *et al.*, 2019] or ELMO [Peters *et al.*, 2018]) brought huge change to the field of word representation. These models allow each token – each occurrence of a word – to have a vector representation that depends on its context. When pre-trained on large datasets, they improve the state-of-the-art on numerous NLP tasks. Similarly, contextualised embeddings can be used for better semantic change detection.

It was first used in a supervised way [Hu *et al.*, 2019]: for a set of polysemic words, a representation for each of their sense is learned using BERT. Then a pre-trained BERT model is applied to a diachronic corpus, extracting token embeddings and matching them to their closest sense embedding. Finally, the proportions of every sense is computed at each successive time slice, revealing the evolution of the distribution of senses for a target word. However, this method requires to know the set of senses of all target words beforehand. Another possibility is to use clustering on all token representations of a word, to automatically extract its set of senses [Giulianelli *et al.*, 2019; Martinc *et al.*, 2020a]. Our analysis in this paper derives from this last set of methods.

3   Model and Pipeline

We briefly describe the model BERT [Devlin *et al.*, 2019] and present the pipeline of detection and interpretation of word use variation.

3.1   Contextualised Embeddings Model: BERT

BERT stands for Bidirectional Encoder Representations from Transformers. It is a method for pre-training language representations that gets state-of-the-art results in a large variety of NLP tasks. The main idea relies on the principle of transfer learning: pre-training a neural network model on a known task with a substantial amount of data before fine-tuning it on a new task.

The architecture of BERT is a multi-layer bidirectional Transformer encoder [Vaswani *et al.*, 2017], a recent and popular attention model, applied to language modelling. The key element to this architecture is the bidirectional training, which differs from previous approaches. It is enabled by a new training strategy, Masked Language Model: 15% of the tokens in each input sequence are selected, from which 80% are replaced with a [MASK] token. The model is trained to predict the original value of these selected tokens using the rest of the sequence. A second training strategy is used, named Next Sentence Prediction (NSP): a set of pairs of sentences is generated for input, with 50% beings pairs of successive sentences extracted from a document, and 50% being two random sentences from the corpus. The model is trained to predict if the two sentences are successive or not.

BERT is mostly used in the literature as a pre-trained model before being fine-tuned on the task of interest, by adding a task-specific layer to the architecture (Sentiment Classification, Named Entity Recognition...). On the contrary, what we are interested in when using BERT is the pre-trained language understanding model which, applied to any sequence, allows to extract contextualised representations for each token (feature-based approach).

3.2 Detecting Variations

We consider a corpus where each sequence is labelled with the time it was written, and the person who wrote it. The author can be characterised by several dimension (the community he belongs to, its geographical location...) that are the synchronic dimensions for the analysis.

We apply a pre-trained BERT model on this corpus; To get a vector representation of all tokens of a sequence, we concatenate the top four hidden layers of the pre-trained model, as advised by Devlin *et al.*[2019]. Thus, we obtain a vector representation for each token of each sentence.

In order to identify the various types of usages of a word, we want to apply a clustering algorithm to the set of token embeddings. Previous works using BERT rely on hand-picking a small amount of target words for semantic change analysis [Giulianelli *et al.*, 2019; Hu *et al.*, 2019; Martinc *et al.*, 2020b]. Our goal is to detect in the full vocabulary which words undergo a variation of usage; however, the clustering step is computationally heavy and can not be computed for a large vocabulary. Thus, we use a preliminary step to detect high-variation words, by extending the approach of [Martinc *et al.*, 2020a] to synchronic analysis.

For a given target word, we compute a variation metric for each of its dimensions of variation. First, we calculate the average token embedding on the full corpus, and the average token embedding for each class of the dimension (for example, for each author or for each year). Then, we take the mean of the cosine distance between each average class embedding and the full corpus average embedding.

We sort the vocabulary according to the variation measures, and select a limited list of target words from the top ranking words. For each selected word, we apply a clustering on all its token representations across the full corpus.

3.3 Clustering Token Embeddings

We use two clustering methods: K-Means and affinity propagation. The affinity propagation algorithm, less common than K-Means, is chosen for two reasons:

First, it has proven its efficiency in the literature for word sense induction [Alagić *et al.*, 2018], a task very close to what we want to achieve.

Second, it does not require the number of clusters to be selected manually, which is convenient for our task where the number of usages varies a lot depending on the word and is tricky to determine. Indeed, this number does not necessarily match the number of senses of the target word. As BERT does not induce perfectly semantic representations, the contextualised representations are heavily influenced by syntax [Coenen *et al.*, 2019]. Thus, the clusters obtained from the representations of a word do not naturally reflect the different senses of the word; more widely, it only reflects the different ways it is used.

Affinity propagation is an iterative clustering algorithm. The main idea is that all data points communicate by sending messages about their relative attractiveness and availability, using the opposite of the euclidean distance as similarity measure. Eventually, clusters of similar points emerge.

This algorithm often leads to a high number of clusters. This allows a very precise distinction of the different types of contexts the words appears in; however, in such situation with a high number of small clusters, it is much harder for a financial analyst to provide an interpretation of the different clusters and of the variation of word usage.

3.4 Analysing Clustering Results

After the clustering, all the occurrences of a word are distributed into clusters. Each token is labelled by its diachronic dimension (the time slice where the token appears), and its synchronic dimension (the class of the document).

We construct the probability distributions of the types of usages of a target word for each class of a dimension. For example, in the case of the time dimension, each token is associated with one time slice of our corpus. For each time slice, we extract the distribution of usages of the word across the clusters. We normalise it by the number of tokens. We obtain the probability distributions of clusters through the time dimension. The process is the same in the synchronic case.

We can compare these distributions together to extract several pieces of information:

1. How much the distributions of usages vary for the word through the dimension?

2. At what time a usage drift happens (for the diachronic dimension); which actor has a different usage distribution compared to the other ones?

3. What is the change about, which usages of the word are involved? How to make an interpretation of this change?

For the first element we use the Jensen-Shannon divergence (JSD), a metric to compare two probability distributions, and its generalisation to n probability distributions $d_1, d_2, \ldots, d_n$ [Ré and Azad, 2014]. With H being the entropy function, the generalised JSD is:

$$\mathrm{JSD}(d_1, d_2, \ldots, d_n) = H\left(\frac{\sum_{i=1}^{n} d_i}{n}\right) - \frac{\sum_{i=1}^{n} H(d_i)}{n} \quad (1)$$

It is applicable in both synchronic and diachronic cases.

For the second element, we compare each distribution with the average distribution of the full dimension. For example, in the diachronic case, we average the distributions for all the time slices element-wise. Then, we compute the Jensen-Shannon divergence with the global average distribution.

In order to capture the clusters involved in the variation, we identify the ones that have an uneven distribution across all the elements of the dimension. It allows for example to find the clusters specific to a given actor, the clusters that vary the most, or the ones that appear or disappear through time.

Finally for the third element, once the clusters of interest are identified, we can get an interpretation of the usages associated with them using two methods. One the one hand, we identify the centroids of the clusters: the example (in our case, the sentence) that is the closest to the centroid is assumed to be representative of the context of the tokens inside the cluster. Thus, we observe these central sentences to get a preliminary idea of the word usages in context. On the other hand, we set up a keyword detection method to characterise the different clusters in relation to one another. Relying on the tf-idf (Term Frequency - Inverse Document Frequency) principle, each cluster containing a set of sentences, we consider them as documents and the set of clusters as a corpus. The goal is to identify the most discriminant words for each cluster. The stop-words and the words appearing in more than 50% of the clusters are excluded from the analysis. We compute the tf-idf score of each word in each cluster. The words with the highest score in a cluster are the most important for the analysis of this cluster: they are used as keywords to ease its interpretation.

4   Experiments

We apply the word usage variation detection pipeline to two financial corpora across several dimensions in addition to time. For our experiments, we use the English BERT-base-uncased model from the library `Transformers`[1] with 12 attention layers, an output layer of size 768 and 110M parameters.

4.1   Data

We use two financial corpora spanning two decades: a corpus of annual financial reports (10-K) of U.S. companies extracted from the Securities Exchange Commission database (SEC-Edgar), and a corpus of central bank statements.

The SEC-Edgar filings were extensively studied in the literature. From the diachronic point of view, Purver *et al.* [2018] extract subsets of the annual reports of 30 companies from the Dow Jones Industrial Average (DJIA) from 1996 to 2015. They manually select a set of 12 financial terms and investigate changes in lexical associations, by looking at the evolution of the similarity between pairs of two terms. More recently, [Desola *et al.*, 2019] fined-tune BERT separately on two corpora of SEC-EDGAR filings (from years 1998-1999 and years 2017-2019). For three selected words (*cloud, taxes* and *rates*), they compare the embeddings from the two periods using cosine similarity. None of these works are fully unsupervised.

We scrape[2] the SEC-EDGAR reports[3] from the 500 biggest companies in the US, between 1998 and today. Similarly to [Purver *et al.*, 2018], we extract the Part I and the Items 7 and 7A from the Part II of the 10-K annual reports. These sections mainly describe the activity of the company and its operations and management. We exclude the year 2019 from the analysis, as many documents of that year are not available yet. We end up with 8676 documents spanning 20 years. It amounts to a total of 7.3 million sentences.

This corpus is very rich for synchronic analysis. Each document is written by one company, and for each company, we extract additional data: its stock exchange (NYSE, NASDAQ,

	Time	Source
1	households	measures
2	labor	committee
3	holdings	rate
4	securities	employment
5	accomodative	developments
6	sectors	support
7	monetary	pressures
8	housing	price
9	sales	stability
10	loan	market

Table 1: Top 10 words with highest variation measure (from section 3.2) for the time dimension and the source dimension on the Central Bank Statements corpus

OTC) and its Standard Industrial Classification[4] (SIC) code. The latter indicates the business line of the company; the classification is divided into 7 Offices and sub-divided into 444 Industries. Thus, we can detect drifts across several dimensions, from the most to the least fine-grained: by company, by Industry, by Office, and by Stock Exchange.

The second corpus assembles all the official statements of two central banks, the European Central Bank (ECB) and the US Federal Reserve Bank (Fed) from June 1998 to June 2019[5]. These statements report the economic situation and expose the policy decisions of the central banks. This corpus was previously studied through sentiment analysis [Buechel *et al.*, 2019]. It is composed of 230 documents from the ECB and 181 from the Fed, and contain a total of 14604 sentences; it is heavily unbalanced towards the ECB (more than 75% of sentences), as the Fed statements are usually shorter.

Both corpora are divided into 20 yearly time steps. Stop-words are removed and we build the vocabulary with all words having at least 100 occurrences in the corpus.

4.2   Selecting Target Words

For both corpora, we conduct the preliminary step on the full vocabulary.

On the SEC-Edgar corpus, the frequency of some words is very high (for example the word *million* appears 1.4 million times). To speed up the process, we sample 3000 sentences for each word. We extract the embedding of the target word using BERT. Then, we compute the variation measures from section 3.2 by year, by company, by Industry, by Office, and by Stock Exchange. We do the same in the Central Banks Statements corpus, by year and by source.

As an example, the words with highest variation for the time dimension and the source dimension on the Central Bank Statements corpus are showed in Table 1. For the source dimension, we keep only the words with a threshold of presence of at least 50 occurrences per source. Words such as *labor* are absent from the FED statements because of orthographic divergence between UK English and US English.

---

[1]Available at https://huggingface.co/transformers/

[2]Using https://github.com/alions7000/SEC-EDGAR-text

[3]Extracted from https://www.sec.gov/edgar.shtml

[4]Described in https://www.sec.gov/info/edgar/siccodes.htm

[5]We thank Sven Buechel from Jena University Language & Information Engineering (JULIE) Lab for sharing the corpus with us.

Method	S-score	JSD-synchronic	JSD-diachronic
Aff-prop	0.267	0.829	2.519
KMeans3	0.213	0.342	0.523
KMeans5	0.215	0.467	0.856
KMeans7	0.218	0.537	1.088

Table 2: The average values of silhouette score, JSD by source and JSD by year for all the target words

Source:	KM2	KM3	KM5	KM7	KM10
	0.389	0.484	0.579	0.596	0.630
Time:	KM2	KM3	KM5	KM7	KM10
	0.325	0.328	0.289	0.282	0.282

Table 3: For both dimensions, the correlation between the JSD from affinity propagation clustering and the JSD from K-Means (KM) with different k.

For each dimension, we select the 10% words with highest variation measure as target words for the clustering step.

4.3 Comparison of the Clustering Algorithms

We apply both K-Means and affinity propagation on the set of token embeddings of each target word. In the case of K-Means, for each word we try different values of the number of clusters k ranging in $[2 : 10]$. To evaluate the quality of a clustering, we compute its silhouette score for each target word. Then, we extract the probability distributions across each dimension (for example the distribution of each year for the time dimension). We apply the generalised Jensen-Shannon Divergence (JSD) on the set of probability distributions to measure the level of usage variation of the word.

We focus on the Central Bank Statements Corpus to analyse the results of the clustering. The average values of silhouette score, JSD by source and JSD by year for all target words of this corpus for different algorithms are in Table 2. It should be recalled that the silhouette score takes values between 0 and 1, a value close to zero signalling a low clustering quality. Plus, while the JSD between two distributions takes values between 0 and 1, the generalised version to n dimensions is restricted by $\log_2(n)$. For example for the temporal dimension in the Central Bank Statements corpus, the 20-years period leads to an upper bound being equal to $\log_2(20) \approx 4.32$.

According to Table 2, the average silhouette score is the highest for the affinity propagation algorithm. Moreover, the average JSD for both dimensions increases with the number of clusters for the algorithm K-Means. The correlation between the number of clusters (k from 2 to 10) and the average JSD at each k, is high and positive (0.962 for the JSD by source and 0.986 for the JSD by year). We also inspect the number of clusters for the affinity propagation algorithm. It ranges from 4 to 450, with an average number of 61 clusters. However, the correlation between the number of clusters and the JSD is not significant. On the contrary, the correlation between the number of clusters of the affinity propagation algorithm and the silhouette score is -0.29: words with very

Label	Description	%
0	Office of Energy & Transportation	15.1
1	Office of Finance	12.5
2	Office of Life Sciences	14.7
3	Office of Manufacturing	19.7
4	Office of Real Estate & Construction	8.2
5	Office of Technology	13.1
6	Office of Trade & Services	16.7

Table 4: Label and proportion of business line with SIC classification in the SEC-Edgar corpus

diversified usages are associated with a clustering of lower quality. Finally, one can evaluate the accordance between the affinity propagation and K-Means algorithms by computing the correlation between their respective JSD for all words. According to Table 3, the correlation between affinity propagation JSD and K-Means JSD increases with k for the Source dimension, while it is relatively stable for the Time dimension.

4.4 Interpreting the Clusters

We focus on the SEC-Edgar Corpus for this last step. We present one example for the diachronic dimension and one for the synchronic dimension, in order to show the different possibilities in terms of interpretation.

For the synchronic dimension, we study the distribution of usages of the word *client* by Office (business line). It is one of the words with the highest JSD for this dimension. The silhouette score is the highest using K-Means algorithm with $k = 4$. All the Offices are listed in Table 4; The normalised distributions of clusters for each of them are in the left part of Figure 1. We apply our interpretation pipeline to identify the clusters that have an uneven distribution, and the Offices that are involved. Using the keyword extraction method, we select the most representative words for each cluster (Table 5, left). The cluster 1 is the most unevenly distributed, and appears mostly in documents belonging to the Real Estate & Construction Office. The keywords associated with this cluster involve the idea of paying (*cost*, *fees*) and negativity (*risk*, *loss*). On the contrary, the clusters 2 and 3 are relatively similarly allocated in the different Offices. Their keywords correspond to the classical definition of a client in a company. Finally, the cluster 0 is characterised by vocabulary from the semantic field of digital technologies (*server*, *applications...*): the clustering algorithm was able to identify this specific meaning of the target word.

For the diachronic dimension, we study the distribution of usages of the word *crisis* by year (Figure 1, right). The highest silhouette score corresponds to the K-Means algorithm with $k = 5$. The keywords for these 5 clusters can be found in Table 5 (right side). We can identify clear temporal tendencies in the figure. The proportions of the clusters 0 and 4 are decreasing through time, while the clusters 1 and 2 are growing. The extraction of keywords allows to differentiate the 5 usages of the word *crisis*. For example, the cluster 1 is associated with vocabulary of the domain of marketing and media. It is almost non-existent before the year 2004, and

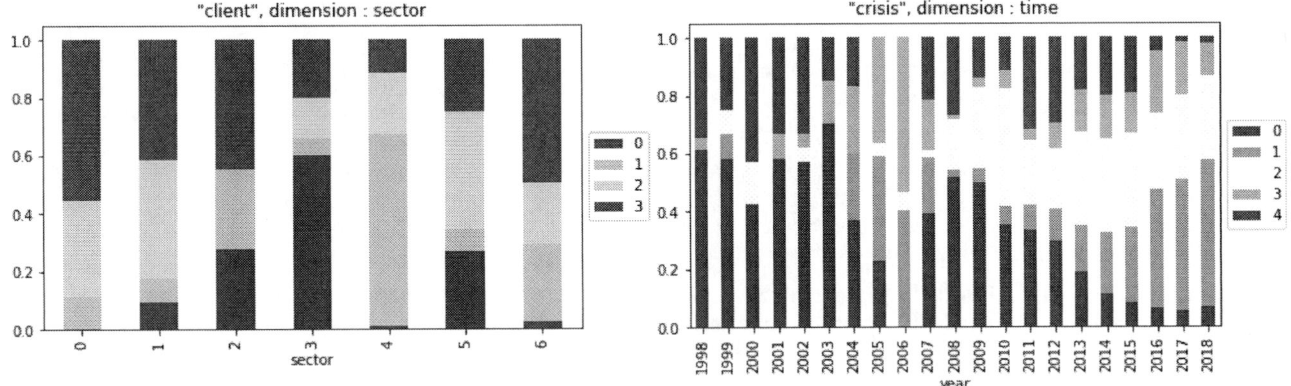

Figure 1: Distribution of clusters per Office for the word *client* (left) and per year for the word *crisis* (right) in the SEC-Edgar corpus. The Offices are described in Table 4

N^o	Keyword examples - Word = *client*
0	server, products, data, applications, services, systems
1	revenue, contract, risk, costs, loss, business, fees
2	assets, funds, cash, interest, balances, investment
3	services, business, revenue, growth, management, products

N^o	Keyword examples - Word = *crisis*
0	liquidity, funding, contingency, cash, collateral, outflows
1	marketing, business, management, design, advertising, media
2	european, debt, credit, sovereign, countries, eurozone, banks
3	financial, accident, capital, regulatory, loss, liquidity, funding
4	credit, financial, global, markets, debt, european, recession

Table 5: List of clusters and keyword examples for the words *client* (left) and *crisis* (right) in the SEC-Edgar Corpus

is rapidly growing. The cluster 2 is related to the crisis of the debt of the European countries; it appears and grows after 2008. The cluster 3 can be found across all the period; it is associated with slightly negative words (*accident* and *loss*), similarly to the cluster 4 (associated with *debt* and *recession*) whose proportion decreases since 2010.

However, one has to be wary of the selection of the number of clusters using the silhouette score. Sometimes, it leads to choose a low amount of clusters that may hide some valuable information. For example, for the target word *insurance*, the silhouette score is maximum for K-means with $k = 2$. However, using $k > 5$, a cluster appears that belong mostly to sector 4 (Office of Real Estate Construction); it is associated with the keywords *property* and *investment*, showing a new aspect of the concept of insurance specific to this sector.

Overall, the disparities in vocabulary and connotation between clusters are encouraging. The clustering allows to identify variations in meaning as well as usage. In particular, the ability to detect clear temporal tendencies in the cluster distributions could allow a financial analyst to link these clusters with real-world events, and have a deeper understanding of the phenomenons behind them.

5   Discussion

In this paper, we investigate the ability of the contextualised embeddings model BERT to detect meaningful synchronic and diachronic word use change in a financial corpus. We showed that using contextualised embeddings associated with clustering allows to automatically detect variations in the use of a word across any dimension. However, even though the keyword extraction method allows to gain insight on the interpretation of the clusters, it still requires some domain-specific knowledge. A crucial next step is to build on this pipeline to propose an evaluation method.

To this end, we would like to link the detected word usage variations with numerical indicators. On the one hand, it would offer a better understanding of the implications of the variations of word usage and complement their interpretations. On the other hand, it would allow a form of evaluation of our method. For example, we can analyse the correlation between the cluster distributions of the token embeddings of the word *unemployment* by Office in the SEC-Edgar reports with the real unemployment curve by Office on the same time period.

To fully leverage the ability of this pipeline to detect and to interpret word usage variations, our method can straightforwardly be extended in a streaming way. Any new document can be included in the analysis, be it a new central bank statement, company report, or in a classical streaming data situation such as daily financial news or tweets. The new document has to be tokenised and the contextualised embeddings extracted; then, the clustering can be updated using incremental clustering methods. For example, several incremental affinity propagation algorithms, adapted to streaming data, are proposed in the literature [Ajithkumar and Wilson, 2017]. The new token embeddings can either be added to an existing cluster, thus modifying the distribution, or creating a new cluster.

References

[Ajithkumar and Wilson, 2017] S. Ajithkumar and Praveen K Wilson. A survey paper on clustering data using incremental affinity propagation. In *IOSR Journal of Computer Engineering (IOSR-JCE)*, 2017.

[Alagić *et al.*, 2018] Domagoj Alagić, Jan Šnajder, and Sebastian Padó. Leveraging lexical substitutes for unsupervised word sense induction. In *Thirty-Second AAAI Conference on Artificial Intelligence*, 2018.

[Buechel *et al.*, 2019] Sven Buechel, Simon Junker, Thore Schlaak, Claus Michelsen, and Udo Hahn. A time series analysis of emotional loading in central bank statements. In *Proceedings of the Second EcoNLP Workshop*, pages 16–21, Hong Kong, November 2019.

[Coenen *et al.*, 2019] Andy Coenen, Emily Reif, Ann Yuan, Been Kim, Adam Pearce, Fernanda B. Viégas, and Martin Wattenberg. Visualizing and measuring the geometry of bert. In *NeurIPS*, 2019.

[Desola *et al.*, 2019] Vinicio Desola, Kevin Hanna, and Pri Nonis. Finbert: pre-trained model on sec filings for financial natural language tasks. 08 2019.

[Devlin *et al.*, 2019] Jacob Devlin, Ming-Wei Chang, Kenton Lee, and Kristina Toutanova. Bert: Pre-training of deep bidirectional transformers for language understanding. In *NAACL-HLT*, 2019.

[Frermann and Lapata, 2016] Lea Frermann and Mirella Lapata. A Bayesian model of diachronic meaning change. *Transactions of the Association for Computational Linguistics*, 4:31–45, 2016.

[Giulianelli *et al.*, 2019] Mario Giulianelli, Raquel Fernandez, and Marco Del Tredici. Contextualised word representations for lexical semantic change analysis. In *EurNLP*, 2019.

[Gulordava and Baroni, 2011] Kristina Gulordava and Marco Baroni. A distributional similarity approach to the detection of semantic change in the google books ngram corpus. In *Proceedings of the GEMS 2011 Workshop*, pages 67–71, 2011.

[Hamilton *et al.*, 2016] William L. Hamilton, Jure Leskovec, and Dan Jurafsky. Diachronic word embeddings reveal statistical laws of semantic change. In *Proceedings of the 54th Annual Meeting of the Association for Computational Linguistics*, pages 1489–1501, 2016.

[Hu *et al.*, 2019] Renfen Hu, Shen Li, and Shichen Liang. Diachronic sense modeling with deep contextualized word embeddings: An ecological view. In *Proceedings of the 57th Annual Meeting of the Association for Computational Linguistics*, pages 3899–3908, Florence, Italy, July 2019.

[Kim *et al.*, 2014] Yoon Kim, Yi-I Chiu, Kentaro Hanaki, Darshan Hegde, and Slav Petrov. Temporal analysis of language through neural language models. In *Proceedings of the ACL 2014 Workshop on Language Technologies and Computational Social Science*, pages 61–65, 2014.

[Martinc *et al.*, 2020a] Matej Martinc, Syrielle Montariol, Elaine Zosa, and Lidia Pivovarova. Capturing evolution in word usage: Just add more clusters? In *Companion Proceedings of the Web Conference 2020*, WWW '20, page 343–349, New York, NY, USA, 2020. Association for Computing Machinery.

[Martinc *et al.*, 2020b] Matej Martinc, Petra Kralj Novak, and Senja Pollak. Leveraging contextual embeddings for detecting diachronic semantic shift. In *LREC*, 2020.

[Mikolov *et al.*, 2013] Tomas Mikolov, Ilya Sutskever, Kai Chen, Greg S Corrado, and Jeff Dean. Distributed representations of words and phrases and their compositionality. In *Advances in Neural Information Processing Systems 26*, pages 3111–3119. Curran Associates, Inc., 2013.

[Peters *et al.*, 2018] Matthew E. Peters, Mark Neumann, Mohit Iyyer, Matt Gardner, Christopher Clark, Kenton Lee, and Luke Zettlemoyer. Deep contextualized word representations. *ArXiv*, abs/1802.05365, 2018.

[Purver *et al.*, 2018] Matthew Purver, Aljosa Valentincic, Marko Pahor, and Senja Pollak. Diachronic lexical changes in company reports : An initial investigation. In *Proceddings of the First Financial Narrative Processing Workshop (FNP 2018)*, 2018.

[Ré and Azad, 2014] Ma Ré and Rajeev Azad. Generalization of entropy based divergence measures for symbolic sequence analysis. *PloS one*, 9:e93532, 04 2014.

[Schlechtweg *et al.*, 2019] Dominik Schlechtweg, Anna Hätty, Marco Del Tredici, and Sabine Schulte im Walde. A wind of change: Detecting and evaluating lexical semantic change across times and domains. In *Proceedings of the 57th Annual Meeting of the Association for Computational Linguistics*, pages 732–746, Florence, Italy, 2019.

[Shoemark *et al.*, 2019] Philippa Shoemark, Farhana Ferdousi Liza, Dong Nguyen, Scott Hale, and Barbara McGillivray. Room to Glo: A systematic comparison of semantic change detection approaches with word embeddings. In *Proceedings of the 2019 EMNLP-IJCNLP Conference*, pages 66–76, Hong Kong, China, 2019.

[Tahmasebi *et al.*, 2018] Nina Tahmasebi, Lars Borin, and Adam Jatowt. Survey of computational approaches to diachronic conceptual change. *CoRR*, 1811.06278, 2018.

[Tredici and Fernández, 2017] Marco Del Tredici and Raquel Fernández. Semantic variation in online communities of practice. In *IWCS 2017 - 12th International Conference on Computational Semantics*, 2017.

[Vaswani *et al.*, 2017] Ashish Vaswani, Noam Shazeer, Niki Parmar, Jakob Uszkoreit, Llion Jones, Aidan N. Gomez, Lukasz Kaiser, and Illia Polosukhin. Attention is all you need. In *31st Conference on Neural Information Processing Systems (NIPS 2017), Long Beach, CA, USA*, 2017.

[Wiedemann *et al.*, 2019] Gregor Wiedemann, Steffen Remus, Avi Chawla, and Chris Biemann. Does bert make any sense? interpretable word sense disambiguation with contextualized embeddings. In *Proceedings of KONVENS 2019*, Erlangen, Germany, 2019.

Detecting Omissions of Risk Factors in Company Annual Reports

Corentin Masson [1*], **Syrielle Montariol**[1,2*]

[1] Université Paris-Saclay, CNRS, LIMSI, 91400, Orsay, France.
[2] Société Générale, Paris, France

`corentin.masson@limsi.fr, syrielle.montariol@limsi.fr`

Abstract

Regulators require most companies to publish yearly reports, describing their activities, results, future plans, and risk factors. Sometimes a risk factor can be omitted in a document, possibly – voluntarily or not– misleading the readers. In this paper, we introduce a task for detecting omitted risk factors in Annual Reports. This new task requires to catch the risks mentions in multiple sentences, and to identify the ones that are specific to a sector or a period. To address it, we use a neural architecture to extract risk sentences from documents and cluster the risk factors from these sentences. Finally, we generate synthetic risk factor omissions and propose a metric to evaluate the omission detection method.

1 Introduction

Risk analysis is a popular task in Business and Management research. While usually approached through expert knowledge and quantitative inputs [Kaplan and Garrick, 1981], it can benefit from the use of unstructured data such as legal and regulatory documents. One of the associated tasks is the automatic extraction of risk sentences.

Theoretically, a risk can be defined as a hazard with a potential for damage to an entity. Its meaning differs from the notion of uncertainty; in the former, one is able to quantify precisely the probability of occurrence and its potential impacts [Altham, 1983]. Therefore, a risk can be defined as a triplet composed of the potential event characterized as a risk, its quantitative counterparts such as the probability of occurrence, and its possible consequences [Kaplan and Garrick, 1981]. Thus, risk evocations can be identified by a topic-oriented summarization system able to detect occurrences of these triplets from natural language written documents such as Annual Reports (ARs).

Listed companies are regulated by the Financial Market in which their value is most traded in, often inducing the obligation to regularly publish information documents. ARs are supposed to exhaustively describe a company's current well-being, perspectives and the risks it is facing. In France, nearly

190 ARs are released each year from CAC40, CAC60 and CAC90 indexes (the principal French stock indexes from Euronext.).

To the best of our knowledge, few authors tackle risk sentences extraction from non-HTML indexed ARs [Liu *et al.*, 2018]; they often rely on XBRL[1]-indexed 10-K filings to identify risk factors markers [Huang and Li, 2011]. However, automatic analysis of such raw long documents can be beneficial for the Financial and Regulatory sectors. These documents represent the vast majority of ARs disclosed worldwide and are composed of an average of 3500 sentences with various sections and topics [AMF, 2020]. As for now, little has been done on extracting specific sections from Annual Reports or indexing them. In this paper, we focus on extracting and analysing the risk factors from these ARs.

In France, the financial market is regulated by the Financial Market Authority (AMF). In particular, disclosure of ARs depends on the "Code Monétaire et Financier" and on the "Doctrine" [2]. Companies must release every year a report containing all the requested information. If an element that might be important for a potential investor is missing from an AR, the company runs the risk of being accused of voluntarily omitting information, which is a specific kind of fraud.

From the extracted risk sentences, it is therefore possible to identify the possible omission of a risk in an AR by comparing its risk distribution to other ARs from the same sector and year. Therefore, in this paper, (1) we propose a new task for omitted risk factors detection from the DoRe Corpus [Masson and Paroubek, 2020], composed of European Companies ARs; and (2) we present a resolution method based on Neural Risk Sentences Extraction and Unsupervised Risk Factors Clustering. We hope to gather people to make the task grow.[3]

2 Related Works

The literature on corporate ARs analysis is plentiful in the financial research community. However, from the NLP perspective, research is more scarce and much more recent, while offering a wide range of applications from stock markets volatility prediction [Kogan *et al.*, 2009] to fraud detection. Today, financial reporting for companies faces a con-

---

*The authors contributed equally to this research.

[1]https://www.xbrl.org/the-standard/what/ixbrl/

[2]AMF guidance for righteous behavior on the market.

[3]Please contact us by email for access to the corpus.

tradiction: the huge increase in volume leads to more and more need of solution from the NLP community to analyse this unstructured data automatically. However, more reporting from more companies leads to more diversity in the shape of the documents; this lack of standardization and structure makes the analysis tougher and requires more complex methods [Lewis and Young, 2019].

For investors and regulators, risk sections are important parts of ARs, as they contain information about the risks faced by the companies and how they handle it. [Mandi *et al.*, 2018] extract risk sentences from legal documents using Naive Bayes and Support Vector Machine on paragraph embeddings. [Dasgupta *et al.*, 2016] explore project management reports from companies to extract and map risk sentences between causes and consequences, using hand-crafted features and multiple Machine Learning methods. [Ekmekci *et al.*, 2019] performed a multi-document extractive summarization on a news corpus for a risk mining task. As it has not yet been done, we experiment extractive summarization on risk extraction task in ARs.

Automatic text summarization is the task of producing a concise and fluent summary while preserving key information and overall meaning. In recent years, approaches to tackle this difficult and well-known NLP problem make use of increasingly complex algorithms ranging from dictionary-based approaches to Deep Learning techniques [Xiao and Carenini, 2019]. The current research trend deviates from general summarization to topic-oriented summarization [Krishna and Srinivasan, 2018], targeting a specific subject in the document such as risks in ARs in our case.

Focusing on detecting risk factors in ARs, topic modeling has been extensively used for this task in the literature [Zhu *et al.*, 2016; Chen *et al.*, 2017]. The evaluation is mostly done using intrinsic measures and by looking at the topics manually. Only [Huang and Li, 2011] manually define 25 risk factor categories, relying on ARs from the Securities Exchange Commission.

3 Pipeline

We propose a pipeline including a Risk Sentence Extractor module with Active Learning labeling framework and a Topics Modeling module to identify omitted risk factors.

3.1 Risk Sentences Extraction

As presented in Figure 1, each sentence in the document is processed sequentially using a fine-tuned French version of BERT [Devlin *et al.*, 2019] named Flaubert [Le *et al.*, 2020]. The goal is to compute the probability for each sentence to be a risk sentence using three modules: a Sentence Encoder, a Document Encoder and a Sentence Classifier.

Data Description

ARs are often disclosed in PDF format, which requires a lot of pre-processing (a notable exception are the 10-K filings [Kogan *et al.*, 2009]). ARs are extremely long documents: they contain an average of 3500 sentences and 27 different sub-sections. Due to the large size of each document, completely labeling a set of reports would take a considerable

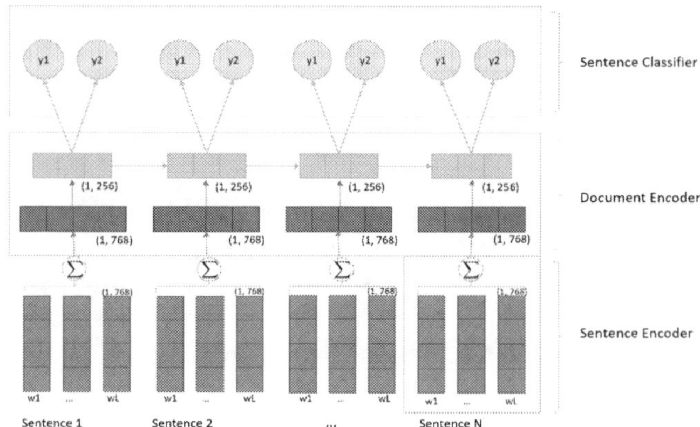

Figure 1: Risk Sentences Extraction architecture overview.

amount of time. To handle this, we propose to split the document into a set of disjoint sub-documents and label by hand a randomly selected subset of these sub-documents.

Model Architecture

The first module is a Sentence Encoder; its goal is to embed each sentence into a k-dimensional space without the information from the surrounding sentences. Due to the limited amount of labeled data, we use a FlauBERT pre-trained Language Model and fine-tune it for the extraction task, allowing it to get a good approximation of basic syntax and semantic features in higher layers [Jawahar *et al.*, 2019]. With N_D being the number of sentences in a document $D = (S_1, S_2, ..., S_{N_D})$ and M_i being the length of the sentence $S_i = (w_1, w_2, ..., w_{M_i})$, $SentEnc_i$ is the sum of the token embeddings computed by the fine-tuned FlauBert:

$$SentEnc_i = \sum_{j=1}^{M_i} \text{BERT}_{TokenEmb_j}(S_i)$$

We also experiment with a version where the sentence embeddings $SentEnc_i$ are computed using the [CLS] token from the FlauBert model. In both cases, each sentence is mapped into a v dimensional vector.

Risk evocations are often split into multiple sentences. For example, in Figure 2, the first sentence displays the risk factor while the second depicts the uncertainty with *'if'* and *'might'* along with the potential impact (*'affect its market share in a near future'*).

The sector is driven by innovation from newcomers. If the Group does not keep with the process, it might affect its market share in a near future.

Figure 2: Example of risk evocation.

We want our model to be able to extract all parts of the risk evocation. In order to extract sentence embedding taking into account the surrounding sentences (context sentences), we apply a forward LSTM layer at the document level, each sentence being considered as a token whose embedding comes from the Sentence Encoder. We take the hidden state of each sentence as the context sentence embedding.

$$DocEnc_i = LSTM(SentEnc_1, SentEnc_2, ..., SentEnc_{M_i})$$

As decoder, we add one linear layer with dropout for regularization. Its input comes directly from the contextualized sentence embeddings computed through the Document Encoder module, followed by a softmax layer to compute probabilities.

$$P(y_i = 1) = Softmax(Linear(DocEnc_1, ..., DocEnc_{N_D}))$$

For training, our loss function is a L2-penalized binary cross-entropy loss.

$$\mathcal{L} = -\sum_{d=1}^{N}\sum_{i=1}^{N_d}(y_i log(p_i) + (1 - y_i)log(1 - p_i)) + \frac{\lambda}{2}||\mathbf{w}||_2^2$$

Active learning
To our knowledge, there is no freely available dataset for risk sentences extraction in French nor in English, leaving us with a considerable labeling task. Randomly selecting sub-documents to label would be biased toward non-risk sentences and therefore would make the dataset asymmetric. Thus, we implement a Pool-Based Query-By-Committee [Settles, 2010] Active Learning approach using dropout masks for committee models generation and compute stochastic predictions for each sentence [Tsymbalov *et al.*, 2018]. It allows to select the most informative sub-documents to label and increase the accuracy of the model for these sentences which are near the segmentation frontier.

With $L = \{D_1^L, D_2^L, ..., D_{N_L}^L\}$ the set of labeled sub-documents and $U = \{D_1^U, D_2^U, ..., D_{N_U}^U\}$ the set of unlabeled sub-documents, the framework – or Learner, as called in the Active Literature – looks for x^*, the most informative sentence with the selected query strategy. Our committee $H = \{h_1, h_2, ..., h_T\}$ is composed of T models. At each Active Learning iteration, a model is trained on the already labeled data. Then, T different dropout masks are applied on the classification layer of the Sentence Classifier module in order to generate T different model. They are used to compute stochastic predictions for each sentence in each sub-document.

Using the predictions for each sentence, we can compute the uncertainty score. As the Least Confidence, Sample Margin and Entropy measures are equivalent in the binary case, we compute the approximated Least Confidence measure using votes from the committee H for probability estimation p_i for each sentence. The uncertainty measure of a given sub-document is the average uncertainty score of all its sentences.

$$LS(D) = \frac{1}{N_D^U}\sum_{i=1}^{N_D^U}|p_i - 0.5|$$

$$\text{where } p_i = P(y_i = 1|X_i)$$

The learner ranks sub-documents by decreasing uncertainty measure and queries the M most informative sentences

to the Oracle following : $x^* = \arg\max_{D^U} LS(D^U)$. The process is then iterated until a stop criterion is met, such as an insufficient increase of accuracy between two iterations.

3.2 Risk Omission Detection

We use the set of risk sentences extracted from the ARs to detect if a risk factor was omitted in a document.

Motivation & Pipeline
All companies describe different types of risks in their ARs, often through a "risk factors" section. To detect if an AR is missing a risk factor that should have been reported, we would need to define a list of risks factors for all the companies. However, the regulators do not enforce any normalisation nor provide a list of risks to report. Thus, the number and the type or risks reported vary a lot in the different documents. Consequently, we have to use unsupervised methods to capture them.

From the sets of risk sentences, we create a mapping of the risks depending on the sector and the year of the ARs. The distribution of risks per year can also allow to identify emerging risks, while the distribution per sector allows to identify the risks that are specific to a sector. We can either work on the data at the sentence level using sentence clustering or at the document level by doing topic modeling. We present the two approaches in the following section.

Sentences clustering
We cluster the risk sentences of all documents together to identify the types of risks across the full corpus. We use the sentence representations from the risk sentence extraction step using FlauBERT.

Moreover, we can assume that successive sentences, or sentences that are close in the document, have a high probability to deal with the same risk factor. Thus, the surrounding sentences as well as their distance to the target sentence can add valuable information to the clustering. We use the representation of the surrounding sentences as features for the clustering, by doing element-wise sum with the representation of the main sentence, weighted by a factor of their distance to the main sentence. The distance is computed according to the number of sentences: two successive sentences have a distance $d = 1$, etc. Then, the weight of each sentence is computed as the inverse of its distance to the main sentence augmented by one: $w = \frac{1}{d+1}$.

For the clustering, we use the K-means algorithm. The number of clusters k is chosen according to the literature on risk factors in ARs. To ease the interpretation of the different clusters of risk sentences, we use a method to detect keywords in the clusters. We consider each cluster of sentences as a document and the set of clusters as a corpus. To identify the most representative words in a cluster, we compute the tf-idf (Term Frequency - Inverse Document Frequency) score of each word in the clusters. We exclude stopwords and words that can be found in 50% of the clusters or more. The words with the highest score in each cluster are used to label it.

Topic Model on Documents
We challenge the previous method using a popular topic modeling algorithm: the Latent Dirichlet Allocation (LDA) [Blei

et al., 2003]. Each document is characterised by a probability distribution over a set of topics, while each topic is characterised by a probability distribution over all the words of the vocabulary. Therefore, the top words per topic are used as a set of keywords to describe it. The number of topics is the same as the number of clusters for the sentence clustering with K-Means.

Intrinsic Evaluation Measures
We compute several measures, all relying on a list of keywords characterising each topic or cluster.

First, the Normalized Point-wise Mutual Information (NPMI) [Aletras and Stevenson, 2013] measures the topic coherence. It relies on word co-ocurrences to measure the level of relatedness of the top k words characterizing each topic. We also use external knowledge – pre-trained Word2Vec embeddings [Mikolov *et al.*, 2013] [4] – to evaluate topic coherence. Similarly to [Ding *et al.*, 2018], we compute the pairwise cosine similarity between the vectors of the top k words characterizing each topic, and average it for all topics. We call this second topic coherence measure TC-W2V. For the two measures, we use a relatively low k ($k = 10$). A high NPMI or TC-W2V measure indicates an interpretable model.

These two measures are completed by a topic uniqueness (TU) measure [Nan *et al.*, 2019] for the top k keywords, representing the diversity of the topics. For a given topic t, with $cnt(i)$ being the number of times the word i appears in the top words of all the topics, the TU is computed as:

$$TU_t = \frac{1}{k} \sum_{i=1}^{k} \frac{1}{cnt(i)}$$

We take the global TU measure as the average TU for all topics. The higher the TU measure is (close to 1), the higher the variety of topics. We use $k = 25$ for this measure.

Risk Omission Detection Task
The extrinsic evaluation is done using the detection of omissions as downstream task. We want to detect if a company omitted or under-reported a risk in one of its reports, by observing the risks reported in the document, and comparing it with the ones reported in other documents of the same year and the same sector.

First, we generate synthetic risk omissions in our corpus. We randomly sample a small set of ARs, manually select a section of each document describing one type of risk, and remove it. Our goal is double: to detect that a risk factor is missing in the altered document, and to identify the risk associated with the removed section.

To tackle this problem, we compute a measure relying on a binarized version of the topic distribution of a document. Indeed, both the topic model and the sentence clustering methods output a distribution of risks (respectively topics or cluster) for each document. We consider that a document includes a topic (or a cluster) if the proportion of the topic (or the number of sentences belonging to the cluster) is higher than a threshold ϵ. Below this threshold, we consider that the

document does not report the risk characterised by that topic. Then, for each sector and for each year, we extract the set of "typical" topics: the ones that are present in most documents for that sector or year, and therefore are expected to appear in all documents of the same sector and year.

First, we count the number of documents mentioning each risk. Then, we binarize it: if the number of documents mentioning the risk is lower than half of the total number of documents in the sector/year, then the risk is considered as not important for the sector/year and we do not select it. We compare this list of "expected" topics with the list of topics reported in each document. It allows to identify the documents where a risk is absent but should have been reported, because it is a risk common to most documents for that sector or year.

For the second step, we check whether the missing topic detected by our method is the same as the one removed from the selected document. We use the fitted LDA and the fitted K-Means algorithm to predict the topics (the clusters) which can be found in the set of sentences that were removed from the selected documents. If there is at least one topic in common between the set of "missing" topics in the document, and the set of topics predicted from the removed sections, we consider that the omission has been correctly detected.

In order to evaluate the ability of our methods to tackle the task, we define the accuracy measure as the proportion of correctly detected omissions among the 20 altered documents. This measure can be computed by using the documents of the same sector or of the same year as comparison; we name it *Binary-sector* and *Binary-year* accuracies. We also compute a joint measure, taking into account both the expected topics from the year and the ones from the sector: *Binary-all*.

4 Experiment

4.1 Data Preparation

Preparation for Risk Extraction
For labeling, we selected a random subset of 50 ARs from the whole DoRe Corpus containing French and Belgian companies with large, mid and small capitalization from various sectors. These documents are converted from PDF to TXT format using MuPDF [5], some were unusable and excluded after conversion, such as the 2018 AR from AIR LIQUIDE. We then extracted start and end offset of sentences from these documents using Stanza[6] from StanfordNLP team; we chose it for its accuracy and relative speed. All of these pre-processing steps induce errors; that is why we add some custom rules to filter out unusable sentences based on number of letters / sentence length ratios and counts of line-breaks in a sentence. To handle the cold start of our Active Learning approach, we label up to 1000 sentences in successive groups of 5 from the 4 first documents in the random sample. The labeling rule is to label a sentence as Risk sentence if it includes the notion of uncertainty, and if at least one other element from the Risk triplet is present. We take into account the surrounding sentences to check whether the missing element

---

[4]We use pre-trained French word embeddings on the Wikipedia Corpus: http://fauconnier.github.io

[5]https://mupdf.com/
[6]https://stanfordnlp.github.io/stanza/

	Accuracy	F1	Recall
Iteration 1	0.8412	0.7373	0.7236
Iteration 2	0.8002	0.6403	0.6863
Iteration 3	0.8331	0.7483	0.6771
Iteration 4	0.8721	0.7767	0.8034
Iteration 5	0.8845	0.8158	0.7723
Iteration 6	**0.8969**	**0.8269**	**0.8216**

Table 1: Performance measures for each active learning iteration.

	Accuracy	F1	Precision	Recall
BERT CLS	0.8398	0.7679	**0.8968**	0.6715
BERT Sum	**0.8969**	**0.8269**	0.8323	**0.7723**

Table 2: Final results of both models after the final Active Learning iteration.

from the triplet is present in a sentence around the current one; if it is the case, we also label this second one as risk.

The initial set of 200 sub-documents is composed of groups of 5 successive sentences. We apply zero-padding to those with less than 5 sentences. We are unable to label a set of risk sentences representative of all potential risk topics from different sectors due to the dimensionality of the data; to evaluate the ability of the algorithm to detect risks even outside the sectors it has seen previously, we split the dataset into two parts and put sub-documents from two of the four first labeled ARs into the test set. This test set containing 70 sub-documents is used to follow the evolution of the performance metrics at each Active Learning iteration. It also allows the metrics during the Active Learning to be less sensitive to randomness of the split due to the low amount of data.

Active Learning

From these selected data, we train the first model in our Active Learning pipeline. The parameters for our Query-By-Committee approach are the dropout probability of classification layers weights set to $p = 0.5$ and the number of models in the committee H set to $T = 15$ for computation feasibility.

We iterate 6 times and have 39% of risk sentences in the labeled sample. We can see in Table 1 that the metrics globally increase during iterations while it is still subject to instability due to the lack of data. A solution to stabilize the results could be to add a cross-validation step, but it is computationally expensive.

Preprocessing for risk clustering

We focus on the CAC40 companies. We have 388 annual reports from 40 companies, spanning 12 sectors and 12 years (from 2008 to 2019). From the risk sentences extraction step, we have for each document, a set of risk-related sentences and their position in the document. On average, the extracted risk-related sentences correspond to 3.6% of the full document (minimum proportion = 1.3%, maximum = 14.1%). Each document is associated with a year and a company, which belongs to one of the 12 sectors. For both the topic modeling and the sentence clustering methods, the number of topics can be chosen by relying on the literature. Following [Huang and Li, 2011], we use $k = 25$ topics.

We apply a heavy processing step to all the risk sentences, in order to get a document as clean as possible to extract the most important keywords for each topic more efficiently. From the set of risk sentences, we first clean all errors resulting from the transition from pdf to text (divided words, merged characters...). Then, we exclude the sentences that have less than 60% of letters (too many symbols, spaces or digits in a sentence usually means that a portion of a data table was extracted). We delete numbers and symbols from the remaining sentences. We also remove French stopwords, words of less than 2 characters, words found in less than 15 documents and words found in more than 80% of the documents. Finally, we lemmatize all the words. [7]

4.2 Results

Risk Sentence Classification

We train two models for risk sentences classification, differing in the method to compute non-contextualized sentence embeddings. The first one (BERT Sum) is computed from the sum of the hidden-states of the last attention layer from the fine-tuned FlauBert model. The second model (BERT CLS) uses the CLS token, even though the Extractive Summarization literature tends to conclude that the second attempt is less accurate [Xiao and Carenini, 2019]. Regarding the architecture, we set the Document Encoder LSTM hidden-states to 256, the Classifier Linear layer dropout probability to 0.5, the L2 penalization parameter of the loss function to 0.01 and the learning rate to 1.e⁻5. The model is optimized by Adam-Optimizer for 150 epochs with batch size of 16. We keep as best model the one having the best validation accuracy, and test it on the previously created test set (not used during Active Learning nor training).

Table 2 presents the final results of both models after the last Active Learning iteration. Even if the (BERT CLS) Precision is better (0.8968), the increase in the recall (+0.1008) for (BERT Sum) makes it the best model for the task with the current amount of data. Table 1 shows the results of the Active Learning step, increasing the F1 score by 0.0785 (10% increase in only 5 iterations). We believe that with a greater amount of data, the model can still increase its performance and gain a better capacity to identify unknown risk factors.

For each document, the risk sentences extracted by the model from each sub-document are concatenated to create the topic-oriented summary.

Risk Clustering

In order to identify the different risk factors from the topic-oriented summary, we use the unsupervised methods described in section 3.2.

On the one hand, we apply Online LDA [Hoffman *et al.*, 2010][8] to the set of risk sentences after preprocessing. On

---

[7]For lemmatization, we use the `LefffLemmatizer()` from `Spacy`: https://pypi.org/project/spacy-lefff/

[8]Using `Gensim` implementation: https://radimrehurek.com/gensim/models/ldamulticore.html

	NPMI (k=10)	TC-W2V (k=10)	TU (k=25)
LDA	**-0.153**	0.175	**0.691**
KM	-0.240	**0.186**	0.652

Table 3: Intrinsic measures of topic modeling and sentence clustering quality.

	LDA	KM	KM2	KM4
Binary - sector	0.2	0.7	**0.8**	**0.8**
Binary - year	0.2	**0.55**	0.4	0.4
Binary - all	0.4	0.75	**0.8**	**0.8**

Table 4: Accuracy measures for the risk omission detection task on the manually altered documents.

Risk factor	Example of keywords
reputation	agency, advertiser, publicity, affect, negatively
patent	property, intellectual, licence, brand, software
energy	oil, exploration, hydrocarbon, well, damage

Table 5: Translation of keywords examples using LDA with 25 topics, and manually associated risk factor.

the other hand, we apply K-Means to the set of sentence embeddings extracted from the Sentence Encoder. We experiment with K-Means of sentences embeddings (KM), Augmented K-Means using weighted embeddings of surrounding sentences with window = 2 (KM2), and Augmented K-Means with window = 4 (KM4). As a preliminary measure of quality, we compute the silhouette score of the K-Means clusterings. The score is the highest for the Augmented K-Means with a window of 4 sentence (score = 0.178), slightly lower with a window of 2 sentences (score = 0.162), and even lower for the standard K-means (score = 0.147).

From the LDA, we have a set of keywords describing each topic. Some topic examples along with an interpretation of the associated risk factor are presented in Table 5. To be able to compare it with the sentence clustering, we extract keywords from the sentence clusters from the K-Means algorithm, using the aforementioned tf-idf method (section 3.2. Then, we compute the three intrinsic measures for both LDA and K-Means to evaluate the quality of the topic model and the clustering (Table 3). The measures for the Augmented K-Means are almost the same as for the standard K-Means.

The measures show that the sentence clustering method leads to a higher extrinsic topic coherence (TC-W2V) than the topic model, but lower intrinsic topic coherence (NPMI). Moreover, the TU measure is lower for K-Means, meaning that the clusters are less diversified.

Risk Omission Detection

We use the same models for the risk omission detection task. In order to generate synthetic omissions in ARs, we randomly sample and alter 20 ARs of the CAC40 companies, by manually removing a section describing one risk factor; and we add these altered documents to our corpus. We choose risk sections of different sizes, describing different types of risks; for example, we remove the *System security and cyber attack* section in the 2018 AR from ATOS, and the *Risk of delay and error in product deployment* section in the 2017 report from DASSAULT SYSTEMES.

After fitting the LDA and the K-Means on the corpus, we obtain the distribution of risks in the altered documents and the average distribution of risks for each sector and year. According to the method described in section 3.2, we binarize these vector and compare them in order to identify the list of missing topics in the altered documents. Then, using the topic model and clustering fitted on the full corpus, we predict the distribution of risks in the sections that were removed from the selected documents. Finally, we can compute the accuracy measures described in section 3.2 using the LDA, the standard K-Means and the Augmented K-Means with windows of size 2 and 4 (Table 4).

Augmenting the K-Means algorithm by using the surrounding sentences, even though it improved the silhouette score, does not lead to a clear improvement for this task. However, the LDA leads to much lower accuracy compared to the K-Means algorithm. It might be linked with the low extrinsic topic coherence of the LDA compared to K-Means.

5 Conclusion

In this paper, we introduced the task of risk omission detection and proposed a pipeline to tackle it. First, we extract risk sentences from company annual reports using an Encoder-Classifier architecture on top of contextualised embeddings from the BERT model. Then, we use unsupervised methods to extract the risk distribution of each annual report.

We generate synthetic risk factor omissions in a sample of ARs in a straightforward way, propose a method to detect them, and a metric to evaluate the method. We conclude that a sentence-level analysis, by clustering sentence representation extracted with BERT, is more adapted than LDA to address the task. Augmenting the sentence clustering by using a weighted sum of the representations of the surroundings of a sentence can further increase its quality. The low performance of the LDA might be overcame using more advanced topic modelling methods [Nan et al., 2019], possibly relying on word embeddings [Dieng et al., 2019].

However, the risk sentence extraction step could be improved with more Active Learning iterations, for the model to learn more about the notions of uncertainty and the impacts than about the risk factors that has already been observed during training. It could also be improved by increasing the number of sentences in each sub-document and transferring information between consecutive sub-documents in an AR.

Acknowledgments

We address our deepest thanks to François Hu (ENSAE-CREST, Société Générale) for his valuable advices on Active Learning, to Patrick Paroubeck (LIMSI-CNRS) and Alexandre Allauzen (ESPCI, University Paris-Dauphine) for their support and comments on the paper.

References

[Aletras and Stevenson, 2013] Nikolaos Aletras and Mark Stevenson. Evaluating topic coherence using distributional semantics. In *IWCS 2013*, pages 13–22, Potsdam, Germany, March 2013. ACL.

[Altham, 1983] J. E. J. Altham. Ethics of risk. *Proceedings of the Aristotelian Society*, 84:15–29, 1983.

[AMF, 2020] AMF. Annual report regulation, February 2020. AMF indications on information submission.

[Blei *et al.*, 2003] David M. Blei, Andrew Y. Ng, and Michael I. Jordan. Latent dirichlet allocation. *J. Mach. Learn. Res.*, 3:993–1022, March 2003.

[Chen *et al.*, 2017] Yu Chen, Md Rabbani, Aparna Gupta, and Mohammed Zaki. Comparative text analytics via topic modeling in banking. In *2017 IEEE Symposium Series on Computational Intelligence (SSCI)*, pages 1–8, 11 2017.

[Dasgupta *et al.*, 2016] Tirthankar Dasgupta, Lipika Dey, Prasenjit Dey, and Rupsa Saha. A framework for mining enterprise risk and risk factors from news documents. In *COLING 2016*, pages 180–184, Osaka, Japan, December 2016. The COLING 2016 Organizing Committee.

[Devlin *et al.*, 2019] Jacob Devlin, Ming-Wei Chang, Kenton Lee, and Kristina Toutanova. BERT: Pre-training of deep bidirectional transformers for language understanding. In *NAACL 2019*, pages 4171–4186, Minneapolis, Minnesota, June 2019. ACL.

[Dieng *et al.*, 2019] Adji B. Dieng, Francisco J. R. Ruiz, and David M. Blei. Topic modeling in embedding spaces. 2019.

[Ding *et al.*, 2018] Ran Ding, Ramesh Nallapati, and Bing Xiang. Coherence-aware neural topic modeling. In *EMNLP 2018*, pages 830–836, Brussels, Belgium, October-November 2018. ACL.

[Ekmekci *et al.*, 2019] Berk Ekmekci, Eleanor Hagerman, and Blake Howald. Specificity-based sentence ordering for multi-document extractive risk summarization, 2019.

[Hoffman *et al.*, 2010] Matthew D. Hoffman, David M. Blei, and Francis Bach. Online learning for latent dirichlet allocation. In *NeurIPS 2010*, page 856–864, Red Hook, NY, USA, 2010. Curran Associates Inc.

[Huang and Li, 2011] Ke-Wei Huang and Zhuolun Li. A multilabel text classification algorithm for labeling risk factors in sec form 10-k. *ACM Trans. Management Inf. Syst.*, 2:18, 10 2011.

[Jawahar *et al.*, 2019] Ganesh Jawahar, Benoît Sagot, and Djamé Seddah. What does BERT learn about the structure of language? In *ACL 2019*, pages 3651–3657, Florence, Italy, 2019. ACL.

[Kaplan and Garrick, 1981] Stanley Kaplan and B. John Garrick. On the quantitative definition of risk. *Risk Analysis*, 1(1):11–27, 1981.

[Kogan *et al.*, 2009] S. Kogan, D. Levin, B.R. Routledge, J.S. Sagi, and N.A. Smith. Predicting risk from financial reports with regression. ACL, 2009.

[Krishna and Srinivasan, 2018] Kundan Krishna and Balaji Vasan Srinivasan. Generating topic-oriented summaries using neural attention. In *the NAACL 2018*, pages 1697–1705, New Orleans, Louisiana, June 2018. ACL.

[Le *et al.*, 2020] Hang Le, Loïc Vial, Jibril Frej, Vincent Segonne, Maximin Coavoux, Benjamin Lecouteux, Alexandre Allauzen, Benoît Crabbé, Laurent Besacier, and Didier Schwab. Flaubert: Unsupervised language model pre-training for french. In *LREC*. ACL, 2020.

[Lewis and Young, 2019] Craig Lewis and Steven Young. Fad or future? automated analysis of financial text and its implications for corporate reporting. *Accounting and Business Research*, 49(5):587–615, 2019.

[Liu *et al.*, 2018] Yu-Wen Liu, Liang-Chih Liu, Chuan-Ju Wang, and Ming-Feng Tsai. RiskFinder: A sentence-level risk detector for financial reports. In *NAACL 2018*, pages 81–85, New Orleans, Louisiana, June 2018. ACL.

[Mandi *et al.*, 2018] Jayanta Mandi, Dipankar Chakrabarti, Neelam Patodia, Udayan Bhattacharya, and Indranil Mitra. Use of artificial intelligence to analyse risk in legal documents for a better decision support. In *TENCON 2018*, Jeju, Korea (South), 10 2018.

[Masson and Paroubek, 2020] Corentin Masson and Patrick Paroubek. Nlp analytics in finance with dore: A french 250m tokens corpus of corporate annual reports. In *LREC 2020*, pages 2254–2260, Marseille, France, May 2020. European Language Resources Association.

[Mikolov *et al.*, 2013] Tomas Mikolov, Ilya Sutskever, Kai Chen, Greg S Corrado, and Jeff Dean. Distributed representations of words and phrases and their compositionality. pages 3111–3119. NIPS, 2013.

[Nan *et al.*, 2019] Feng Nan, Ran Ding, Ramesh Nallapati, and Bing Xiang. Topic modeling with Wasserstein autoencoders. In *ACL 2019*, pages 6345–6381, Florence, Italy, July 2019. ACL.

[Settles, 2010] Burr Settles. Active learning literature survey. Technical report, University of Wisconsin, Madison, July 2010.

[Tsymbalov *et al.*, 2018] Evgenii Tsymbalov, Maxim Panov, and Alexander Shapeev. Dropout-based active learning for regression. pages 247–258, Cham, 2018. Springer.

[Xiao and Carenini, 2019] Wen Xiao and Giuseppe Carenini. Extractive summarization of long documents by combining global and local context. In *EMNLP-IJCNLP 2019*, pages 3011–3021, Hong Kong, China, 2019. ACL.

[Zhu *et al.*, 2016] Xiaodi Zhu, Steve Yang, and Somayeh Moazeni. Firm risk identification through topic analysis of textual financial disclosures. In *2016 IEEE Symposium Series on Computational Intelligence (SSCI)*, pages 1–8, 12 2016.

A Semantic Approach to Financial Fundamentals

Jiafeng Chen[*1,2] , **Suproteem K. Sarkar**[*†1]

[1]Harvard University
[2]Harvard Business School
{jiafengchen, suproteemsarkar}@g.harvard.edu,

Abstract

The structure and evolution of firms' operations are essential components of modern financial analyses. Traditional text-based approaches have often used standard statistical learning methods to analyze news and other text relating to firm characteristics, which may shroud key semantic information about firm activity. In this paper, we present the Semantically-Informed Financial Index (SIFI), an approach to modeling firm characteristics and dynamics using embeddings from transformer models. As opposed to previous work that uses similar techniques on news sentiment, our methods directly study the business operations that firms report in filings, which are legally required to be accurate. We develop text-based firm classifications that are more informative about fundamentals per level of granularity than established metrics, and use them to study the interactions between firms and industries. We also characterize a basic model of business operation evolution. Our work aims to contribute to the broader study of how text can provide insight into economic behavior.

1 Introduction

Firm operations are key components of financial analyses, but fine-grained data about business characteristics are often stored in unstructured corpora. Text analysis has been used over the past decade in the study of firms and their characteristics, though most of these studies have used manual labels or simple word-based metrics [Tetlock, 2007; Loughran and McDonald, 2016]. Recently, [Hoberg and Phillips, 2016] introduced a method for clustering firms by taking the cosine similarity of bag-of-words of 10-Ks, annual reports filed by firms to the SEC, and [Ke et al., 2019] introduced a topic model-based approach to modeling sentiment and returns.

With the recent growth of large transformer models [e.g. Devlin et al., 2018; Radford et al., 2019; Brown et al.,

2020], semantically-informed approaches to domain-specific language tasks have become more tractable. While there is a preliminary literature on using pre-trained language models to measure sentiment [Hiew et al., 2019], a more consistent measure of fundamentals may instead lie in descriptions of actual firm operations. We use pre-trained language models to study business descriptions on firm filings, which are legally required to be accurate. This paper presents the following contributions:

- We introduce the Semantically-Informed Financial Index (SIFI), a quantitative representation of business operations that can be interpreted alongside existing industrial classifications of firms.

- We compare our index to existing business classifications, including those based on text, and find our measure can be more informative and queryable.

Our index allows us to measure the structure and evolution of firms and industries over time. With this semantically-informed approach, we seek to develop rich information sources for broader financial applications.

1.1 Paper Organization

In Section 2, we discuss the methods used to develop the SIFI index. In Section 3, we probe the interpretability of our index, relating it to existing classification schemes and analyzing how it can track industry-level trends. Finally, in Section 4, we quantitatively measure the expresiveness of our index compared to existing benchmarks.

2 Developing SIFI

Recent advances in natural language processing have contributed to a growing literature of transfer learning-based applications using large pre-trained transformer models [Vaswani et al., 2017], with models based on BERT [Devlin et al., 2018] achieving state-of-the-art results in a variety of domains and tasks. Transformers in particular [Vaswani et al., 2017] allow for modeling of long-range dependencies, since their architecture allows for massively parallelizable operations on GPUs—in contrast to RNN models, where evaluation is iterative along the length of the text. BERT is a transformer pre-trained on a series of self-supervised tasks on a large dataset—and can be used to learn a representation

---

*Equal Contribution.

†Sarkar gratefully acknowledges the support of a National Science Foundation Graduate Research Fellowship.

Proceedings of the Second Workshop on Financial Technology and Natural Language Processing

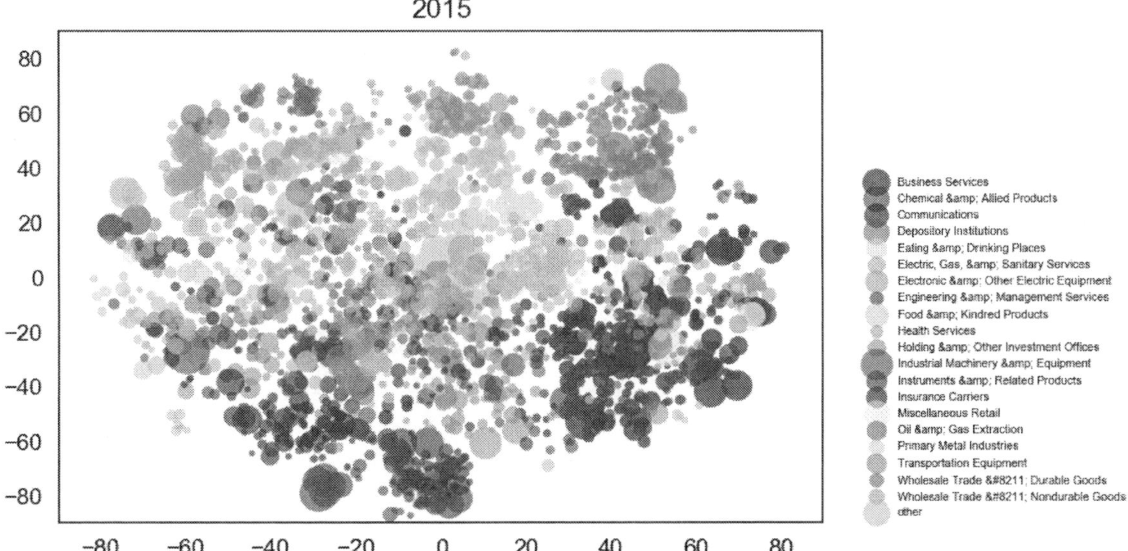

Figure 1: t-SNE decomposition of business section embeddings in 2015, labeled by SIC industry code. The size of each bubble reflects the market capitalization of each firm.

of language which allows for downstream fine-tuning [Liu, 2019].

In this paper, we build on these advances to generate concise document embeddings that capture important features of financial documents. Compared to traditional approaches using word embeddings [Mikolov et al., 2013], the semantic embeddings generated by BERT are context dependent, and can capture long-range dependencies bidirectionally [Jawahar et al., 2019]. Therefore, we believe transformer-based embeddings hold particular promise for processing financial documents, which are often long, complex, and context-dependent.

Our data encompasses the universe of Form 10-K filings to the Securities and Exchange Commission (SEC) from 2006 to 2018 collected by [Loughran and McDonald, 2016],[1] which consists of 93,480 firm-years, with an average of 7,191 firms represented per year. 10-Ks are annual filings to the SEC in which a firm's management discusses business operations and financial performance in the recent fiscal year. These documents are legally required to be correct, and contain rich information about each firm's operations, as shown in Figure 2. We use regular expressions to collect only the *Business Section* of the filing, which provides a description of firms' operations and products.

We use pre-trained uncased BERT-large (24-layer, 340 million parameters) implemented by Huggingface in PyTorch in order to compute our embeddings.[2] We break each document into 512-word segments and pass into the pre-trained transformer. We then mean-pool over the resulting word-level embeddings over the entire document, and save the resulting

---

Figure 2: An excerpt from the business section of Alphabet's 2019 10-K.

vector as the document embedding. Our approach is entirely zero-shot, since the model is not fine-tuned on the specific dataset, though we still find interpretable and meaningful results. In this vein, we believe these findings can be interpreted as a lower bound of the power of using transformers for financial applications. Our approach can be extended in future work by fine-tuning the model on meaningful financial targets, including fundamentals and trading metrics, which we anticipate may lead to even greater separation across the semantic components that are most relevant for the financial metrics we aim to identify.

3 Querying the Index

In this section, we present a series of experiments describing the validity and interpretability of our index.

---

[1]https://sraf.nd.edu/data/stage-one-10-x-parse-data/
[2]https://github.com/huggingface/transformers

Table 1: Industries most similar to
Heavy Construction (16)

Industry	Distance (L2)
Engineering & Management Services (87)	0.8578
Rubber & Miscellaneous Plastics Products (30)	0.8720
Industrial Machinery & Equipment (35)	0.8870
Instruments & Related Products (38)	0.9055
Wholesale Trade & Durable Goods (50)	0.9158
Electronic & Other Electric Equipment (36)	0.9237
Business Services (73)	0.9254
Printing & Publishing (27)	0.9406
Transportation Equipment (37)	0.9432
Oil & Gas Extraction (13)	0.9517

Table 2: Industries most similar to
Depository Institutions (60)

Industry	Distance (L2)
Holding & Other Investment Offices (67)	0.7101
Insurance Carriers (63)	0.7898
Instruments & Related Products (38)	0.8808
Wholesale Trade & Durable Goods (50)	0.8965
Real Estate (65)	0.9121
Security & Commodity Brokers (62)	0.9491
Electronic & Other Electric Equipment (36)	0.9677
Oil & Gas Extraction (13)	1.0147
Engineering & Management Services (87)	1.0262
Business Services (73)	1.0327

3.1 Industry Characteristics

After computing embeddings for all firms in our sample period, we can plot relationships between firm-years for our sample. In Figure 1, we plot a t-SNE [Maaten and Hinton, 2008] decomposition of all firms in the 2015 sample, first transforming each firm embedding into 50-component PCA space. We label each firm by its 2-digit SIC classification code, which is an established classification scheme for businesses and has been used to evaluate industry-level operations [Fertuck, 1975].

Our results mirror those encoded by SIC classifications, separating into clusters that map onto 2-digit codes. Note that we do not introduce additional information about SIC codes to the model, so this clustering is based on the pre-trained corpus. Therefore, Figure 1 suggests our vectors separate in a similar manner as existing SIC classifications without relying on the metric during the development of the index—this leads us to believe that our embedding-based approach may mirror actual operational differences at the industry-wide scale.

Furthermore, we report the minimum-distance cluster centroids to the Heavy Construction (Table 1) and Depository Institution (Table 2) SIC classification centroids. We note that many of these SIC-2 clusters employ similar operations as their respective targets, including "Engineering & Management Services" and "Rubber & Miscellaneous Plastics Products" for "Heavy Construction," as well as "Holding & Other Investment Offices" and "Insurance Carriers" for "Depository Institutions." The cluster similarities mirror what one might expect for similar industries, but do not exclusively reside in the same 1-digit classification as the SIC index, which may reflect the evolving nature of business operations since the introduction of SIC in the 1930s. The results suggest that our embeddings may also capture semantic information about operations at a broad, industry level.

3.2 Firm Characteristics

We also query our firm space by projecting firm embeddings onto components reflecting the direction between two given firms. For example, projections onto axes from CVS Health to Amgen and CVS Health to Amazon components are reported in Figure 3. This decomposition allows us to query how the semantic embeddings of firms' operations change as

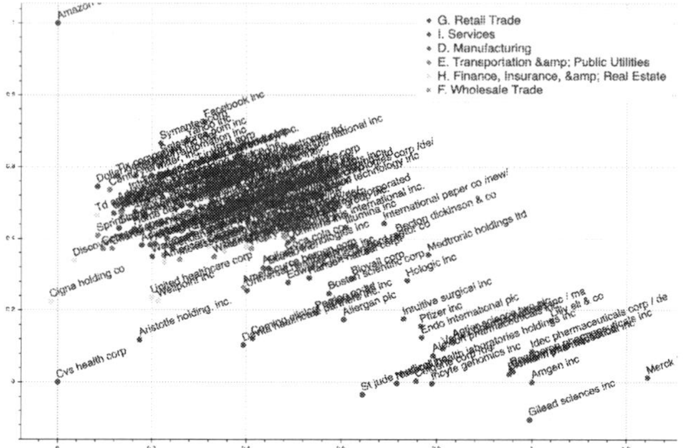

Figure 3: Projections of firm embeddings onto CVS Health-Amgen and CVS Health-Amazon components.

they move across the latent space. Note that as firms move toward Amazon they lean toward tech (e.g. Facebook, Yahoo), and as they move toward Amgen they lean toward biotech (e.g. Celgene and Regeneron). Furthermore, although firms along each axis do not neatly fall in the same 2 broad industrial classifications, they do exhibit similar focuses (e.g. St. Jude Medical and Incyte Genomics, which both have health-related operations, fall across the CVS Health-Amgen axis, even if they are not in the same broad SIC code), which suggests that the rigid boundaries of the SIC classification system do not necessarily account for all the ways that firm operations may coincide. These analyses suggest that meaningful semantic information about operations is also being captured at the firm level in our index.

3.3 Industry Dynamics

Since our sample contains filing information across several years, we can also use our document embeddings to explore the evolution of firms and industries over time. In Figure 4, we plot the within cluster mean sum of squares of the Depository Institutions and Motion Picture Industry SIC codes over time in the SIFI embeddings. The motivation behind this particular analysis is to broadly study how operations are different from one another over time. The trends in the dispersion

Table 3: Across-industry variation for each index, holding granularity fixed across learned clusters. OI denotes operating income and MV denotes market value. A higher standard deviation indicates greater informativeness for that particular fundamental. The higher variation of SIFI compared to SIC-3 and TNIC suggests that it is capturing important semantic information, which allows for greater separation of firms across business operations that are associated with fundamentals.

Across-Industry Std. Dev.	OI / Assets	OI / Sales	MV / Assets	MV / Sales	OI / MV
SIC-3	0.429	19.104	4.191	85.963	13.251
TNIC	0.971	20.736	10.055	83.692	14.457
SIFI	**1.271**	**41.088**	**11.350**	**147.763**	**23.310**

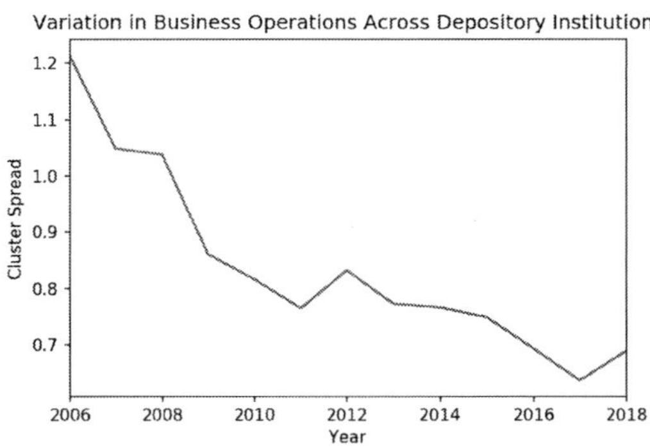

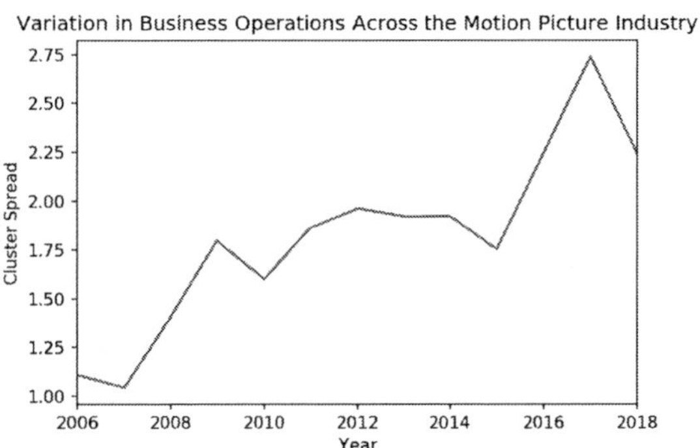

Figure 4: Business operation dispersion across selected industries over time, measured using within-cluster mean sum of squares.

of operations mirror what we might expect from the evolution of product mixes in these industries, particularly given consolidation in banks, which supports the claim that semantic embeddings may also be useful for documenting changes in operations over time.

4 Evaluating SIFI

In this section, we compare the informativeness of our index with related classifications, using metrics explored elsewhere in the literature.

4.1 Index Informativeness

An important metric for evaluating SIFI is its relative informativeness compared to existing indices. In their development of Text-Based Network Industries (TNIC), [Hoberg and Phillips, 2016] use across-industry variation in fundamentals to measure the informativeness of their index. Specifically, they cluster firms that have small pairwise distances between their respective latent space vectors. Next, they take the standard deviation of selected financial fundamentals across their mean values in each of these clusters' centers.

In Table 3, we report this measure for SIFI, TNIC, and 3-digit SIC codes across a series of fundamentals that are scale-invariant. We hold the granularity of SIFI and TNIC fixed to have the same number of clusters as the SIC-3 classification, which is also done in the informativeness calculations in [Hoberg and Phillips, 2016], in order to put our index on the same playing field as the less granular SIC index. We find that SIFI maintains the highest level of across-industry

variation across different types of fundamentals, for example in predicting the ratio of operating income to sales, which is also queried by [Hoberg and Phillips, 2016].

The higher measured across-industry variation suggest that SIFI is meaningfully capturing differences in fundamentals across firms, even when it is limited to a coarser scale. This implies that using semantically-informed measures of firm operations may contribute additional information about the ways that fundamentals of related firms behave.

5 Discussion

In this paper, we develop a semantically-informed index of firm operations sourced from the business section of firm filings, which are legally required to be accurate. We demonstrate how the index can be used to understand the characteristics and dynamics of firms and industries, both at a large, industry-wide level and a smaller, firm-specific level. We further evaluate how our index might be useful for evaluating operational trends within industries, as well as for analyzing fundamentals. This paper is a step in our efforts to develop more targeted, semantically-informed measures of operations to augment the financial data toolbox. In this paper, we employed a raw pre-trained model to form embeddings, and future research would benefit from fine-tuning on operationally meaningful targets, including financial fundamentals and market shares, which may produce even better separation across fundamental types.

The universe of semi-structured firm filings provides an ideal application for transformer models, which have allowed us to dig deeper into the structure of firm operations than pre-vious methods based on text. Through our approach, we have sought to introduce more robust and principled approaches to knowledge discovery from semi-structured financial data, and to contribute useful metrics to the broader research community in finance and computer science.

References

[Brown et al., 2020] Brown, T. B., Mann, B., Ryder, N., Subbiah, M., Kaplan, J., Dhariwal, P., Neelakantan, A., Shyam, P., Sastry, G., Askell, A., et al. (2020). Language models are few-shot learners. *arXiv preprint arXiv:2005.14165*.

[Devlin et al., 2018] Devlin, J., Chang, M.-W., Lee, K., and Toutanova, K. (2018). Bert: Pre-training of deep bidirectional transformers for language understanding. *arXiv preprint arXiv:1810.04805*.

[Fertuck, 1975] Fertuck, L. (1975). A test of industry indices based on sic codes. *Journal of Financial and Quantitative Analysis*, 10(5):837–848.

[Hiew et al., 2019] Hiew, J. Z. G., Huang, X., Mou, H., Li, D., Wu, Q., and Xu, Y. (2019). Bert-based financial sentiment index and lstm-based stock return predictability. *arXiv preprint arXiv:1906.09024*.

[Hoberg and Phillips, 2016] Hoberg, G. and Phillips, G. (2016). Text-based network industries and endogenous product differentiation. *Journal of Political Economy*, 124(5):1423–1465.

[Jawahar et al., 2019] Jawahar, G., Sagot, B., and Seddah, D. (2019). What does bert learn about the structure of language?

[Ke et al., 2019] Ke, Z. T., Kelly, B. T., and Xiu, D. (2019). Predicting returns with text data. *University of Chicago, Becker Friedman Institute for Economics Working Paper*.

[Liu, 2019] Liu, Y. (2019). Fine-tune bert for extractive summarization. *arXiv preprint arXiv:1903.10318*.

[Loughran and McDonald, 2016] Loughran, T. and McDonald, B. (2016). Textual analysis in accounting and finance:: A survey. *Journal of Accounting Research*, 54(4):1187–1230.

[Maaten and Hinton, 2008] Maaten, L. v. d. and Hinton, G. (2008). Visualizing data using t-sne. *Journal of machine learning research*, 9(Nov):2579–2605.

[Mikolov et al., 2013] Mikolov, T., Sutskever, I., Chen, K., Corrado, G. S., and Dean, J. (2013). Distributed representations of words and phrases and their compositionality. In *Advances in neural information processing systems*, pages 3111–3119.

[Radford et al., 2019] Radford, A., Wu, J., Child, R., Luan, D., Amodei, D., and Sutskever, I. (2019). Language models are unsupervised multitask learners.

[Tetlock, 2007] Tetlock, P. C. (2007). Giving content to investor sentiment: The role of media in the stock market. *The Journal of finance*, 62(3):1139–1168.

[Vaswani et al., 2017] Vaswani, A., Shazeer, N., Parmar, N., Uszkoreit, J., Jones, L., Gomez, A. N., Kaiser, L., and Polosukhin, I. (2017). Attention is all you need. In *Advances in neural information processing systems*, pages 5998–6008.

Learning Company Embeddings from Annual Reports
for Fine-grained Industry Characterization

Tomoki Ito[1*] , **Jose Camacho Collados**[2] , **Hiroki Sakaji**[1] , **Steven Schockaert**[2]

[1]Graduate School of Engineering, The University of Tokyo, Japan
[2]School of Computer Science & Informatics, Cardiff University, UK

Abstract

Organizing companies by industry segment (e.g. artificial intelligence, healthcare or fintech) is useful for analyzing stock market performance and for designing theme base investment funds, among others. Current practice is to manually assign companies to sectors or industries from a small predefined list, which has two key limitations. First, due to the manual effort involved, this strategy is only feasible for relatively mainstream industry segments, and can thus not easily be used for niche or emerging topics. Second, the use of hard label assignments ignores the fact that different companies will be more or less exposed to a particular segment. To address these limitations, we propose to learn vector representations of companies based on their annual reports. The key challenge is to distill the relevant information from these reports for characterizing their industries, since annual reports also contain a lot of information which is not relevant for our purpose. To this end, we introduce a multi-task learning strategy, which is based on fine-tuning the BERT language model on (i) existing sector labels and (ii) stock market performance. Experiments in both English and Japanese demonstrate the usefulness of this strategy.

1 Introduction

Investing in individual companies carries a high risk to investors, as stock prices can move in highly unpredictable ways. A popular alternative is to reduce this idiosyncratic risk by instead investing in funds that track the performance of a particular index (i.e. weighted set of companies). While most indices have traditionally been designed to capture particular geographic regions (e.g. S&P 500 for the US market), in recent years, funds that track a particular industry segment have been gaining in popularity. For instance, such funds allow investors who believe that technology companies will continue to outperform to specifically target that segment of the economy. However, investment companies who want to offer such industry-specific funds are faced with the problem of

choosing or defining a suitable index to track. Currently, this is predominately achieved by relying on standardized sets of sector or industry labels, such as those from the Global Industry Classification Standard (GICS). However, such labels are often not sufficiently fine-grained. For instance, while they allow us to define an Information Technology or Health Care index, they do not allow us to do the same for more specific domains such as Fintech or Artificial Intelligence (AI). Moreover, such labels are hard assignments, whereas the exposure of a given company to a domain such as AI tends to be a matter of degree. Finally, these labels do not allow us to quickly adapt to changes in the market (e.g. a major company deciding to create a high profile AI-lab). Similar problems arise when we want to analyze stock market performance. While the existing categorization of companies allows us to analyze which sectors and geographic regions have performed well or poorly over a given time period, doing such analysis at a fine-grained industry level is currently not straightforward.

To address these limitations, in this paper we introduce a method for automatically developing vector representations of companies that can be useful for searching or categorizing companies at a fine-grained industry level. While there has been some previous work on predicting industry segments of companies [Chen *et al.*, 2018; Lamby and Isemann, 2018], in this paper we specifically focus on annual reports of companies as a source of information. Compared to the use of news stories [Lamby and Isemann, 2018], this has several advantages. First, the information captured in news stories can be heavily biased. For instance, a company such as Facebook is frequently mentioned in the news in relation to their AI research, whereas from an economic perspective, the performance of the AI sector might only be weakly correlated to that of Facebook. Moreover, representations learned from news stories can capture what companies have focused on in the past, but it is more difficult to capture changes in company strategy from such sources. In contrast, annual reports are authoritative documents, which explicitly describe the sectors in which the company is currently active.

In particular, we consider the problem of learning company embeddings from annual reports, such that the embedding of a given company characterizes the industries in which it is active. Learning such embeddings from annual reports is challenging, however, since only a small fragment of these reports is typically devoted to describing the industry in which

---

*Contact Author: m2015titoh@socsim.org

Proceedings of the Second Workshop on Financial Technology and Natural Language Processing

the company is active. This clearly differentiates our problem from the general problem of learning entity embeddings from descriptions [Jameel and Schockaert, 2016; Xie *et al.*, 2016; Wang *et al.*, 2019b], as approaches for the latter problem have focused on learning representations that reflect the entire description. To solve this challenge, we propose a method for fine-tuning a pre-trained neural language model [Devlin *et al.*, 2019]. Since we do not have access to annotations of fine-grained industry labels, we rely on a number of distant supervision signals, including the broad industry sector label of the company as well as its recent stock market performance. Our main contributions are as follows:

1. We introduce a new dataset[1] for the problem of characterizing industries from annual reports.

2. We propose several evaluation tasks for quantitatively evaluating the performance of these embeddings. On the one hand, these tasks aim to analyze to what extent companies with similar vector representations are active in similar industries. On the other hand, we also focus on a zero-shot learning setting, where the aim is to use company vectors to find companies that are active in a given industry, given only the name of that industry.

3. We introduce a model for learning company embeddings from annual reports, which is based on a multi-task learning set-up for fine-tuning the BERT language model [Devlin *et al.*, 2019].

4. We analyze the effectiveness of the considered distant supervision signals, as well as the general strengths and weaknesses of the learned embeddings.

2 Related Work

The general problem of learning vector space representations of entities has been widely studied in recent years. Such methods can be categorized based on the kind of information that is used. For instance, a large number of graph embedding methods have been proposed [Perozzi *et al.*, 2014; Tang *et al.*, 2015; Grover and Leskovec, 2016], which learn vector representations of entities based on their local neighbourhood in an associated graph, e.g. a social network of users or a citation graph of academic papers. As another example, there is a popular line of research which learns embeddings of knowledge graphs [Bordes *et al.*, 2013; Trouillon *et al.*, 2017; Balazevic *et al.*, 2019], which can for instance be useful to inject knowledge from such resources into Natural Language Processing (NLP) architectures. Most closely related to this paper, there have been several models that aim to combine entity descriptions with structured information, and knowledge graphs in particular [Wang *et al.*, 2014; Camacho-Collados *et al.*, 2016; Xie *et al.*, 2016; Wang *et al.*, 2019b]. One important difference with our setting is that these models assume that all the information in the given text descriptions is relevant, whereas our main challenge is to distill the relevant information for characterizing industries.

While there is considerable work on learning general entity representations, and recent work leveraging NLP techniques

to model financial market dynamics [Xing *et al.*, 2018], the specific problem of learning company embeddings has only received limited attention thus far. Chen *et al.* [2018] introduced a model called Company2Vec, which learns company embeddings based on the intuition that companies are likely to be similar if employees tend to transition from one to the other. For our setting, this approach has two drawbacks. First, it relies on proprietary and sensitive personal data from the LinkedIn platform. Second, the corresponding notion of similarity is clearly skewed by factors such as geographic location. In [Lamby and Isemann, 2018], an analysis is carried out to assess to what extent industry sectors can be predicted from standard word embeddings, finding that such embeddings indeed capture a non-trivial amount of industry information. While achieving promising results, the method falls short when considering low-frequency companies and it does not consider ambiguity (e.g. the word *apple* can be a company but it also has other meanings).

3 Method

In this section we describe our method for learning vector representations of companies (i.e. company embeddings).

3.1 Fine-tuning BERT

Let x_i be a document about company i. In our experiments x_i will be the latest annual report of the company, although the same model could be used with other kinds of financial documents. The main strategy is to learn a mapping from such documents x_i to a corresponding company vector $\mathbf{h_i}$ by fine-tuning the BERT [Devlin *et al.*, 2019] language model.

Neural language models such as BERT are deep neural networks, which have been pre-trained in an unsupervised way on large amounts of text, typically by learning to predict masked words in sentences. Because of this pre-training process, they capture a large amount of knowledge about the meaning of words and phrases, and the typical syntactic structure of sentences. We can exploit this knowledge in applications, by fine-tuning a pre-trained language model on task-specific training data, rather than learning a neural network from scratch. This strategy has led to substantial performance gains across a wide range of Natural Language Processing (NLP) tasks [Wang *et al.*, 2019a]. Most closely related to our work, BERT has been shown to be effective for learning embeddings of entities from their description [Logeswaran *et al.*, 2019; Wang *et al.*, 2019b]. Formally, we have:

$$\boldsymbol{h}_i = \text{BERT}(x_i)$$

where x_i is the textual description of company i and $\boldsymbol{h}_i \in \mathbb{R}^e$ is the resulting embedding. Specifically, $\text{BERT}(x_i)$ refers to the mean vector of the token-level embeddings that are predicted by BERT. We also tried using the vector predicted for the [CLS] token, as is common in the literature [Wang *et al.*, 2019a], but found this to be less effective.

3.2 Multitask Learning

As we will see in the experiments, without fine-tuning the embeddings learned by BERT are not particularly useful for our setting. Among others, this is because annual statements

---

[1] Our preprocessed dataset and code is available at https://github.com/itomoki430/Company2Vec.

contain information beyond descriptions of the industry in which the company is operating. For this reason, we consider a multi-task learning set-up, allowing us to fine-tune BERT on three tasks: predicting the sector labels, capturing stock market performance and modelling sector names. The overall loss thus takes the following form:

$$\mathcal{L} = \mathcal{L}^{sec} + \mathcal{L}^{stock} + \mathcal{L}^{sn} \tag{1}$$

We now discuss each of these components in more detail.

Sector Category Loss

As a first supervision signal, we consider the task of predicting which sector of the economy company i belongs to. Note that while sector labels are coarser-grained that the industry segments which we want to model, the assumption is that by learning to extract sector-level information from the document x_i, the model will also extract finer-grained information. The advantage of using sector labels is that they are readily available. Let us write d_i^{sec} for the one-hot encoding of the sector of company i. We define $\mathcal{L}^{sec}$ as follows:

$$y_i^{sec} = \text{Softmax}(W^{sec} h_i + b^{sec})$$
$$\mathcal{L}^{sec} = \sum_{i \in \Omega} CE(d_i^{sec}, y_i^{sec})$$

where we write CE for the cross-entropy and Ω is the set of all considered companies.

Stock Performance Loss

Research has shown that companies from the same industry tend to exhibit similar stock price fluctuations [Gopikrishnan *et al.*, 2000]. Inspired by this finding, we also consider the following component in the loss function:

$$\mathcal{L}^{stock} = \sum_{i \in \Omega} \sum_{j \in \Omega} \| h_i^T \cdot h_j - Sim(v_i^{stock}, v_j^{stock}) \|$$

where Sim is the cosine similarity and v_i^{stock} denotes a vector containing the monthly stock return value for company i, for the last five years, i.e.:

$$v_i^{stock} := [r_i(t_1), r_i(t_2), \cdots, r_i(t_{60})],$$

with $r_i(t_j)$ the monthly stock return value for company i for j months ago. In case stock price data is not available for both companies over the full period, the longest period for which data is available is used instead.

Sector Name Loss

The third component of the loss function is aimed at fine-tuning BERT such that it maps the name of a given sector onto the correct index of that sector. Let us write $\mathcal{S}$ for the set of all sectors. For $j \in \mathcal{S}$, we write sn_j for the name of sector j (e.g. "Healthcare"). As before, we write d_j^{sn} for the corresponding one-hot encoding. Then we have:

$$s_j = \text{BERT}(sn_j)$$
$$y_j^{sn} = \text{Softmax}(W^{sn} s_j + b^{sn})$$
$$\mathcal{L}^{sn} = \sum_{j \in \mathcal{S}} CE(d_j^{sn}, y_j^{sn})$$

The reason why we include this component is because we want to be able to use the trained model to identify companies that belong to a given industry given only a text description of that industry. For instance, if the input is *Artificial Intelligence* then the model should be able to predict what part of the vector space contains AI companies, despite not having seen any training examples of such companies. The loss $\mathcal{L}^{sn}$ encourages the model to make such predictions for sector names, where the assumption is that this ability will also transfer to descriptions of more specific industry segments.

4 Experimental Setting

To evaluate the performance of our method we propose two tasks for which we construct a dataset. In the following we describe the construction of the datasets and the experimental evaluation details.

4.1 Datasets

To test our methodology we constructed two datasets: one English-language dataset about the US stock market and one Japanese-language dataset about the Japanese stock market. The US dataset includes the financial annual reports, stock return data, and sector label data for 2,462 US companies (see below for details). The Japanese dataset includes the same information for 3,016 Japanese companies. We split the datasets into train, validation, and test fragments, containing respectively 1800, 262, and 400 companies for the US dataset, and 2200, 316, and 500 companies for the Japanese dataset. For companies in the test splits, stock return data and sector labels are not used during training.

Text Corpora. For the US dataset, we used the financial annual reports (i.e., Form 10-K documents) of listed companies in the US stock market, focusing in particular on those that were published in 2019. We were able to obtain 2,462 such reports from http://www.annualreports.com in September 1st, 2019. For the Japanese dataset, we used the financial annual reports of listed companies in the Tokyo Stock Exchange, focusing on those that were published in 2018 (which is the most recent year for which reports were available). These documents are written in Japanese. We were able to obtain 3,016 reports from https://github.com/chakki-works/CoARiJ. For these datasets we make use of the business description section that contain a summary of the activities of the company, and thus typically contains the most relevant information for learning the embeddings.

Stock Data. For the $\mathcal{L}^{stock}$ loss, we need monthly return data. For both datasets we used data from a period of five years. In particular, for the US companies, we used data for April 2014 to March 2019, while for the Japanese companies, we used data for April 2013 to March 2018.

Sector Labels. For the sector loss $\mathcal{L}^{sec}$ and sector name loss $\mathcal{L}^{sn}$, we utilized the sector labels provided by annualreports.com[2] in the case of the US dataset. For the Japanese companies, we used the 17 sector labels that were assigned by the Tokyo Stock Exchange (TSE)[3].

---

[2]http://www.annualreports.com/Browse?type=Industry
[3]https://www.jpx.co.jp/markets/statistics-equities/misc/01.html

4.2 Training

For the US companies, we used the BERT-base-uncased model[4] [Devlin *et al.*, 2019], whereas we used a Japanese BERT pre-trained model[5] for the Japanese companies. An important difference between these two models is that the English BERT model was trained on general purpose text (i.e. Wikipedia and the Books and Movie Corpus [Zhu *et al.*, 2015]), whereas the Japanese BERT model was trained on three million Japanese business news articles[6]. In both cases we utilized the first 512 tokens of the business description section in each report as textual data for the embedding. To adapt both models to the language that is used in the annual reports, we first fine-tuned them on our text corpus, using the standard masked word and next sentence prediction tasks [Devlin *et al.*, 2019]. After this step, we trained our model on the loss function (1) using the Adam optimizer [Kingma and Ba, 2015] for 30 epochs with early stopping.

4.3 Evaluation Tasks

We evaluated our method on two tasks, namely a related company extraction test and a theme-based extraction test.

Task 1: Related Company Extraction Test

The aim of this task is to assess to what extent companies with similar vectors are similar in terms of the industries to which they belong. To this end, for each company X, we first obtain the K most similar companies, in terms of the cosine similarity between their embeddings. Then we evaluate to what extent the categories to which these companies belong are the same as the category of X. Following the work in [Yu *et al.*, 2012], we used the Mean Average Precision at K (MAP@K) evaluation metric, where $K = 5, 10, 50$.

For the US companies, we use two types of categories, corresponding to the sector labels and the industry labels provided by annualreports.com. Out of the 11 sector labels, only 9 appeared in the test data. The industry labels are essentially a finer-grained version of the sector labels. In the test set, a total of 140 different industry labels appeared, all of which were used for this evaluation. For the Japanese companies, we used the TOPIX-17 sector labels and TOPIX-33 sector labels, as defined by TSE[7], as the categories. TOPIX-33 sector labels are a refinement of the TOPIX-17 sector labels. For example, companies of "ENERGY RESOURCE" sector in TOPIX-17 are divided into "Mining" or "Oil and Coal Products" in TOPIX-33. The US sector labels and TOPIX-17 labels are the same ones that were used for training, which clearly makes the task easier than if previously unseen categories were used. Therefore, we will also report results for configurations of our model in which only a small number of sector labels are used during training. This will allow us to analyze to what extent the model is able to capture categories which it has not seen during training.

Task 2: Theme-Based Extraction Test

In this task, we evaluate to what extent our method is able to find companies that are relevant to a given theme, given only the name of that theme. As theme names, for the US dataset, we used the same 140 industry labels from Task 1. For the Japanese dataset, we used a finer-grained classification involving 274 themes, which we extracted from https://minkabu.jp/screening/theme. Note that while each US company has a unique industry label, companies in the Japanese dataset may belong to multiple themes. We believe the latter setting is more realistic, but we were not able to obtain a similar dataset for the US stock market. We again treat this problem as a ranking task. In particular, for each theme Y, we first determine the K most relevant companies, by comparing the company vectors to the vector that was predicted by our fine-tuned BERT model for the theme name Y.

4.4 Baselines

To our knowledge, there are no previous models that have specifically been proposed for learning company vectors from annual reports. As baselines, we thus use two standard document representation methods. First, we consider the bag-of-words representation of the annual report (BOW), using term frequency weights.[8] For Task 2, we similarly use a BOW representation of the theme descriptions. For both tasks, companies are ranked based on cosine similarity.

As a second baseline, we used the mean vector of the skip-gram Word2Vec word embedding (SG) [Mikolov *et al.*, 2013] that was trained on all financial documents. To learn this skip-gram embedding, we utilized the 200-dimensional word embedding vectors that were trained on the corpus of US annual reports and Japanese annual reports, respectively, using a window size of 5. For Task 2, Hirano *et al.* [2019] already proposed an approach based on word vectors for Japanese, which we use as an additional baseline. This baseline first searches for synonyms of each theme name, using both the similarity based on word embeddings and the similarity based on co-occurrence in annual reports. Then, it extracts the companies related to the theme using the frequency of the theme name, and each of its discovered synonyms, in each annual report. For this method, we rely on the same skip-gram embedding as for the SG baseline. We also tried the same method for English but could not obtain any meaningful results.

5 Results

In this section we present the results in Task 1 (i.e. Related Company Extraction) and Task 2 (i.e. Theme-Based Extraction) and a qualitative analysis of the results provided by our model.

5.1 Related Company Extraction

The results for Task 1 are shown in Table 1 for the US dataset and in Table 2 for the Japanese dataset. In addition to the results of our full model and the baselines, the tables contain an ablation analysis, showing results for configurations where some components were removed from the loss function. The

---

[4]Available at https://github.com/huggingface/transformers

[5]Available at https://drive.google.com/drive/folders/1iDlmhGgJ54rkVBtZvgMlgbuNwtFQ50V-

[6]https://qiita.com/mkt3/items/3c1278339ff1bcc0187f

[7]https://www.jpx.co.jp/english/markets/indices/line-up/files/e_fac_13_sector.pdf

[8]To allow for a direct comparison, for the baselines we used the same 512 tokens as for the BERT-based methods.

	US (SECTOR)			US (INDUSTRY)		
	MAP@5	MAP@10	MAP@50	MAP@5	MAP@10	MAP@50
BOW	0.177	0.127	0.066	0.184	0.177	0.182
SG	0.216	0.167	0.084	0.179	0.174	0.173
BERT$_{\text{CLS}}$	0.115	0.083	0.041	0.152	0.144	0.143
BERT	0.324	0.270	0.152	0.243	0.242	0.238
BERT + Stock	0.471	0.419	0.242	0.325	0.328	0.338
BERT + Sector	0.569	0.544	0.501	0.313	0.324	0.349
BERT + Stock + Sector	0.590	0.567	0.509	0.328	0.337	0.365
BERT + Sector + Sector Name	**0.613**	**0.582**	**0.545**	0.331	0.337	0.369
BERT + Stock + Sector + Sector Name	**0.613**	0.578	0.530	**0.349**	**0.359**	**0.388**
BERT + Sect. (2 labels) + Sect. Name	0.459	0.412	0.260	0.290	0.288	0.294
BERT + Sect. (5 labels) + Sect. Name	0.540	0.499	0.389	0.326	0.330	0.350
BERT + Stock + Sect. (2 labels) + Sect. Name	0.485	0.435	0.259	0.322	0.327	0.337
BERT + Stock + Sect. (5 labels) + Sect. Name	0.531	0.487	0.379	0.319	0.327	0.349

Table 1: Results for Task 1 (Related company extraction) on the US dataset.

	JAPAN (TOPIX-17)			JAPAN (TOPIX-33)		
	MAP@5	MAP@10	MAP@50	MAP@5	MAP@10	MAP@50
BOW	0.368	0.302	0.220	0.295	0.243	0.188
SG	0.281	0.228	0.150	0.199	0.153	0.101
BERT$_{\text{CLS}}$	0.128	0.097	0.058	0.081	0.056	0.032
BERT	0.202	0.156	0.098	0.145	0.108	0.068
BERT + Stock	0.405	0.330	0.216	0.338	0.274	0.199
BERT + Sector	0.654	0.618	0.568	0.542	0.503	0.448
BERT + Stock + Sector	**0.675**	**0.636**	**0.577**	0.557	0.521	0.458
BERT + Sector + Sector Name	0.660	0.622	0.556	0.547	0.508	0.445
BERT + Stock + Sector + Sector Name	0.672	0.633	0.561	**0.576**	**0.534**	**0.464**
BERT + Sect. (2 labels) + Sect. Name	0.420	0.360	0.268	0.337	0.282	0.221
BERT + Sect. (5 labels) + Sect. Name	0.462	0.389	0.310	0.387	0.318	0.262
BERT + Stock + Sect. (2 labels) + Sect. Name	0.486	0.418	0.335	0.410	0.354	0.294
BERT + Stock + Sect. (5 labels) + Sect. Name	0.472	0.405	0.325	0.396	0.338	0.272

Table 2: Results for Task 1 (Related company extraction) on the Japanese dataset.

	US			JAPAN		
	MAP@5	MAP@10	MAP@50	MAP@5	MAP@10	MAP@50
BOW	0.165	0.172	0.189	0.116	0.099	0.088
SG	0.030	0.032	0.043	0.066	0.054	0.050
BERT$_{\text{CLS}}$	0.004	0.003	0.008	0.019	0.015	0.013
BERT	0.094	0.108	0.124	0.024	0.020	0.019
[Hirano *et al.*, 2019]	-	-	-	0.118	0.101	0.093
BERT + Stock	0.164	0.177	0.196	0.030	0.025	0.027
BERT + Sector	0.188	0.208	0.238	0.114	0.100	0.099
BERT + Stock + Sector	0.174	0.192	0.221	0.106	0.090	0.087
BERT + Sector + Sector Name	0.215	0.238	0.268	0.175	0.150	0.133
BERT + Stock + Sector + Sector Name	0.194	0.210	0.241	0.160	0.143	0.136
BERT + Sect. (2 labels) + Sect. Name	0.141	0.151	0.166	0.101	0.089	0.085
BERT + Sect. (5 labels) + Sect. Name	0.190	0.208	0.238	0.161	0.148	0.136
BERT + Stock + Sect. (2 labels) + Sect. Name	0.199	0.220	0.238	0.125	0.122	0.120
BERT + Stock + Sect. (5 labels) + Sect. Name	**0.234**	**0.254**	**0.279**	**0.176**	**0.161**	**0.144**

Table 3: Results for Task 2 (Theme-based extraction).

Company	Sector	Industry	Company	Sector	Industry
US LIME & MINERALS	INDUSTRIAL GOODS	GENERAL BUILDING MATER.	WHITING PETROLEUM	BASIC MATERIALS	OIL & GAS DRILL. & EXPLR.
Freeport-McMoRan Copper&Gold	Basic Materials	Copper	Halcon Resources	Basic Materials	Oil & Gas Drill. & Explr.
United State Antimony	Basic Materials	Industrial Metals & Minerals	Callon Petroleum Company	Basic Materials	Independent Oil & Gas
Approach Resources	Basic Materials	Oil & Gas Drill. & Explr.	Cimarex Energy Co.	Basic Materials	Independent Oil & Gas
XENIA HOTELS & RESORTS	FINANCIAL	REIT - HOTEL/MOTEL	VIKING THERAPEUTICS	HEALTHCARE	BIOTECHNOLOGY
Ashford Hospitality Prime	Financial	REIT - Hotel/Motel	Adaptimmune Therapeutics	Healthcare	Biotechnology
LaSalle Hotel Properties	Financial	REIT - Hotel/Motel	Sage Therapeutics	Healthcare	Biotechnology
RLJ Lodging Trust	Financial	REIT - Hotel/Motel	Celldex Therapeutics	Healthcare	Biotechnology
TELEPHONE & DATA SYSTEMS	TECHNOLOGY	WIRELESS COMMS.	TANDY LEATHER FACTORY	CONSUMER GOODS	TEXTILE-APPAREL FOOTW.&ACC.
Verizon Communications	Technology	Telecom Services - Domestic	Steve Madden	Consumer Goods	Housewares & Accessories
Sprint Corp	Technology	Wireless Comms.	Vince Holdings	Consumer Goods	Textile - Apparel Clothing
U.S. Cellular	Technology	Telecom Services - Foreign	Vera Bradley	Consumer Goods	Textile - Apparel Footw. & Acc.

Table 4: Three nearest neighbours for selected companies in the test set in the vector space resulting from our full BERT multitask model.

full method is shown as BERT + Stock + Sector + Sector Name. On the last four rows, we furthermore show results for a more challenging setting where only 2 or 5 sector labels were used during training, instead of the full set of sector labels from the dataset (see Section 4.1).

As can be seen in Table 1, BERT already outperforms the BOW and SG baselines on the US dataset, even without incorporating any of the three supervision signals. For comparison, we also show results of BERT when using the [CLS] output vector instead of averaging the token-level vectors, which performs substantially worse. Incorporating stock performance and sector labels clearly helps, with further performance gains being achieved when incorporating the sector name loss. When only 2 or 5 sector labels are available for training, as expected, the performance drops. However, for the industry labels, the drop is surprisingly small, which shows that the model learns to identify which parts of the annual reports contain the most relevant information, rather than simply learning to predict particular sector labels. The Japanese results in Table 2 broadly follow a similar pattern, although a larger drop in performance is seen for the configurations in which only 2 or 5 sector labels are used during training. Moreover, the BOW and SG baselines are also stronger in this case, outperforming the BERT configuration.

5.2 Theme-Based Extraction

Table 3 summarizes the results for Task 2. This task is clearly more challenging than Task 1, especially considering the fine-grained nature of the considered themes, which is reflected in the overall scores. The BOW baseline performs surprisingly well on this task. In terms of our model, the sector name component of the loss function now clearly plays an important role, which is not surprising, given that this component specifically trains BERT to map category names onto the embedding space. Surprisingly, the variant where only 5 sectors are used during training actually leads to the best results for the US and Japan. This reflects the fact that learning a mapping from sector names to the embedding space is most important for this task; including fewer sector names allows the model to focus more on the segment name component.

5.3 Qualitative Analysis

To analyze the company embeddings qualitatively, Table 4 shows the nearest neighbours for selected companies from the US test set (for the full BERT multitask model). As can be observed, in some cases, the neighbors have the same sector and industry labels (*Xenia Hotels & Resorts* and *Viking Therapeutics*). The case of *Viking Therapeutics* provides an example where the industry segment captured by the embedding is finer-grained than the pre-defined industry labels, given that all neighbors are specifically concerned with therapeutics. Even in cases where the industry labels are different, the nearest neigbors are often meaningful. For instance, the neighbors of *Tandy Leather Factory* are all focused on products made with leather (i.e. shoes for *Steve Madden* and *Vince Holdings* and handbags for *Vera Bradley*). This shows the potential of our vectors for capturing themes that cut across the traditional classification of industry segments. In the case of *US Lime & Minerals*, the nearest neighbors belong to a different sector. However, *US Lime & Minerals* is clearly related to the Basic Materials sector, as they focus on the processing of limestone. This illustrates the potential benefit of vector representation in identifying borderline cases, or more generally, for estimating the degree to which a company is exposed to a given sector or industry segment.

6 Conclusion

This paper addresses the problem of learning company embeddings from annual reports, such that the embedding of a given company characterizes the industries in which it is active. To achieve this end, we introduce a multi-task learning strategy, which is based on fine-tuning the BERT language model on (i) existing sector labels and (ii) stock market performance. Experiments in a newly constructed dataset of US and Japanese companies (in English and Japanese language, respectively) demonstrated the usefulness of this strategy. The proposed distant supervision signals were effective to improve the performance in several tasks. Finally, given the flexibility of our multitask model framework, in future work, it would be interesting to incorporate other sources of business information, such as Price Earnings Ratio (PER) and Price Book-value Ratio (PBR). Similarly, it would be useful to analyze how the authoritative information that is contained in annual reports can be complemented with more informal sources, such as news stories and company websites.

Acknowledgements. Jose Camacho Collados and Steven Schockaert have been supported by ERC Starting Grant 637277. Tomoki Ito was Supported by JSPS KAKENHI Grant Number JP17J04768.

References

[Balazevic *et al.*, 2019] Ivana Balazevic, Carl Allen, and Timothy M. Hospedales. TuckER: Tensor factorization for knowledge graph completion. In *Proceedings of EMNLP*, pages 5184–5193, 2019.

[Bordes *et al.*, 2013] A. Bordes, N. Usunier, A. Garcia-Duran, J. Weston, and O. Yakhnenko. Translating embeddings for modeling multi-relational data. In *Proceedings of NIPS*, pages 2787–2795, 2013.

[Camacho-Collados *et al.*, 2016] José Camacho-Collados, Mohammad Taher Pilehvar, and Roberto Navigli. Nasari: Integrating explicit knowledge and corpus statistics for a multilingual representation of concepts and entities. *Artificial Intelligence*, 240:36–64, 2016.

[Chen *et al.*, 2018] Xi Chen, Yiqun Liu, Liang Zhang, and Krishnaram Kenthapadi. How linkedin economic graph bonds information and product: applications in linkedin salary. In *Proceedings of SIGKDD*, pages 120–129, 2018.

[Devlin *et al.*, 2019] Jacob Devlin, Ming-Wei Chang, Kenton Lee, and Kristina Toutanova. BERT: pre-training of deep bidirectional transformers for language understanding. In *Proceedings of NAACL-HLT*, pages 4171–4186, 2019.

[Gopikrishnan *et al.*, 2000] Parameswaran Gopikrishnan, Bernd Rosenow, Vasiliki Plerou, and H Eugene Stanley. Identifying business sectors from stock price fluctuations. *arXiv preprint cond-mat/0011145*, 2000.

[Grover and Leskovec, 2016] Aditya Grover and Jure Leskovec. Node2vec: Scalable feature learning for networks. In *Proceedings of SIGKDD*, pages 855–864, 2016.

[Hirano *et al.*, 2019] Masanori Hirano, Hiroki Sakaji, Shoko Kimura, Kiyoshi Izumi, Hiroyasu Matsushima, Shintaro Nagao, and Atsuo Kato. Related stocks selection with data collaboration using text mining. *Information*, 10, 2019.

[Jameel and Schockaert, 2016] Shoaib Jameel and Steven Schockaert. Entity embeddings with conceptual subspaces as a basis for plausible reasoning. In *Proceedings of ECAI*, pages 1353–1361, 2016.

[Kingma and Ba, 2015] D.P. Kingma and L.J. Ba. Adam: A method for stochastic optimization. In *Proceedings of the International Conference on Learning Representations (ICLR)*, 2015.

[Lamby and Isemann, 2018] Martin Lamby and Daniel Isemann. Classifying companies by industry using word embeddings. In *International Conference on Applications of Natural Language to Information Systems*, pages 377–388, 2018.

[Logeswaran *et al.*, 2019] Lajanugen Logeswaran, Ming-Wei Chang, Kenton Lee, Kristina Toutanova, Jacob Devlin, and Honglak Lee. Zero-shot entity linking by reading entity descriptions. In *Proceedings of ACL*, pages 3449–3460, 2019.

[Mikolov *et al.*, 2013] Tomas Mikolov, Kai Chen, Greg Corrado, and Jeffrey Dean. Efficient estimation of word representations in vector space. *CoRR*, abs/1301.3781, 2013.

[Perozzi *et al.*, 2014] Bryan Perozzi, Rami Al-Rfou, and Steven Skiena. Deepwalk: Online learning of social representations. In *Proceedings of SIGKDD*, pages 701–710, 2014.

[Tang *et al.*, 2015] Jian Tang, Meng Qu, Mingzhe Wang, Ming Zhang, Jun Yan, and Qiaozhu Mei. Line: Large-scale information network embedding. In *Proceedings of WWW*, pages 1067–1077, 2015.

[Trouillon *et al.*, 2017] Théo Trouillon, Christopher R. Dance, Éric Gaussier, Johannes Welbl, Sebastian Riedel, and Guillaume Bouchard. Knowledge graph completion via complex tensor factorization. *J. Mach. Learn. Res.*, 18:130:1–130:38, 2017.

[Wang *et al.*, 2014] Zhen Wang, Jianwen Zhang, Jianlin Feng, and Zheng Chen. Knowledge graph and text jointly embedding. In *Proceedings of EMNLP*, pages 1591–1601, 2014.

[Wang *et al.*, 2019a] Alex Wang, Yada Pruksachatkun, Nikita Nangia, Amanpreet Singh, Julian Michael, Felix Hill, Omer Levy, and Samuel R. Bowman. Superglue: A stickier benchmark for general-purpose language understanding systems. *arXiv preprint arXiv:1905.00537*, 2019.

[Wang *et al.*, 2019b] Xiaozhi Wang, Tianyu Gao, Zhaocheng Zhu, Zhiyuan Liu, Juanzi Li, and Jian Tang. Kepler: A unified model for knowledge embedding and pre-trained language representation. *arXiv preprint arXiv:1911.06136*, 2019.

[Xie *et al.*, 2016] Ruobing Xie, Zhiyuan Liu, Jia Jia, Huanbo Luan, and Maosong Sun. Representation learning of knowledge graphs with entity descriptions. In *Proceedings of AAAI*, 2016.

[Xing *et al.*, 2018] Frank Z Xing, Erik Cambria, and Roy E Welsch. Natural language based financial forecasting: a survey. *Artificial Intelligence Review*, 50(1):49–73, 2018.

[Yu *et al.*, 2012] Kuifei Yu, Baoxian Zhang, Hengshu Zhu, Huanhuan Cao, and Jilei Tian. Towards personalized context-aware recommendation by mining context logs through topic models. In *Proceedings of PAKDD*, 2012.

[Zhu *et al.*, 2015] Yukun Zhu, Ryan Kiros, Rich Zemel, Ruslan Salakhutdinov, Raquel Urtasun, Antonio Torralba, and Sanja Fidler. Aligning books and movies: Towards story-like visual explanations by watching movies and reading books. In *Proceedings of the IEEE International Conference on Computer Vision*, pages 19–27, 2015.

Unsupervised Discovery of Firm-Level Variables in Earnings Call Transcript Embeddings

Daniel Edmiston*, **Ziho Park**
[1]University of Chicago, Chicago, IL, USA
{danedmiston, zpark}@uchicago.edu

Abstract

In this paper, we repurpose an algorithm from the computational biology literature to detect the extent to which modern document embedding methods are sensitive to financial and micro-economic variables. The contributions are two-fold. First, we provide a novel application of methods from an outside field and show its usefulness for unsupervised discovery of economic information in high-dimensional embeddings of financial documents. Second, we use the quantitative output of the algorithm to compare different embedding methods across different economic variables.

1 Introduction

The financial and economic worlds have never suffered for want of data, a fact which holds even more true in the modern era of big-data. In recent years, these worlds have seen a further explosion in the amount of data in the form of unstructured text. These new sources of data can be social-media interactions, internet news-stories, etc., in addition to the traditional text data available in the form of, for example, annual 10k filings and earnings call transcripts. Naturally, given the competitive advantage offered by the ability to better process data in all forms, considerable work in the economics and finance literature has gone into researching methods of processing these texts [Loughran and McDonald, 2016] to automatically detect and leverage the information contained therein, with a large portion of methods relying on discrete counts of words in documents.

In the somewhat far removed field of Natural Language Processing (NLP), researchers have gradually moved away from discrete, count-based methods since the early 2000's [Bengio *et al.*, 2003], all but eschewing them in modern research. Instead, virtually all current work in NLP is conducted representing linguistic entities (such as words, documents, etc.) with continuous, high-dimensional representations ($\in \mathbb{R}^n$), commonly referred to as embeddings. In addition to the advantages offered by the topology of the continuous space vs. a discrete one, researchers have also moved away from count-based methods altogether, instead favoring prediction-based approaches [Baroni *et al.*, 2014].

Given the applicability of modern NLP methods to text data in the financial world, it is perhaps surprising that these methods have not yet gained a foothold in mainstream finance and economics research. This is perhaps due to the fact that many of the variables (micro-)economists concern themselves with appear readily amenable to the simpler, and far-more interpretable count-based methods still popular in financial text-analytics. For example, [Hassan *et al.*, 2019] show that simple word counts from conference call transcripts provide an adequate proxy for political risk and associated sentiment, well correlated with other micro-economic variables. Conversely, in spite of the effectiveness of high-dimensional continuous embeddings for traditional NLP tasks, these representations remain opaque, and it is not clear how to mine them for economic information.

This paper hopes to provide a first step towards the discovery of economic information in high-dimensional embeddings, suggesting that it is indeed possible to discover information related to micro-economic variables within the seemingly opaque representations common in NLP. To do this, we build a graph structure based on the topology of embeddings built from earnings call transcripts, and apply the Spatial Analysis of Functional Enrichment (SAFE) algorithm [Baryshnikova, 2016] to this graph structure. The SAFE algorithm, originally developed in the computational biology literature, detects regions in a graph which show statistically high concentrations of values for a variable. The presence of high concentrations of values in a graph built on the topology of embeddings suggests that the embedding method used to create the graph is sensitive to that variable, and this is reflected in the partitioning of the space.

This paper then has the following as contributions. First, we repurpose an algorithm from the computational biology literature to show that the kind of firm-level variables (micro-)economists care about are reflected in the high-dimensional embeddings produced by modern NLP methods. This takes us a step closer to the interpretability of count-based methods, with the added advantages of a rich, continuous embedding space. Second, by using the quantitative output of the algorithm, we compare different document embedding strategies, showing that some methods capture certain economic variables better than others.

---

*Contact Author

Proceedings of the Second Workshop on Financial Technology and Natural Language Processing

It is our hope that work in this vein will serve as an encouragement to those in the finance/economic fields that modern document representation methods have value for their field, and we also hope to show the potential of the SAFE algorithm to the NLP field at large for the unsupervised discovery of information in high-dimensional embeddings.

2   Related Work

2.1   Text Mining in Economics

Text analysis in Finance/Economics has a long history, and a useful summary of methods in the field can be found in [Loughran and McDonald, 2016]. Here, we focus on the recent trend of mining textual data and treating the result as a proxy for economic variables. Such a method is exemplified in e.g. [Baker *et al.*, 2016], where the authors measure economic policy-related uncertainty via a word count-based index over newspaper articles. This proxy correlates with measured economic variables, such as observed political instability, and the proxy count variable is shown to peak at times of instability in the world at large, for example Brexit, and the election of Donald Trump as president of the United States.

Other exemplars of the kind of work often done in financial/economics text-analytics are [Hassan *et al.*, 2019] and [Hassan *et al.*, 2020], wherein the text-based variables the authors compute not only exemplify modern text-analysis research in the economics literature, but also use the same dataset as this study.[1] These studies employ count-based methods on bag-of-words text-representations to create proxy variables for risk/uncertainty and sentiment with relation to politics and the COVID-19 pandemic. As an illustration of their methods, the authors of [Hassan *et al.*, 2020] use the following formula to measure firm-level exposure to a disease (e.g. COVID-19).

$$Risk_{i,t}^{d} = \frac{1}{B_{i,t}} \sum_{b=1}^{B_{i,t}} \{ \mathbb{1}[b \in Disease_d] \times \mathbb{1}[|b - r| < 10] \}$$

Here, $Risk_{i,t}^{d}$ measures the risk associated with disease d for firm i at time t, as measured by parsing firm i's earnings call transcript at time t. $B_{i,t}$ is the length of firm i's transcript at time t, and b ranges over the unigrams in the transcript. $\mathbb{1}$ is the indicator function, and $Disease_d$ is a dictionary of synonyms for disease d.[2] Finally, r is the nearest position of a word deemed synonymous with 'risk' or 'uncertainty', as determined by Oxford English Dictionary. The term $|b - r|$ then signals how close the nearest risk-meaning word is to current unigram b. In words, $Risk_{i,t}^{d}$ counts the number of occurrences of a unigram denoting virus d within a window of 10 words of a word denoting risk or uncertainty, and then normalizes for the size of the transcript.

In spite of the simple bag-of-words based methods employed by the authors, it is shown that these variables serve as reliable proxies correlating well with economic variables.

---

[1]Strictly speaking, we make use of only a subset of their dataset.

[2]For example, *coronavirus* and *COVID* would be treated as synonyms for the COVID-19 virus.

Given the effectiveness of these methods for the variables in question (e.g. exposure to political risk), economics researchers can perhaps feel vindicated in their continued use of less linguistically sophisticated techniques.

While a large portion of mainstream literature in financial/economics text analytics does proceed with bag-of-words, count-based methods, there has been slight movement towards adopting the more modern methods as studied in the NLP literature. For example, [Araci, 2019] makes use of the recent trend of leveraging pre-trained language models [Devlin *et al.*, 2018] and applying them to sentiment analysis in the financial domain with encouraging results. [Hiew *et al.*, 2019] similarly use a pre-trained language model for sentiment analysis, further using the output for the task of stock-price prediction.

While there is no question that modern, continuous representations of linguistic units are superior for practical downstream tasks, it has yet to be shown that they are useful for the sort of text analytics e.g. [Baker *et al.*, 2016] practices. We reiterate our hope with this work to take the first step of showing that these continuous representations can also be interpreted as reflecting micro-economic variables.

2.2   Document Embeddings

As mentioned in the introduction, modern NLP research has all but abandoned discrete, count-based methods for representing linguistic entities in favor of continuous embedding methods, most often trained by neural networks. This holds true for representation of linguistic entities from the character level through to the document level. In this study, we examine three methods of embedding earnings call transcripts into continuous high-dimensional space, meaning that embeddings at the level of document are the focus of this study. While the literature on document embeddings has grown vastly in recent years, we restrict ourselves to discussing only the models relevant to this study. Specifically, we look at one count-based method of high-dimensional embedding, and two neural network-based methods.

The first method is Latent Semantic Analysis (LSA) [Deerwester *et al.*, 1990], which is based on the truncated Singular-Value Decomposition (SVD) of a matrix consisting of TF-IDF values [Jones, 1972]. This is the only count-based method investigated here, but due to the dimensionality reduction of the truncated SVD, the result is opaque continuous embeddings for each document in the corpus. TF-IDF/LSA can often serve as a strong baseline for document representation [Wang and Manning, 2012], and has the principled interpretation of document embeddings being projections of their weighted unigram word counts onto the principal directions of variation in the corpus.

The second method we examine is the Doc2Vec (D2V) method of [Le and Mikolov, 2014], which trains a document embedding by optimizing a vector to predict the words which appear in that document. This method, which can be considered a document-level extension of Word2Vec [Mikolov *et al.*, 2013], comes in two varieties, one which trains word-embeddings in tandem with the document embedding, and one which trains only the document embedding. The former generally shows better results, however the concatenation of two embeddings (one from each variant) consistently showed the best results per [Le and Mikolov, 2014].

The third and final method of embedding documents is a variant of the Transformer architecture [Vaswani *et al.*, 2017], specifically Longformer [Beltagy *et al.*, 2020], which is an extention of the popular BERT model [Devlin *et al.*, 2018]. The principal modification of Longformer is a more memory efficient self-attention mechanism, allowing the model to more easily handle long documents such as the ones we deal with here. In this paper, we make use of two variants of Longformer. The first is a pre-trained model *as-is*, meaning we simply use the model with its pre-trained model weights and no additional fine-tuning. The second is the same model further fine-tuned on the TriviaQA dataset [Joshi *et al.*, 2017].

While BERT-style models have set the standard in recent years with regard to virtually every downstream task in NLP, one significant limitation of these models is their restriction to modeling sequences of fixed length. As this fixed length is typically 512 tokens,[3] BERT-style models are generally regarded as being less suitable for modeling long-form documents. Efforts to extend the fixed length are hampered by the fact that the self-attention mechanism on which the model relies is quadratic in both time and memory with respect to sequence length. To get around this, rather than attending to the entire sequence as self-attention typically does, the Longformer model uses a sliding window approach (*cf.* [Child *et al.*, 2019]) in addition to using sparse global attention. This way, longer sequences can be modeled, while no individual applications of self-attention extend past a reasonable limit (further details on the embeddings follow in Section 3.2).

Using these four methods to embed our corpus of earnings call transcripts, we hope to use the algorithm described in Section 3.1 to (i) show that micro-economic level variables can be discovered in them, and (ii) compare results between models and across variables as a first approximation of what kind of information might be available. Insofar as we are successful on these fronts, we will have shown that we can have the benefits of high-dimensional continuous embeddings (e.g. not requiring hand-crafted dictionaries [Loughran and McDonald, 2011], capturing rich semantic information, etc.), while maintaining some interpretability with regard to economic variables.

3 Experiment Preliminaries

3.1 SAFE Algorithm

In this paper, we make use of the Spatial Analysis of Functional Enrichment (SAFE) algorithm [Baryshnikova, 2016]. This graph algorithm was originally designed to detect the functional organization of large biological networks such as those representing relationships between genes. Here, we repurpose it to work over graphs constructed from document embeddings so as to ascertain the extent to which these embedding methods are sensitive to the information we're interested in.

The input to the SAFE algorithm is a graph $\mathcal{G} = (V, E)$ wherein each node $v_i \in V$ has associated with it a set of variables $\mathcal{X} = \{X_k\}$; write $X_{k,j}$ as the value of the kth variable on the jth node. Given such an input, the SAFE algorithm provides a means of identifying neighborhoods in the graph with statistically high concentrations of either low-values or high-values for variables X_k.

The node-level output of SAFE for variable X_k is a "neighborhood enrichment score"($\in \mathbb{R}$) which is calculated in the following way. For node v_i, define the neighborhood of v_i as $N(v_i) = \{v_j \in V \mid d(v_i, v_j) < \varepsilon\}$, where $\varepsilon \in \mathbb{R}^+$, and $d(\cdot, \cdot)$ is a distance metric on $\mathcal{G}$, e.g. shortest path. Define the observed score for variable X_k at node v_i as $O_k(v_i) = \sum_{v_j \in N(v_i)} X_{k,j}$. That is, $O_k(v_i)$ is the sum of values of variable X_k at nodes v_j for each node v_j in the neighborhood of v_i. Compare $O_k(v_i)$ with $n = 1,000$ random shufflings of the values of X_k across the nodes in the graph, thus producing a p-value for $O_k(v_i)$, call it $P_k(v_i)$. The neighborhood enrichment score of node v_i, denoted $NES_k(v_i)$, is the negative log transform of this p-value, i.e. $NES_k(v_i) = -log_{10}(P_k(v_i))$. Intuitively, nodes whose neighborhoods have scores for a variable resembling a random distribution will have high p-values, and accordingly low neighborhood enrichment scores. Alternatively, nodes whose neighborhoods commonly have very high (or very low) values will have relatively low p-values, and therefore high neighborhood enrichment scores.

Given node-level scores, one can describe a variable's distribution throughout the network with the score described in Equation 1. Total SAFE score, as a sum of all nodes' neighborhood enrichment scores, measures the extent to which a sample variable has high values or low values concentrated in specific neighborhoods in a graph. One refers to a variable with high (*resp.* low) SAFE scores as being highly (*resp.* poorly) enriched in a network. We interpret an embedding method as sensitive to a particular variable when that variable is highly enriched, and not so otherwise.

$$\text{Total SAFE Score}_k = \sum_{v_i \in V} NES_k(v_i) \qquad (1)$$

3.2 Embedding Details

Given a corpus of 1,408 earnings call transcripts from the first quarter of 2020, we use the four models discussed above for embedding these documents into continuous, high-dimensional space. In the case of LSA, the TF-IDF vectors are calculated and then reduced via truncated SVD to a dimension of 800. For the Doc2Vec vectors, each document is trained for 10 epochs for each of the two variants of Doc2Vec (see Section 2.2), each in 400 dimensions. Each document is then represented as the concatenation of the resulting vectors from these variants, resulting in 800 dimensional embeddings, per the suggested specifications of [Le and Mikolov, 2014]. Finally for Longformer, both the pre-trained and fine-tuned models are BERT-Large variants, meaning they embed into 1,024 dimensions. To do the embedding, documents are split into chunks $c_1, ..., c_t$, each of 4096 tokens (except perhaps the last) with a stride of 500. Global attention is placed on the special [CLS] for each chunk, and the final embedding is the average of these [CLS] tokens.

---

[3]Tokens are roughly equivalent to words, though uncommon words are sometimes broken into multiple tokens.

For each of the models, we also compare a random baseline where the variables are permuted randomly throughout the network. It is sometimes common to evaluate models against a random baseline in which the embeddings themselves are randomized. However, as the output of SAFE is sensitive to graph structure, we use the same embeddings to ensure the same graph, and only randomly permute the variable values.

4 Experiment Design

4.1 Graph Construction

Given embeddings of the corpus documents, the first step is to construct a graph which reflects the topology of the distribution of the embeddings in the continuous space. Graph construction is done via an ϵ-radius graph; i.e. given document embeddings $X = \{x_1, ..., x_{1,408}\}, x_i \in \mathbb{R}^d$, construct graph $\mathcal{G} = (V, E)$ such that there is a bijection $f : V \rightarrow X$, and for $v_i, v_j \in V$, $(v_i, v_j) \in E$ iff $d(f(v_i), f(v_j)) < \epsilon$, where $d(\cdot, \cdot)$ is Euclidean distance in $\mathbb{R}^d$. In other words, there is a one-to-one correspondence between vertices in the graph and document embeddings, and there is an edge between vertices just in case their representative document embeddings are closer in $\mathbb{R}^d$ than ϵ.

The choice of ϵ is not arbitrary, but is again chosen to reflect the topology of the underlying embeddings. Specifically, ϵ is chosen such that resulting graph $\mathcal{G}$ has the "correct" number of connected components, where the number of connected components is decided by the *eigengap* heuristic [Von Luxburg, 2007].[4] The graph $\mathcal{G}$ is fed as input to SAFE for experimentation.

4.2 Discovering Micro-economic Variables

The experiment we describe here makes use of data collected from Computstat for the first quarter of 2020, in line with the timing of our earnings call transcripts. While the number of potential variables to experiment with from this data is large (in the thousands), here we focus on a subset of the variables, as listed in Table 1.

Along with the graph output discussed above, the values for these variables serve as input to the SAFE algorithm. The task is then to obtain $NES_k(v_i)$ for each variable k and transcript embedding represented by v_i, allowing us to calculate the Total SAFE score discussed in Section 3.1. This score can be taken as a measure for how much an embedding model has a tendancy to partition its embedding space by value of the respective variable. A low SAFE score indicates that the dispersion of the values of the variable is close to what would be expected by random assignment of values to nodes, whereas a high SAFE score indicates that certain nodes have neighborhoods which have significantly higher (or lower) values than would be expected by random assignment.

As a simple coarse measure of how much different embedding models reflect microeconomic information (at least for

---

[4]That is, given the eigendecomposition of the laplacian of an affinity matrix (e.g. as given by a Gaussian kernel), sort the eigenvalues in ascending order and determine the number of clusters—or in this case, connected components—as k such that the gap between eigenvalues k and $k + 1$ is large.

Compustat abbr.	Description
actq	Current assets
altoq	Long-term Assets
chq	Cash
ciderglq	Derivatives gains/losses
cshtrq	Common shares traded
dlcchy	Changes in current debt
dlttq	Long-term debt
epsf12	Earnings per share
fincfy	Net cash flow
ivstchy	Short-term investments (change)
revtq	Total revenue

Table 1: Variables of interest for experiment. Abbreviations used as in Compustat database.

the variables chosen), we can average the Total SAFE scores for all relevant variables. The results of this experiment are in Table 2, along with the random baselines discussed above which serve as a control. For a more fine-grained analysis, we examine the Total SAFE scores for each of the individual variables. These results are in Table 3.

We stress that due to the lack of context with regard to SAFE scores—this being the first application of the method outside of biology, to the authors' knowledge—it is best to interpret model scores relative only to how they fare when compared against their random baselines. This is especially the case because SAFE scores are sensitive to the graph structure they're calculated on, and thus only models which share the same graph structure are directly comparable. As such, absolute SAFE scores are less informative for our purposes than the ratio of trained model performance to random model performance, as indicated in Tables 2-3. We interpret scores significantly higher than the random baseline as evidence of the information being reflected in the embeddings.

5 Results

Table 2 houses the scores for each model, along with its random baseline control where the values of the variables are permuted as discussed above. The results in the table are the Total SAFE Scores averaged over all variables. Again, this can be taken as a coarse measure of the embedding models' sensitivity to the variables.

Model	Trained	Random	Ratio
Latent Semantic Analysis	841	578	1.46
Doc2Vec	1909	751	2.54
Longformer	569	613	0.93
Longformer-finetuned	522	473	1.10

Table 2: Average Total SAFE Score across all considered variables. SAFE scores rounded to nearest integer, ratios to two decimal places. Red score indicates trained model below random baseline.

In three of the four cases, the trained model outscores its random baseline, but in the case of the non-finetuned Longformer, this is not the case. Doc2Vec, meanwhile, performs the best. Speculation as to why Doc2Vec performed the

Model	LSA			D2V			LF			LF-finetuned		
Variable	Trained	Random	Ratio	Trained	Random	Ratio	Trained	Random	Ratio	Trained	Random	Ratio
actq	970	558	1.74	2480	867	2.86	352	519	0.68	675	454	1.49
altoq	1246	614	2.03	2396	387	6.19	811	644	1.26	466	534	0.87
chq	1029	589	1.75	1663	945	1.76	567	599	0.95	683	286	2.39
ciderglq	420	491	0.86	1430	614	2.33	338	445	0.76	708	617	1.15
cshtrq	785	556	1.41	3360	583	5.76	641	755	0.85	711	665	1.07
dlcchy	351	643	0.55	1213	919	1.32	560	401	1.40	355	79	4.49
dlttq	914	659	1.39	1498	1125	1.33	420	636	0.66	211	200	1.06
epsf12	1115	534	2.09	2651	632	4.19	487	864	0.56	294	258	1.14
fincfy	412	619	0.67	828	498	1.66	916	602	1.52	171	125	1.37
ivstchy	709	510	1.39	470	386	1.22	686	635	1.08	843	1674	0.50
revtq	1295	593	2.18	3004	1302	2.31	478	643	0.74	629	306	2.06

Table 3: Total SAFE Score for each of the eleven variables of interest. All scores rounded to the nearest integer, ratios to two decimal places. Red denotes trained score for a model is below random baseline.

best and why the non-finetuned Longformer underperforms is withheld till Section 6.

In Table 3 are housed the Total SAFE Scores for each model and for each variable. This more fine-grained view of the scores shows that non-finetuned Longformer consistently produces scores near its random baseline. The LSA model and finetuned-Longformer models perform near-random on some variables, while showing strong results on others (e.g. *dlcchy*, 'Changes in current debt' for finetuned-Longformer). Doc2Vec on the other hand, outperforms its random counterpart on every variable, and significantly so in many cases, appearing particularly sensitive to *cshtrq*, 'Common shares traded.'

6 Discussion

Though the results are preliminary, it would appear that at least in some cases it is possible to show that high-dimensional embeddings have distributions correlated with micro-economic variables. For example, the topology of Doc2Vec embeddings seems to reflect the distribution of variables like *epsf12*, 'Earnings per share.' It stands to reason that if any type of economic information would be identifiable in these embeddings it would be the sort of variable referenced in conversation between shareholders and management. The issue of earnings per share for the quarter, along with topics like total revenue (variable *revtq*), are likely to be broached in earnings calls. Note that we do not interpret this as Doc2Vec being directly sensitive to values of variables like the number of shares traded, rather we interpret this as Doc2Vec (and similarly well performing models) being sensitive to language which likely correlates with variables like the ones discussed here.

As for relative performance of the models, it is not surprising that Doc2Vec outperforms the others. First, that it would outperform LSA is expected, as it has been shown that models trained on prediction tasks (like Doc2Vec) generally outperform those based on counts [Baroni *et al.*, 2014]. That said, even more traditional methods like LSA show potential for mining economic variables directly from high-dimensional vectors, as it showed strong performance on variables *revtq*, 'Total revenue,' and *epsf12*, 'Earnings per share'.

With regard to the two transformer-based models, it is a noted weakness of these models that they are not ideal at representing long sequences without fine-tuning on a downstream task. Particularly, it has been noted that the [CLS] token is likely not a good representation of the entire sequence without further task-specific training. As such, that the non-finetuned model would underperform its finetuned counterpart is to be expected.

As for the finetuned Longformer, its better-than-random performace is encouraging. This is because even though this model was finetuned on a general language understanding dataset, it resulted in embeddings which showed increased sensitivity to economic variables; i.e. finetuning is an effective means of creating representations more sensitive to the types of variables economists care about. Furthermore, it is likely the case that if a Longformer model had the benefit of further in-domain pre-training, it would significantly enhance the quality of the embeddings for this task [Gururangan *et al.*, 2020]. As such, we caution the reader against treating Longformer's poor performance relative to Doc2Vec as an indictment against Transformer models for this sort of task. Transformers have shown themselves invaluable for virtually every downstream task NLP practitioners care about, and with the proper training regimen it is entirely possible models like Longformer would be more competitive; we leave this for future work.

7 Conclusion

In this paper, we have hoped to show that the high-dimensional continuous representations common in NLP have potential for mining the sort of variables researched in economics and its neighboring discplines. Specifically, with the results above we have shown that certain continuous embedding models appear to partition their spaces in a way that correlates with certain firm-level variables. We take this as evidence of success with regard to the modest goals set out for this paper. Specifically, we hoped to show that modern algorithms and their representational techniques are sufficiently powerful to reflect the correlations of language as found in financial documents with that of certain economic variables. Furthermore, we have presented an algorithm from an outside field to aid in the resultant representations' interpretation.

References

[Araci, 2019] Dogu Araci. Finbert: Financial sentiment analysis with pre-trained language models. *arXiv preprint arXiv:1908.10063*, 2019.

[Baker *et al.*, 2016] Scott R Baker, Nicholas Bloom, and Steven J Davis. Measuring economic policy uncertainty. *The quarterly journal of economics*, 131(4):1593–1636, 2016.

[Baroni *et al.*, 2014] Marco Baroni, Georgiana Dinu, and Germán Kruszewski. Don't count, predict! a systematic comparison of context-counting vs. context-predicting semantic vectors. In *Proceedings of the 52nd Annual Meeting of the Association for Computational Linguistics (Volume 1: Long Papers)*, pages 238–247, 2014.

[Baryshnikova, 2016] Anastasia Baryshnikova. Systematic functional annotation and visualization of biological networks. *Cell systems*, 2(6):412–421, 2016.

[Beltagy *et al.*, 2020] Iz Beltagy, Matthew E Peters, and Arman Cohan. Longformer: The long-document transformer. *arXiv preprint arXiv:2004.05150*, 2020.

[Bengio *et al.*, 2003] Yoshua Bengio, Réjean Ducharme, Pascal Vincent, and Christian Jauvin. A neural probabilistic language model. *Journal of machine learning research*, 3(Feb):1137–1155, 2003.

[Child *et al.*, 2019] Rewon Child, Scott Gray, Alec Radford, and Ilya Sutskever. Generating long sequences with sparse transformers. *arXiv preprint arXiv:1904.10509*, 2019.

[Deerwester *et al.*, 1990] Scott Deerwester, Susan T Dumais, George W Furnas, Thomas K Landauer, and Richard Harshman. Indexing by latent semantic analysis. *Journal of the American society for information science*, 41(6):391–407, 1990.

[Devlin *et al.*, 2018] Jacob Devlin, Ming-Wei Chang, Kenton Lee, and Kristina Toutanova. Bert: Pre-training of deep bidirectional transformers for language understanding. *arXiv preprint arXiv:1810.04805*, 2018.

[Gururangan *et al.*, 2020] Suchin Gururangan, Ana Marasović, Swabha Swayamdipta, Kyle Lo, Iz Beltagy, Doug Downey, and Noah A Smith. Don't stop pretraining: Adapt language models to domains and tasks. *arXiv preprint arXiv:2004.10964*, 2020.

[Hassan *et al.*, 2019] Tarek A Hassan, Stephan Hollander, Laurence van Lent, and Ahmed Tahoun. Firm-level political risk: Measurement and effects. *The Quarterly Journal of Economics*, 134(4):2135–2202, 2019.

[Hassan *et al.*, 2020] Tarek Alexander Hassan, Stephan Hollander, Laurence van Lent, and Ahmed Tahoun. Firm-level exposure to epidemic diseases: Covid-19, sars, and h1n1. Technical report, National Bureau of Economic Research, 2020.

[Hiew *et al.*, 2019] Joshua Zoen Git Hiew, Xin Huang, Hao Mou, Duan Li, Qi Wu, and Yabo Xu. Bert-based financial sentiment index and lstm-based stock return predictability. *arXiv preprint arXiv:1906.09024*, 2019.

[Jones, 1972] Karen Sparck Jones. A statistical interpretation of term specificity and its application in retrieval. *Journal of documentation*, 1972.

[Joshi *et al.*, 2017] Mandar Joshi, Eunsol Choi, Daniel S Weld, and Luke Zettlemoyer. Triviaqa: A large scale distantly supervised challenge dataset for reading comprehension. *arXiv preprint arXiv:1705.03551*, 2017.

[Le and Mikolov, 2014] Quoc Le and Tomas Mikolov. Distributed representations of sentences and documents. In *International conference on machine learning*, pages 1188–1196, 2014.

[Loughran and McDonald, 2011] Tim Loughran and Bill McDonald. When is a liability not a liability? textual analysis, dictionaries, and 10-ks. *The Journal of Finance*, 66(1):35–65, 2011.

[Loughran and McDonald, 2016] Tim Loughran and Bill McDonald. Textual analysis in accounting and finance: A survey. *Journal of Accounting Research*, 54(4):1187–1230, 2016.

[Mikolov *et al.*, 2013] Tomas Mikolov, Kai Chen, Greg Corrado, and Jeffrey Dean. Efficient estimation of word representations in vector space. *arXiv preprint arXiv:1301.3781*, 2013.

[Vaswani *et al.*, 2017] Ashish Vaswani, Noam Shazeer, Niki Parmar, Jakob Uszkoreit, Llion Jones, Aidan N Gomez, Łukasz Kaiser, and Illia Polosukhin. Attention is all you need. In *Advances in neural information processing systems*, pages 5998–6008, 2017.

[Von Luxburg, 2007] Ulrike Von Luxburg. A tutorial on spectral clustering. *Statistics and computing*, 17(4):395–416, 2007.

[Wang and Manning, 2012] Sida Wang and Christopher D Manning. Baselines and bigrams: Simple, good sentiment and topic classification. In *Proceedings of the 50th annual meeting of the association for computational linguistics: Short papers-volume 2*, pages 90–94. Association for Computational Linguistics, 2012.

Using Extractive Lexicon-based Sentiment Analysis to Enhance Understanding of the Impact of Non-GAAP Measures in Financial Reporting

Stacey Taylor and Vlado Keselj

Dalhousie University, Halifax, Nova Scotia

stacey.taylor@dal.ca and vlado@cs.dal.ca,

Abstract

For some time, there has been significant disagreement as to whether financial measures that do not conform to the Generally Accepted Accounting Principles (GAAP) should be used in communication to stakeholders, as research points to these measures being used both altruistically and opportunistically. In this paper, we present a novel approach of using Sentiment Analysis to measure the impact that non-GAAP measures have on financial communication. We use an extractive approach in conjunction with the sentiment of four well known and robustly established dictionaries: General Inquirer, QDAP, Henry and Loughran-McDonald. We find that the sentiment declines once the non-GAAP measures are extracted with a statistical significance at the $p = 0.01$ level. We believe that this enhances NLP-based investment management and also has important implications for *Know Your Customer* (KYC) and text-based market provisioning.

1 Introduction

Each year, public companies are required to submit regulatory filings to the U.S. Securities and Exchange Commission (SEC) that provide information on the financial and operational health of their company. While the SEC has provided rules regarding information that must be disclosed under the *Generally Accepted Accounting Principles* (GAAP) [U.S. Securities and Exchange Commission, 2017], anything beyond that is at the discretion of the company. This leaves the company open to discuss financial measures that do not adhere to the Genereally Accepted Accounting Principles (GAAP), which means that these measures are not regulated in how they must be calculated, and are therefore not auditable. These *non-GAAP* measures are ubiquitous in the financial world, have been, and continue to be, a major source of disagreement as prior research has shown these measures to be used in beneficial and predatory ways.

There are two main beneficiaries of this research: investors who are not considered finance professionals (which we term the *average investor*) and companies who prepare the financial filings. For clarity, we define the term *finance profes-sional* in this research to broadly include professional investors, investment and financial analysts, and accountants. We also include those with no formal financial training but who have significant experience in finance and the market, as we recognize that experience and knowledge can be commensurate with training in certain cases.

Given this dispute, we designed an experiment to quantitatively determine the effects that the unregulated non-GAAP measures have on financial reports filed with the SEC. We draw on the well established and robustly proven lexica of General Inquirer, QDAP, Henry, and Loughran-McDonald, using the first two as proxies for average investors, and the latter two as proxies for financially savvy investors. We demonstrate that when non-GAAP measure sentences are extracted, the aggregate sentiment of our sample decreases with statistical significance at the $p = 0.01$ level.

To the best of our knowledge, this *extractive* approach has not been used before in sentiment analysis of financial reports. We see this research as an important step to learning how to better protect the average investor from making poor decision based on measures that can easily obfuscate the information presented. We believe that this will contribute to and enhance NLP-based investment management, as well as have important implications for *Know Your Customer* (KYC) and text-based market provisioning.

The rest of our paper is organized in the following manner: Section 2 provides a discussion of the related work; Section 3 addresses our research design, hypotheses, lexical dictionaries used, as well as the distribution of the data; Section 4 discusses our results and why this research is important; and in Section 5, we provide our conclusion and present some directions for future work.

2 Related Work

Even though non-GAAP measures are not regulated, they have become mainstays of the financial narrative used by companies when communicating to stakeholders. One overarching concern is that by further adjusting audited figures, a company asserts that actual performance differed from audited performance — which in some cases can create an unaudited gain out of an audited loss. Consequently, researchers have determined that non-GAAP measures are influential, deceptive, and can fool the average investor [Young, 2014; Fisher, 2016; Asay *et al.*, 2018]. Written corporate

Proceedings of the Second Workshop on Financial Technology and Natural Language Processing

communication is crafted carefully and purposefully in terms of what information is provided or omitted. It is also designed to evoke emotional responses, and guide decision-making — the effects of which the decision-maker, themselves, may be unaware of. Research has also found that companies employ significant latitude in tone to mitigate bad news by reframing it in a positive light [Kang *et al.*, 2018; Li, 2006; Loughran and Mcdonald, 2011].

Most Natural Language Processing (NLP) approaches to finance have been sentiment analysis or other forms of text categorization, based on the use of dictionaries (lexica) — developed word lists of positive, negative, and neutral words, as well as other categories such as uncertainty, litigious, and modal [Henry, 2008; Loughran and Mcdonald, 2011].

Kang *et al.* studied the relationship between firm performance and the tone of the 10-K (SEC filing). One of the foci of their research was determining if there was an "overtone" (inflated positivity) or an "undertone" (less robust positivity) in the text. They used the ordinary least squares regression model and a firm cluster-robust regression model. Their results showed a correlation between sentiment and performance, and that companies that overstate positivity in their financial narratives are less able to deliver on the company's expected future performance. The study also found that investors either do not understand or struggle to fully comprehend the underlying overtone and its true meaning [Kang *et al.*, 2018].

Butler and Keselj evaluated how generating readability indices for corporate annual reports can be used to make class predictions. Using Perl, they created three well known readability indicies for each annual report: Flesch, Flesch-Kinkaid, and Gunning-Fog. Five features were used in the classification — the three readability indices and two financial performance measures from the preceding year. This data was scaled and transformed in order to be used with Support Vector Machines. Results show that their model outperformed previous n-gram techniques and portfolio benchmarks (S&P index), thereby creating more efficient trades. Their approach also offered textual insight related to a company's forecasted performance [Butler and Keselj, 2009].

Jegadeesh *et al.* identified that previous research has considered positive and negative words equal in weighting. To address this, they used the market's reaction to corporate annual reports to determine the weighting that was assigned to each word in an effort to provide a more realistic weighting for each word. They believed this approach provided a much more accurate sentiment evaluation [Jegadeesh and Wu, 2013]. Finally, Sarderlich *et al.'s* work focused on building a novel financial lexcion based on Yahoo Message Stock Boards to determine new weightings for financial terms. They found a strong bias towards positive words — either due to wishful thinking or overconfidence on the part of participants on the message board. Using a sparse vector space model which considers each term in a separate dimension, they developed a "bag of semantic orientation" model that is specific to market terminology (long, short, put call, etc.). In taking this approach, they were able to extend existing lexica and capture both the formal and informal language used in stock trading to better classify documents [Sarderlich and Kazakov,

2018].

3 Research Design

The purpose of this research is to quantitatively measure the effect that non-GAAP measures have on the tone of the Management Discussion and Analysis and Market Risks sections of the annual 10-K and quarterly 10-Q reports filed with the SEC. Our sample dataset comprised 100 randomly selected 10-K and 10-Q reports from each quarter from 1998 to 2019. We drew these samples from the dataset maintained by Bill McDonald [McDonald, 2019]. This gave us a dataset of 10,000 SEC filings.

We followed the main ideas for text pre-processing, extraction, and sentiment analysis from a related *forthcoming* paper [Taylor and Keselj, 2020]. Although the reporting to the SEC is standardized, the format and naming conventions are not. Therefore, parsing out the Management Discussion and Analysis proved to be a significant challenge as it is listed in the Table of Contents, could be listed at the top of each page of the report that contained parts of that section, or could go by other names such as *Financial Review and Analysis, Business Outlook*, or *Management's Financial Discusison*, for example. To address this challenge, we used Python's *file read backwards* package to ensure that the first time Python encountered Management's Discussion and the Market Risks would be the actual section itself, rather than a page header or listing in the Table of Contents.

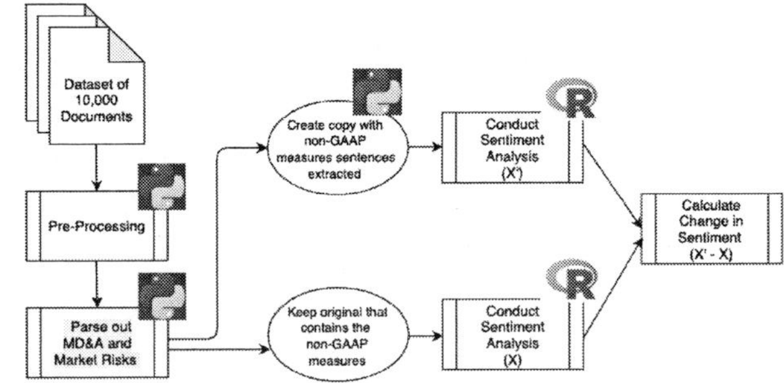

Figure 1: Sentiment Experiment Setup

Sentences that contained any of the following non-GAAP measures were then extracted, using a Python script:

- Revised Net Income
- Earnings Before Interest and Taxes (EBIT)
- Earnings Before Interest, Taxes, and Depreciation (EBITDA)
- Earnings Before Interest, Taxes, Depreciation, Amortization, and Rent/Restructuring (EBITDAR)
- Adjusted Earnings Per Share
- Free Cash Flow (FCF)
- Core Earnings
- Funds From Operations (FFO)
- Unbilled Revenue

- Return on Capital Employed (ROCE)
- Non-GAAP
- Reconciliation

Note: Commonly accepted name variations of these measures, as well as "Adjusted" or "Revised" variations were also included, along with the term "Reconciliation", which is required when companies use non-GAAP measures.

3.1 Lexical Dictionaries and Sentiment Analysis

We used four dictionaries for our sentiment analysis, each providing scores that range from -1 to 1. The first two dictionaries used, the General Inquirer and the QDAP, are all-purpose dictionaries that are not targeted towards any specific domain. As such, we believe that these act as good proxies for the average investor. The remaining two dictionaries, Henry and Loughran-McDonald, are specifically targeted to the domain of finance, and as such, are good proxies for the financially savvy. The change in sentiment between the reports containing the non-GAAP measures and those without was then calculated as $[X' - X]$.

The Harvard-IV General Inquirer is a general psychological dictionary. Financial words such as loans and taxes are considered negative [Zimmerman, 1987] We believe that this is a reasonable proxy for the average investor as they, too, would interpret words such as loans and taxes as negative terms. The other general purpose dictionary that, for similar reasons, we believe is a reasonable proxy for the average investor is QDAP. This dictionary has some degree of overlap with the Harvard dictionary as it includes a subset of the Harvard-IV, but also includes words that target opinion mining, government data, and words by reading level [Rinker, 2018].

We selected two well known financial dictionaries, Henry and Loughran-McDonald, as representative of the financially savvy, who have either significant experience in the market/finance, or who have financial training. The Henry dictionary is very small in comparison to Loughran-McDonald, however, but focuses on descriptive words such as "deteriorate" (negative) or "improved" (positive) to characterize the financial terms [Henry, 2008]. This approach provides a robust bridge between a highly financially oriented dictionary and one that is general purpose. Conversely, Loughran-McDonald's dictionary is quite large and is continually being adjusted to keep up with the evolution and dynamism of language. Words such as loans and taxes are assigned a sentiment of 0 in this dictionary [Loughran and Mcdonald, 2011], as contextualization is needed to determine if these words are negative or positive. As such, we believe that this fairly represents the analytical approach that finance professionals would take. As Henry and Loughran-McDonald each take different approaches to their financial lexica, there is no overlap between the dictionaries.

3.2 Data Distribution

Before conducting any statistical tests, we looked at the histograms to determine if our dataset was parametric or non-parametric, as the result would dictate the statistical testing that could be used.

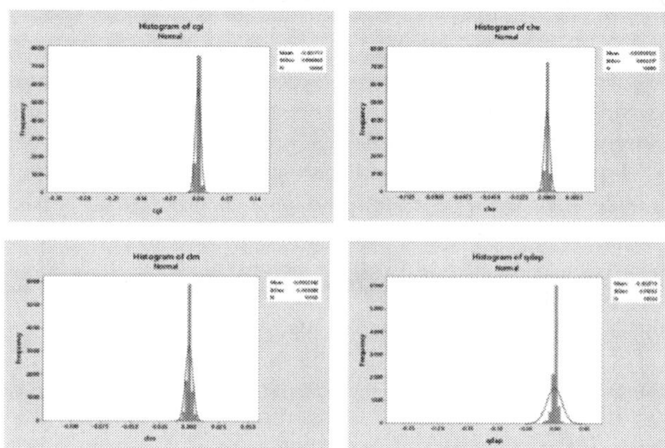

Figure 2: Dataset Histograms for Each Dictionary

As the histograms in Figure 2 showed normal distribution of the data for each dictionary, we were able to use a paired t-test to evaluate the statistical significance for each dictionary.

3.3 Hypotheses

We developed two research hypotheses to examine the effect of the non-GAAP measures:

Hypothesis 1 *Overall Aggregated Tone*

There is a significant body of existing research that supports the perspective that non-GAAP measures are used opportunistically in order to positively impact the tone of the Management Discussion and Analysis and Market Risks in order to influence investor decision-making. If the non-GAAP measures were not as positively influential as researchers have found, we would expect the tone change, calculated as $[X' - X]$, to either be zero (or close to it) or to increase once the sentences containing the non-GAAP measures were removed. We examine this hypothesis on a dictionary-by-dictionary basis, using Harvard-IV and QDAP as proxies for the average investor (without financial training) and Henry and Loughran-McDonald as proxies for those with financial training or significant investment training. Taking this approach allows us to capture how the two different groups of investors will interpret the sentiment of the non-GAAP measures, giving us quantitative insight on how influential (or not) these measures are.

Therefore, when the tone changes for each dictionary have been aggregated for all 10,000 reports, we postulate that the aggregated tone will decrease:
Null Hypothesis: The aggregate tone of the dictionary under evaluation is ≥ 0.
Alternative Hypothesis: The aggregate tone of the dictionary under evaluation is < 0.

Hypothesis 2 *Statistical Significance*

Another aspect to our main research question of quantifying the effects of non-GAAP measures is to determine if the results in our *Aggregated Tone* hypothesis are explainable by chance alone. As we are using two related samples, one with non-GAAP measures and one without, we use a paired t-test to examine the paired observations. If the probability results from the paired t-test are greater than $\alpha = 0.05$, then any differences observed could be explained by chance. If they are equal to or less than $\alpha = 0.05$, then the differences are not from chance alone, and we can, therefore, infer with statistical significance that the difference is a result of removing the non-GAAP measure sentences.

Therefore, we postulate that the aggregated changes in the mean for each dictionary will be less than 0, and will be statistically significant at $\alpha = 0.05$.

Null Hypothesis: After extraction, the mean (μ) of the tone change for the dictionary under evaluation $= 0$.

Alternative Hypothesis: After extraction, the mean (μ) of the tone change for the dictionary under evaluation < 0.

Note: In conducting these tests, we used a 95% confidence interval to evaluate our hypothesis.

4 Results and Why This Is Important

Hypothesis 1: Figure 3 below provides the aggregate totals of the tone change for each dictionary for 10,000 documents over 100 experiments. As can be seen, the *aggregate* tone change for each dictionary is negative, meaning that the sentiment decreased in tone once the non-GAAP measures (and the supporting words) were extracted. The most pronounced negative results are for the two dictionaries that were used as proxies for the average investor. The results show that once the non-GAAP measure sentences have been extracted from the text, the aggregate sentiment score for General Inquirer and QDAP have dropped sharply, as the change in the sentiment scores are -17.57297 and -27.13332 respectively. We can therefore infer that, from the point of view of the average investor, that the text including the non-GAAP measures is much more positive (and therefore influential) than the text that does not include the non-GAAP measures. This also demonstrates that average investors are very sensitive to financially oriented words that are used in conjunction with the discussions of the non-GAAP measures.

It is also notable that change in the sentiment scores for the financially oriented dictionaries of Henry and Loughran-McDonald also show that once the non-GAAP sentences have been extracted, the change in the tone has dropped by -0.81217 and -2.36182 respectively. While this is not as sharp a decrease as for the general purpose dictionaries, it is a decrease nonetheless. These results indicate that even the financially oriented dictionaries recognize that there is inflation of positivity in the text when the non-GAAP measures are included in the text. These results also strongly suggest that savvy investors are not as influenced by non-GAAP measures as average investors.

The results of the Henry dictionary is barely negative which may raise questions as to if the inflationary assertion still holds for the dictionary; we believe it does. The Henry dictionary's focus is on descriptive words that are used in finance such as "growth", "opportunity", "declining", and "deteriorated" [Feuerriegel and Proellochs, 2019], not on the fi-

Experiment Number	Report Quarter	cgi	cqdap	che	clm
100	Q3-18	-0.0101182	-0.0074967	-0.000153	0.002228726
100	Q3-18	-0.00148	0.00104623	-2.52E-05	-0.00411334
100	Q3-18	0.00401739	0.00011235	0.0005106	0.000758538
100	Q3-18	-0.0025215	0.00049252	-0.00172	0.002472894
100	Q3-18	0.00270776	0.00243339	-0.001678	0.000373329
100	Q3-18	0.00246886	-5.053E-05	0.000188	-0.00127438
100	Q3-18	-0.0048782	-0.0050087	-0.000422	0.000396483
100	Q3-18	-0.0080319	-0.0061931	0.000152	0.001665008
AGGREGATE TOTALS		-17.57297	-27.13332	-0.81217	-2.36182

change = X' - X, where:

cgi = change in tone for the General Inquirer;

cqdap = change in tone for the QDAP dictionaries;

che = change in tone for Henry; and

clm = change in tone for Loughran-McDonald

Figure 3: Aggregate Sentiment Results

nancial words themselves such as "debt" or "interest". Based on the evidence of the experiments, these descriptive words have been used as supporting words for non-GAAP measures. We can also infer that, based on the results, that sufficient positive descriptive words have been used with the non-GAAP measures that, when removed, have returned an overall decrease in the sentiment, thereby reinforcing that the inflationary assertion still holds.

We also looked at the distribution of the non-GAAP measures over the 100 experiments performed. We first looked at the distribution of the first half of the dataset, up to the 4th quarter of 2005. As can be seen in Figure 4 below, the three most prevalent non-GAAP measures are Earnings Before Interest, Tax, Depreciation, and Amortization (EBITDA), Earnings Before Interest and Tax (EBIT), and Free Cash Flow (FCF).

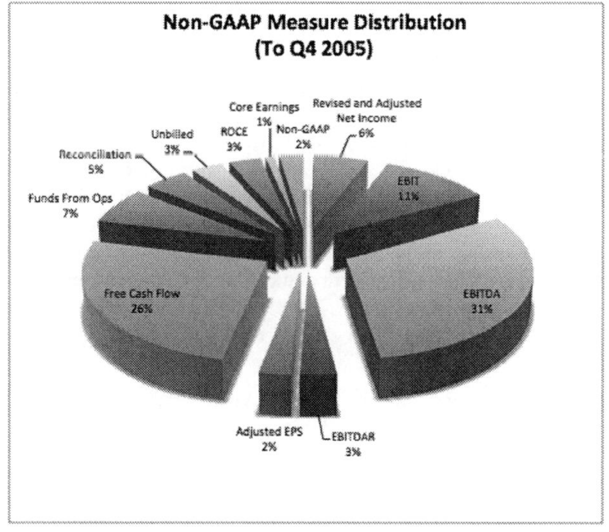

Figure 4: Sentiment Results for the First Half of the Experiments

Over time, however, we see that the use of non-GAAP measures is growing, but the distribution is changing. When we compare the midway results with the overall results (Figure 5), we find that while Earnings before Interest, Tax, Depreciation and Amortization (EBITDA), Earnings before Iterest and Tax (EBIT), and Free Cash Flow (FCF) are still the three main non-GAAP measures used, the percentages for EBITDA and Free Cash Flow have decreased by 6% and 4% respectively, while EBIT has grown by 8%, seen in Figure 5, below.

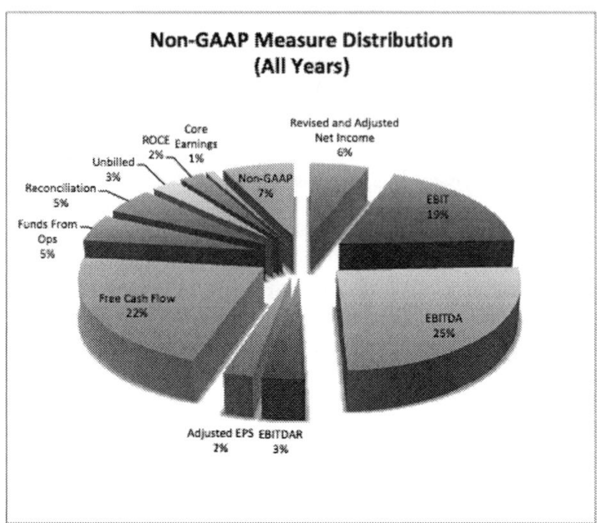

Figure 5: Sentiment Results for All Experiments

The increase in EBIT and simultaneous decrease in EBITDA suggests that companies are changing their communication strategy. In recent years, the SEC has scrutinized the use of EBITDA as companies were including extra adjustments (beyond just interest, tax, depreciation and amortization). Examples include "Further Adjusted EBITDA" or "Structring Adjusted EBITDA" [Scraggs and Powell, 2018]. Therefore, using EBIT instead draws far less attention to the company's reporting than does EBITDA.

With respect to FCF, the SEC has warned companies about using this measure, as it can be very misleading. The word "Free", for example, has a tremendous effect on the average investor, and is seen as a positive word in both General Inquirer and QDAP. The Henry and Loughran-McDonald dictionaries show no effect, as it requires contextualization in order to determine if "Free" is positive or negative. So, we can infer from the drop in the use of FCF that companies are, again, changing their communication strategy in order to draw less regulatory attention.

There are several alternative plausible reasons for the change in the use of these financial measures, however, that should be discussed. The change could be driven by the companies that were included in the random sample. If more capital and intangible intensive companies were included in experiments 50-100, then those types of companies will prefer to use EBIT as it is a better proxy for cash flow. The SEC also requires that companies compare and reconcile the non-GAAP measure with the closest GAAP measure. EBIT is usually compared to the GAAP measure of Net Income, as the reconciliation is straightforward, only needing to show the difference of interest and taxes. Depending on the adjustments a company makes to EBITDA or FCF, though, it can be harder to find a GAAP measure for comparability. So this too could explain the increase in using EBIT as a non-GAAP measure.

PricewaterhouseCoopers LLP (PWC) (2019) has indicated that there has been a substantial increase in the usage of non-GAAP measures when comparing today's reporting with that of twenty years ago. PWC also indicates that nearly all of the companies listed on the Standard & Poor 500 (better known as the S&P 500) use at least one non-GAAP measure. This is consistent with the change that is seen between Figures 4 and 5.

Hypothesis 2:Using the same four dictionaries, we tested the statistical significance using a paired t-test, given that the distribution of the data for each dictionary was normal. We had hypothesized that the change in the mean of each dictionary, when we considered $[X' - X]$, that the change would be negative for each dictionary. As seen below in Table 1, the results for each dictionary were determined to be statistically significant at the 0.01 level, meaning that there is a 1% risk that we could incorrectly conclude that there is a difference where none exists.

Dictionary	Number of Samples	Mean	Std Deviation	T-Value	P-value
GI	10,000	−0.001757	0.006865	−25.6	<0.001*
QDAP	10,000	−0.00272	0.012801	−21.25	<0.001*
HE	10,000	−0.000081	0.002217	−3.66	<0.001*
LM	10,000	−0.000236	0.003083	−7.66	<0.001*

Table 1: Paired T-Test Results

We see that over 10,000 samples, that all of the dictionaries are statistically significant. This draws attention to the importance of language. As we have extracted both the non-GAAP measures as well as the supporting words in the sentence, we see that the non-GAAP measures are having a pronounced effect for both the non-financial and the financial dictionaries, which act as proxies for the two different types of investors we identified. This is an important finding given that regardless of motive for use, there is a quantifiable effect.

This could have tremndous ramifications on NLP-based investment management, touching on all aspects ranging from due diligence to portfolio selection and maintenance, to client reporting, as prominent companies look to natural language processing (NLP) to aid in these tasks [Xy, 2019; Deloitte, nd]. Training data including non-GAAP measures without proper contextualization or understanding of the sentiment could affect the way that the system functions, which could also affect the way that the system is tested and ultimately evaluated [Bender and Friedman, 2019]

4.1 Inter-Domain Integration

Although our paper was focused on NLP-based investment management, in the finance and business domains, non-GAAP measures are ubiquitous. This creates opportunities for our approach to be applied and integrated into different, but highly related streams of the FinTech. The first stream that we believe would benefit from our approach is text-based market provisioning. According to the World Economic Forum (WEF), key disruptive trends centre around Artificial Intelligence, Big Data, and Machine Learning [World Economic Forum and Deloitte, 2015]. Using non-GAAP extraction as we have described can help provide better due diligence on companies, which could improve algorithms used to gain insights into the market, as well as those used for processing machine-readable news feeds [World Economic Forum and Deloitte, 2015]. We have also addressed that market participants fall into two main categories — those with financial expertise and those without. Our extractive technique can also be used in for reducing risk as part of a *Know Your Customer (KYC)* approach. One important aspect to the creation and maintenance of an investment portfolio is risk tolerance. Research has shown that risk tolerance is affected by financial literacy [Caratelli and Ricci, 2011; Gentile *et al.*, 2016; Kramer, 2016], which our paper helps to reinforce. Better understanding the influence of non-GAAP measures on investors' perceptions will help investment managers better meet the needs of clients who lack sufficient financial literacy, as well as help to avoid the inclusion of securities with a high chance of facing a class action lawsuit, thereby reducing risk to the client.

5 Conclusion

In this paper, we have presented a novel use of sentiment analysis that extracts non-GAAP measure sentences in order to quantify the effect that non-rule based accounting measures have on financial reporting in the Management Discussion & Analysis and Market Risks section of the 10-K and 10-Q reports filed with the SEC. We found that once the non-GAAP measure sentences have been removed from our sample, the sentiment declines with a statistical significance at the $p = 0.01$ level. We believe that this enhances NLP-based investment management and also has important implications for Know Your Customer (KYC) and text-based market provisioning.

5.1 Future Work

The approach that we have described has opened up new avenues of research, particularly in the areas of Know Your Customer (KYC) and Text-Based Market Provisioning. We see applying our method to those areas a natural *next step* for our research. Also, as we only applied this to the 10-K and 10-Q filings submitted to the U.S. SEC, we believe that extending this approach to financial filings to regulatory bodies (similar to the SEC) in other countries would be valuable.

References

[Asay *et al.*, 2018] H. Scott Asay, Robert Libby, and Kristina Rennekamp. Firm performance, reporting goals, and language choices in narrative disclosures. *Journal of Accounting and Economics*, 65(2–3):380–398, 2018.

[Bender and Friedman, 2019] E. Bender and B Friedman. Data statements for natural language processing: Toward mitigating system bias and enabling better science. *Transactions of the Association for Computational Linguistics*, 2019.

[Butler and Keselj, 2009] Matthew Butler and Vlado Keselj. Financial forecasting using character n-gram analysis and readability scores of annual reports. In *Proceedings of Canadian AI'2009*, Kelowna, BC, Canada, May 2009.

[Caratelli and Ricci, 2011] M. Caratelli and O. Ricci. *The Relationship between Everyday Practices and Financial Literacy: An Empirical Analysis*, 2011.

[Deloitte, nd] Deloitte. *Artificial intelligence — The next frontier for investment management firms*, n.d.

[Feuerriegel and Proellochs, 2019] Stefan Feuerriegel and Nicolas Proellochs. *Package SentimentAnalysis*, 2019.

[Fisher, 2016] Alex Fisher. *Non-GAAP Measures — A 20-Year Echo*, 2016.

[Gentile *et al.*, 2016] M. Gentile, N. Linciano, and P. Soccorso. *Financial advice seeking, financial knowledge and overconfidence*, 2016.

[Henry, 2008] E. Henry. Are investors influenced by how earnings press releases are written? *The Journal of Business Communication*, 45:363–407, 2008.

[Jegadeesh and Wu, 2013] N. Jegadeesh and D. Wu. Word power: A new approach for content analysis. *Journal of Financial Economics*, 110:712–729, 2013.

[Kang *et al.*, 2018] Taeyoung Kang, Do-Hyung Park, and In-goo Han. Beyond the numbers: The effect of 10-k tone on firms' performance predictions using text analytics. *Telematics and Informatics*, 35(2):370–381, 2018.

[Kramer, 2016] M. Kramer. Financial literacy, confidence and financial advice seeking. *Journal of Economic Behavior & Organization*, 2016.

[Li, 2006] Feng Li. *Do Stock Market Investors Understand the Risk Sentiment of Corporate Annual Reports?*, 2006.

[Loughran and Mcdonald, 2011] Tim Loughran and Bill Mcdonald. When is a liability not a liability? textual analysis, dictionaries, and 10-ks. *The Journal of Finance*, 66(1):35–65, 2011.

[McDonald, 2019] Bill McDonald. *Loughran-McDonald 10X File Summaries*, 2019.

[Rinker, 2018] Tyler Rinker. *Package qdapDictionaries*, 2018.

[Sarderlich and Kazakov, 2018] M. Sarderlich and D. Kazakov. Extending the loughran and mcdonald financial sentiment words list from 10-k corporate filings using social media texts. *Proceedings of the 11th LREC Conference on Language Resources and Evaluation in Workshop on Financial Narratives*, 2018.

[Scraggs and Powell, 2018] Alexandra Scraggs and Jamie Powell. *Structuring adjusted ebitda now exists*, 2018.

[Taylor and Keselj, 2020] Stacey Taylor and Vlado Keselj. e-commerce and sentiment analysis: Predicting outcomes of class action lawsuits. In *Proceedings of the Third EC-NLP Workshop (ACL) on Financial Technology and Natural Language Processing*, 2020.

[U.S. Securities and Exchange Commission, 2017] U.S. Securities and Exchange Commission. *Topic 6 — Foreign Private Issuers & Foreign Businesses*, 2017.

[World Economic Forum and Deloitte, 2015] World Economic Forum and Deloitte. *The Future of Financial Services*, 2015.

[Xy, 2019] Jingya Xy. *How NLP Is Advancing Asset Management*, 2019.

[Young, 2014] Steven Young. The drivers, consequences and policy implications of non-GAAP earnings reporting. *Accounting and Business Research*, 44(4):444–465, 2014.

[Zimmerman, 1987] D. Patrick Zimmerman. Effects of computer conferencing on the language use of emotionally disturbed adolescents. *Behavior Research Methods, Instruments, & Computers*, 19(2):224–230, Mar 1987.

FinSBD-2020: The 2nd Shared Task on Sentence Boundary Detection in Unstructured Text in the Financial Domain

Willy Au, Bianca Chong, Abderrahim Ait Azzi, Dialekti Valsamou-Stanislawski

Fortia Financial Solutions, France

{willy.au, bianca.chong, abderrahim.aitazzi, dialekti.valsamou}@fortia.fr

Abstract

In this paper, we present the results and findings of FinSBD-2020, the 2nd shared task on Sentence Boundary Detection in unstructured text of PDFs in the Financial Domain. This shared task was organized as part of the 2nd Workshop on Financial Technology and Natural Language Processing (FinNLP) of the conference IJCAI-PRICAI 2020. This second edition differs from its predecessor by introducing list structure extraction. Participating systems aimed at detecting boundaries of sentences, lists and list items by marking their beginning and ending boundaries in the text extracted from financial prospectuses. In addition, systems were also tasked to determine the hierarchy level of each item in its list. 5 teams from 4 countries participated (4 of which submitted a paper) in this shared task using different approaches.

1 Introduction

Sentences are arguably the most foundational units of language and are at the core of Natural Language Processing (NLP) architectures. Sentence Boundary Detection (SBD) has become fundamental as the first pre-processing step to high-level tasks in any Natural Language Processing (NLP) application, parsing textual data from a string of characters into linguistic segments (sentences).

Issues around SBD have not received much attention and most research has been confined to clean texts in standard reading formats such as the news and limited datasets such as the WSJ corpus [1] or the Brown corpus [2].

The first FinSBD [3] task aimed to provide further research on the issue of noise in machine-readable formats such as PDFs. The financial sector is one of many that uses PDFs as an integral form of documentation. Most PDF-to-text conversion tools introduce noise in the form of missing, erroneous, unordered characters and obstructing texts (from tables, page footers and page headers). Moreover, financial documents often use full-stop punctuation in various ways. For example, section numbers and enumerated items (e.g. "1.", "2.") and abbreviations (e.g. "S.A.", "LTD.") all contain periods. Consequently, applying out-of-the-box SBD tools can often yield inaccurate sentence boundaries (i.e., Stanford sentence segmenter[4], spaCy[5], NLTK[6]). In order to function optimally, these tools require tinkering with inner heuristics based on punctuation, syntax and sometimes semantics.

However, what the first FinSBD did not address were the obstacles concerning text appearance and physical position within a document, especially in structuring text into units in the form of lists. Lists are a visual hierarchy of information that organizes data-rich documents into more easily read blocks. Simple lists containing two or three enumerated items may be restructured into sentences (Figure 1), but the notion of a "sentence" becomes lost when lists contain multiple sentences, paragraphs, or lists within the list (Figure 2). Boundaries of such structures are often undetectable with simple rule-based approaches that depend on sentence-ending punctuation.

Existing tools of SBD are unreliable when given unstructured text. They do no account for text position within a document page where visual information allows us to understand whether the text belongs to the document structure (e.g. page footers, page headers, footnotes, etc.) or structured information (e.g. lists, tables, titles, etc.). Extraction of such unstructured text results in incomplete sentences or multiple sentences embedded in a sentence. This hinders the performance of NLP application (i.e. POS tagging, information extraction, machine translation, etc.) which expects a well-formatted and grammatical sentence of which boundaries are clear [7].

For this reason, this year's task differs from its predecessor by introducing boundary detection on lists and list items, including a subtask for identifying each item's level in its list. Understanding the position of text in structures such as lists is essential for SBD in segmenting characters not only into sentences but into semantic units.

In this shared task, we first focus on extracting well-segmented sentences, lists and and list items from text originating from financial prospectuses by detecting and marking their beginning and ending boundaries. Secondly, we focus on determining the depth level of each item in its list. These prospectuses are official PDF documents in which investment funds precisely describe their characteristics and investment modalities.

In this paper we report the results and findings of the FinSBD-2020 shared task. The shared task was organized as part of The Second Workshop on Financial Technology and Natural Language Processing (FinNLP)[1], collocated with IJCAI-PRICAI-2020. A total of 5 teams from 4 countries submitted runs and contributed 4 system description papers. All system description papers are included in the FinNLP workshop proceedings and cited in this report.

This paper is structured as follows: Section 2 describes previous work on SBD, Section 3 describes the task, Section 4 describes the shared task data, Section 5 describes the participants and their proposed systems, Section 6 describes the results and discussion and finally, Section 7 finishes the paper with conclusions.

Les revenus sont constitués par :
- les revenus des valeurs mobilières,
- les dividendes et intérêts encaissés au taux de la devise, pour les valeurs étrangères,
- la rémunération des liquidités en devises, les revenus de prêts et pensions de titres et autres placements.

Figure 1: Simple list

Le calcul de la valeur liquidative de la part est effectué en tenant compte des règles d'évaluation précisées ci-dessous :

- Les valeurs mobilières négociées sur un marché réglementé français ou étranger, sont évaluées au prix du marché. L'évaluation au prix du marché de référence est effectuée selon les modalités arrêtées au dernier cours de bourse.

  Les différences entre les cours de Bourse utilisés lors du calcul de la valeur liquidative et les coûts historiques des valeurs mobilières constituant le portefeuille, sont enregistrées dans un compte "Différences d'estimation".

  Toutefois :

  - Les valeurs mobilières dont le cours n'a pas été constaté le jour de l'évaluation ou dont le cours a été corrigé sont évaluées à leur valeur probable de négociation sous la responsabilité de la Société de gestion. Ces évaluations et leur justification sont communiquées au commissaire aux comptes à l'occasion de ses contrôles.

  - Les Titres de Créances Négociables et assimilés sont évalués de façon actuarielle sur la base d'un taux de référence défini ci-dessous, majoré le cas échéant d'un écart représentatif des caractéristiques intrinsèques de l'émetteur :

    - TCN dont l'échéance est inférieure ou égale à 1 an : Taux interbancaire offert en euros (Euribor)
    - TCN swapés : valorisés selon la courbe OIS (Overnight Indexed Swaps)
    - les TCN d'une durée de vie supérieure à trois mois (OPC monétaires) : valorisés selon la courbe OIS (Overnight Indexed Swaps)
    - TCN dont l'échéance est supérieure à 1 an : Taux des Bons du Trésor à intérêts Annuels Normalisés (BTAN) ou taux de l'OAT (Obligations Assimilables du Trésor) de maturité proche pour les durées les plus longues.

    Les Titres de Créances Négociables d'une durée de vie résiduelle inférieure ou égale à 3 mois pourront être évalués selon la méthode linéaire.

    Les bons du Trésor sont valorisés au taux du marché, communiqué quotidiennement par les Spécialistes en Valeurs du Trésor.

  - Les parts ou actions d'OPC sont évaluées à la dernière valeur liquidative connue.

- Les titres qui ne sont pas négociés sur un marché réglementé sont évalués sous la responsabilité de la Société de gestion à leur valeur probable de négociation. Ils sont évalués en utilisant des méthodes fondées sur la valeur patrimoniale et le rendement, en prenant en considération les prix retenus lors de transactions significatives récentes. Les parts ou actions de fonds d'investissement sont évaluées à la dernière valeur liquidative connue ou, le cas échéant, sur la base d'estimations disponibles sous le contrôle et la responsabilité de la Société de Gestion.

Figure 2: Complex list

2   Previous Work on SBD

SBD has been largely explored following several approaches that could be classified into three major classes: (a) rule-based SBD, using hand-crafted heuristics and lists [8]; (b) machine learning approaches such as Naïve Bayes and Support Vector Machine (SVM) based models as reviewed in [2], decision tree classifiers [9] and the Punkt unsupervised model [10]; and more recently (c) deep learning methods [11]. Most of these approaches give fairly accurate results and prove to be highly accurate for most domain language data (e.g. clean collections of news articles). However, these systems are

based on a number of assumptions [8] that do not hold for noisy, unstructured text extracted automatically from PDFs.

Read et al., [7] proposed a survey of publicly-available SBD systems such as CoreNLP, tokenizer, RASP and others. They evaluated several systems on a variety of datasets and report a performance decrease when moving from corpora with formal language to those with less formal language. Such designing and implementation customized to different domains has attracted the attention of several researchers. Griffis et al. [12] evaluated popular off-the-shelf NLP toolkits on the task of SBD for a set of corpora in the clinical domain. López and Pardo [13] tackle SBD on informal user-generated content such as web reviews, comments, and posts. Rudrapal et al,. [14] presented a study on SBD in a social media context. SBD from speech transcriptions has also gained much attention due to the necessity of finding sentential segments in transcripts created by automatized recognition. Carlos-Emiliano et al [15] tackled the problem of SBD as binary classification applied on an expansive written dataset (French Gigaword), an ASR transcription corpus. They focused on deep learning methods such as Convolutional Neural Networks to handle the task.

There are few papers that directly explore the problem of segmenting lists with items. Savelka et al. [16] treated the SBD problem in Adjudicatory Decisions [2], legal documents with a complex structures similar to prospectuses. They also conducted an analysis on tagging strategies of sentences and list of items, proposing several tags with which they then applied rule-base SBD systems such as OpenNLP and other trainable systems such as CRF (Lafferty et al., 2001; Liu et al., 2005; Okazaki, 2007) that prove to perform better on this kind of task. George Sanchez[17] worked on the same dataset, and explored the use of Punkt unsupervised model [10], CRF, and BiLSTM algorithm. They treated the problem as a sequence labeling task to predict the beginning and the end of sentences.

3   Task Description

The FinSBD-2020 shared task is an extension of FinSBD-2019, with the addition of list and list items boundaries. We have included lists and items due to their unique structure and common occurrence in financial documents. The first subtask consists of detecting the boundaries of three types of text segments: sentences, lists and list items. The second subtask requires distinguishing the hierarchy depth level of each item in its list. Each item can be assigned a depth level of 1, 2, 3 or 4.

The shared task provided a corpus of annotated data allowing supervised approaches. The annotated prospectuses were split into a train set and a hidden test set used for evaluating submitted systems. We provided one JSON file for each PDF (i.e. Figure 3) with the following keys:

- **text**: whole text extracted from the document
- **sentence**: boundaries of sentences
- **list**: boundaries of list
- **item**: boundaries of list items

{
    "text": "... The risk management team of the Management Company may impose stricter criteria in terms of financial \nguarantees received and thereby exclude certain types of instruments, certain countries, certain issuers or even \ncertain securities. \n \nc) Level of financial guarantee \n \n The Management Company has put in place a policy which requires a level of financial guarantee based on the \ntype of transactions as follows: \n\uf0a7\n securities lending transactions: 105% of the value of the assets transferred; \n\uf0a7\n repurchase agreements and reverse repurchase agreements: 100% of the value of the assets transferred; \n\uf0a7\n OTC financial derivative instruments: In OTC financial transactions, some sub-funds may cover operations by \nmaking cash margin calls in the currency of the sub-fund in accordance with the restrictions laid down in \nclause 7.1 of the present Prospectus as regards the counterparty risk. ...",

    "sentence": [... {"start": 66281, "end": 66546}, {"start": 66550, "end": 66582} ...],
    "list": [... {"start": 66587, "end": 67246} ...],
    "item": [... {"start": 66753, "end": 66830}, {"start": 66836, "end": 66937}, {"start": 66943, "end": 67246} ...],
    "item1": [... {"start": 66753, "end": 66830}, {"start": 66836, "end": 66937}, {"start": 66943, "end": 67246} ...],
    "item2": [...],
    "item3": [...],
    "item4": [...]
}

Figure 3: Example of a truncated JSON of a simple list with items of depth level 1 (actual JSON is composed of many more boundaries and the whole text from the document)

- **item1**: boundaries of list items of depth 1
- **item2**: boundaries of list items of depth 2
- **item3**: boundaries of list items of depth 3
- **item4**: boundaries of list items of depth 4

A boundary consists of a pair of integer indexes marking the starting and ending character of well-formed text segments (see Figure 3). Item depth level is the hierarchy level of the list to which the item belongs. Subtask 1 focuses on the detection of the boundaries of *sentence*, *list* and *item*. Subtask 2 focuses on detecting the boundaries of *item1*, *item2*, *item3* and *item4*. Note that *item* boundaries are equal to the union of all boundaries of items of different levels, *item = item1 ∪ item2 ∪ item3 ∪ item4*. Therefore, subtask 2 can be formulated as classifying *item* boundaries into 4 classes.

One important detail is that the provided text was not pre-tokenized whereas in the first FinSBD, the text was already pre-tokenized at the word level. We hoped to encourage diverse approaches by not constraining participants to one type of word tokenization. Boundary indexes correspond to the character index and systems should predict pairs of character indexes as boundaries. Coordinates of each character were also provided in a separate JSON file for each PDF to encourage the creation of multi-modal system exploiting both textual and positional information. Each character's coordinates is referenced by its index in the text.

4 Shared Task Data

Next, we discuss the corpora used for the English and French subtasks.

4.1 Corpus annotation

For FinSBD-2019, annotated data for SBD was created by using Pdf2text and Brat tools [3]. Due to the many limitations of Brat (e.g. lack of visual cues, dependency between annotations and Brat), we decided to use a new annotation tool, tagtog[3], which allowed direct annotations on visualized PDF pages. This tool displays each document in its entirety and provides an ergonomic web interface that allows the annotator to select text directly on the PDF document. The visual component of PDFs with unique structures, graphs and images provides annotators valuable information that would otherwise not be available via Pdf2text and Brat. As a result, annotations were no longer dependent on PDF-to-text conversion tools. In addition, the annotation guidelines also had to be reworked to obtain better data with respect to a more linguistic approach.

Financial prospectuses were available both online in PDF format and directly from fund managers. We built a medium-sized dataset consisting 8 English (66 pages on average) and 33 French (26 pages on average) prospectuses.

Three bilingual (English and French) annotators were used to annotate these documents according to SBD's new annotation guidelines. The guidelines define what constitutes a "sentence" in financial documents and more specifically the different types of units and their boundaries that can be found in the text.

Guidelines Our guidelines consisted of 4 types of units: "sentences", "lists", "nesting lists" and "items".

A "sentence" was defined as a set of words that represents a complete and independent thought. A "sentence" usually contains a subject and a predicate along with independent and/or dependent clauses. A "sentence" could also be nominal and verbal groups that took form as a title of a passage of text.

A "list" was defined as an introduction followed by "items" of the same category which are read in a vertical manner. Lists composed of several other embedded lists and levels of items were considered "nesting lists". This nesting of lists can reach

---

[3]https://www.tagtog.net

up to four depth levels. It is important to mention that the typographic occurrence of bullets did not determine whether an enumeration was a list, as it could also simply be a sequence of independent "sentences".

In the corpora, we focused on extracting well-defined sentences, lists and items by detecting their boundaries and discarding non-phrases (figures, images, footers, page headers, etc.).

The annotated corpus was converted into the FinSBD-2020 labels mentioned in Section 3. Annotated sentence boundaries within item of list were not given to participants in order to simplify the shared task.

A total of 41 documents were annotated. To create the ground-truth, each document was annotated independently by two analysts, then reviewed and corrected by a third analyst.

Annotation Challenges Data annotation may have varied due to interpretations of the following ambiguities:

1. Lists were visually distinguished by bullets and numbers, but not always. Some lists did not contain visual indicators (bullets or numbers) of items and appeared to be only sentences.

2. Groups of sentences were sometimes found with bullets that had no semantic relationship and therefore did not make up part of a list.

3. The distinction between a title and items of a list were not always clear. Titles were visually distinguishable from text passages by differences in font types and sizes, bold or italics, underlined words, etc. These titles sometimes appeared to be items in a list.

4. The use of colons was inconsistent. Colons were sometimes used at the end of titles, followed by either grammatically complete or incomplete sentences. The boundaries of a "sentence" in this case becomes unclear.

5. Human errors in the documents such as missing punctuation, incorrect punctuation or incorrect grammar required that each annotator independently interpret what the intended text was.

4.2 Corpus Description

In this section, we provide an analysis of the data used for both subtasks in English and in French.

In Table 1, we report some statistics about the dataset. #Prospectuses indicates the number of financial prospectuses used in each set; #Page the total number of document pages in each set; and finally the number of occurrence each classes #sentence, #list, #item (subtask1) and #item1, #item2, #item3 and #item4 (subtask2).

We also report the percentage of segments ending with a punctuation mark ("?", "!", ";", ".", ":") as well as percentage of segments starting with an uppercase letter to support the claim that SBD cannot solely rely on capital letters and punctuation. In the shared task data, only 75% up to 86% of text segments ended with a punctuation mark and only 28% up to 57% began with a capital letters. This is significantly lower than the numbers reported in FinSBD-2019 and is due to the introduction of list items which boundaries are more subtle than those of sentences. Hence, FinSBD-2020 presented a

	English		French	
	train	test	train	test
# Prospectuses	6	2	23	10
# Page	350	180	624	224
# sentence	8070	2450	13164	4748
# list	249	69	494	173
# item	1111	332	1722	638
# item1	1029	272	1548	570
# item2	78	60	150	60
# item3	4	0	21	8
# item4	0	0	3	0
% Punct. as end	76%	86%	76%	75%
% Uppercase start	45%	28%	56%	57%

Table 1: Distribution of the Training and Testing sets used in the English and French corpora.

non-trivial problem, which had the potential to be solved by novel SBD systems that would leverage richer features, such as syntactic and semantic cues from the text, and features related to the position of the text in its page.

5 Participants and Systems

	# team submissions
subtask 1 EN	6
subtask 2 EN	2
subtask 1 FR	4
subtask 2 FR	1

Table 2: Statistics on the participation in the French and English subtasks.

A total of 18 teams registered in the shared task, of which 5 teams who participated and 4 who submitted a paper to describe of their method. The participants came from 8 different countries and belonged to 18 different institutions. The shared task brought together private and public research institutions including Rakuten, Flipkart Pvt Ltd, Subtl.ai. and Sorbonne University (see Table 3 for more details).

In table 2, we show the details on the submissions per task. One team who submitted boundaries did not send a paper describing their approach.

Participating teams explored and implemented a wide variety of techniques and features. In this section, we give a short summary of the methods proposed by each participating team (for further details, all papers appear in the proceedings of the FinNLP 2020 Workshop).

Team	Affiliation
PublishInCovid19	Flipkart, India
aiai	Rakuten, Japan
Daniel	Sorbonne University, France
Subtl.ai	Subtl.ai, India

Table 3: List of the 4 teams that participated and submitted papers in subtasks English and French of the FinSBD Shared Task.

PublishInCovid19 [18] This team formulated the boundary prediction problem as a sequence labeling task on overlapping windows of words. They first simplified the annotations by removing the recursiveness and hierarchy of items inside lists. Each word was given a beginning or ending label for a type of segment. Then, they compared two neural architectures, namely BiLSTM-CRF and BERT, trained on predicting the boundaries of sentences and simplified items. They used window sizes of 300 and 512 with overlapping of 20 words. Boundaries were post-processed by heuristics to correct missing beginning and ending boundaries. In the second phase, they identified the hierarchy and the recursive relation between items through a rule-based method applied on item boundaries predicted in the first phase. This allowed reconstitution of lists boundaries. The rules were based on visual cues like left-indentation and bullet-style of items. Their submitted system was the BiLSTM-CRF for both subtasks in English which achieved the highest score in the shared task.

aiai [19] This team approached the task as a two-stage text classification problem using two LSTM models with attention. First, they trained a multi-label boundary classifier to determine if a word is inside, outside, starting or ending a text segment. Each word is classified using a window of words, with additional features based on the word position and characters' width and height. They tested different window sizes and chose 21 as the most optimal (10 words before + 10 words after + current word). In a second stage, using these boundaries, they extracted candidate text segment and trained a second multi-label classifier to determine if the segment was a sentence, an item or a list. For both stages, the team used their own trained word embedding using CBOW on the shared task data. They managed to submit their system in English and French for both subtasks.

Daniel [20] This team decided not to use the provided textual representation. Instead, they utilized the "pdf2xml" converter to extract both text content and structural information, from which they extracted PDF structures in a top-down fashion, from higher-level to lower-level structures (i.e. the table of contents, tables, page headers and footers). Therefore, they were able to ignore text from table of contents, tables, page headers and footers. Finally, they created a set of heuristics based on bullet points, text position and font characteristics to identify lists, lists items and paragraphs. They exploited font features thanks to the use of the "pdf2xml" converter. Sentences were extracted from paragraphs by identifying end-sentence punctuation. The team submitted their system in English and French for the first subtask but not for the second subtask.

Subtl.ai [21] This team proposed an architecture combining a two-stage deep learning approach with heuristics. They first used a vocabulary to identify candidate words which could be sentence boundaries. Each candidate word was then represented by two windows of one-hot vectors derived from POS tags from 7 words located before and after. This was used to train a binary classifier, composed of 2 LSTM models, to determine if the candidate word was a true sentence boundary. From these boundaries, candidate segments of words were extracted for training a second LSTM with attention model,

the input of which were pre-trained Glove word embeddings. This model was used to determine whether a segment was a true sentence. Multiple segments were merged if the concatenated sequence was classified as a true sentence. The team submitted their system in English for the first subtask and did not complete the second subtask.

6 Results and Discussion

In this section, we describe the evaluation metrics used in the shared task and we give an analysis of the results obtained for the various submitted systems.

Evaluation Metric Participating systems were ranked based on the macro F1-score of each subtask for each language obtained on a blind test set. A predicted boundary was considered to be true if both starting and ending indexes were correct. Consequently, this metric was more severe than the one used in FinSBD-2019 where a boundary could be considered true even if the corresponding starting or ending boundary was false. For each document, the F1-score was computed by label. Then, the scores of *sentence*, *list* and *item* were averaged as an F1-score of subtask 1 and those of *item1*, *item2*, *item3* and *item4* were averaged as an F1-score for subtask 2. Finally, the mean over all documents was taken as the macro-averaged F1-score to rank systems in each subtask by language.

We provided a starting kit[4] with an evaluation script and a baseline based on spaCy [5] for detecting only boundaries of sentences. Interestingly, low F1-scores of our baseline showed that applying out-of-the-box spaCy's SBD does not yield optimal results for our documents.

Table 4 and Table 5 reports the results by team obtained from FinSBD-2020 in English and French.

	English	
	subtask1	**subtask2**
PublishInCovid19	0.937	0.844
aiai	0.413	0.203
Daniel	0.317	0
Subtl.ai	0.217	0
our baseline	0.208	0
Anuj	0.126	0

Table 4: Ranking of teams according to macro-averaged F1-score for each subtask in English (0 means no submission).

Discussion As stated in Section 2, most previous work on SBD relied on unsupervised approaches based on heuristics derived from punctuation, letter capitalization, abbreviations and so on. This is mainly due to a lack of annotated data on unstructured text from documents. Through FinSBD, thanks to the introduction of annotated boundaries, we offered the opportunity of supervised approaches to tackle SBD given unstructured and noisy text. Each team had a unique approach in solving this problem and all teams who submitted a paper outperformed our baseline.

Most teams trained a supervised system on word-level labels they created by pre-processing the provided character-level

---

[4]https://github.com/finsbd/finsbd2

	French	
	subtask1	subtask2
PublishInCovid19	0	0
aiai	0.471	0.350
Daniel	0.232	0
Subtl.ai	0	0
our baseline	0.161	0
Anuj	0.025	0

Table 5: Ranking of teams according to macro-averaged F1-score for each subtask in French (0 means no submission).

	ranking score
	mean F1-score
PublishInCovid19	0.445
aiai	0.359
Daniel	0.145
Subtl.ai	0.054
our baseline	0.092
Anuj	0.038

Table 6: Ranking of teams by averaging the F1 scores obtained on each subtask for each language.

labels. This allowed application of transfer learning by using existing embeddings and architecture that expect words as input. Each word was assigned a class which served as start or end segments. Moreover, training a word-level model was computationally cheaper than character-level, the latter of which no team attempted.

There were two main approaches. The best performing one, proposed by *PublishInCovid19* [18], was sequence labeling: one multi-label architecture was trained to classify in one-go all words from a window into all different types of boundaries. The second approach, proposed by *aiai* [19] and *Subtl.ai* [21], was a two-stage classification architecture. A first stage model determined whether a word is a boundary given a window of surrounding words. Boundaries are then used in a second stage to create candidate segments, which were then classified by a second model into different types of segment: sentence, list or item. Separating the task into boundary detection and segment-type classification did not yield improvement over sequence labeling.

aiai [19] and *Subtl.aiai* [21] experimented with LSTM-based models with an attention mechanism in order to exploit dependencies between words for SBD for their classification tasks. *PublishInCovid19* [18] also based his model on LSTM layers, but with classic sequence labeling elements such as a CRF layer, bi-directionality and pre-trained word embeddings. Larger windows (300 and 512 words) [18] proved to be quite effective compared to smaller windows (7 and 21 words) [19] [21] for detecting both boundaries and their type. This was due to long dependencies between boundaries, especially of lists, which can span hundreds of words. There were also long dependencies between different types of segments, between lists and items for example, that large windows are better at detecting. Interestingly, *PublishInCovid19* [18]

reported no significant improvement using large pre-trained language model such as transformers, i.e. BERT, compared to a BiLSTM-CRF with pre-trained word embedding. They respectively scored 0.956 and 0.959 weighted F1 scores in a sequence labeling setting, meaning there is little difference between both models. It is possible that there was a lack of sufficient data in order to leverage large transformers. In addition, transformer pre-training already depends on some type of sentence segmentation, which makes transformers ill-suited for predicting sentence boundaries.

All teams resorted in some extent to the use of heuristics based on text position, text appearance and/or punctuation to improve their SBD. *PublishInCovid19* [18] used a set of post-processing rules to resolve erroneous boundaries predicted by his models. *Daniel* [20] was the only team that used solely unsupervised rule-based approaches in their SBD system. Based on positional and syntactical heuristics, they explored a top-down pipeline for structuring PDFs into table of content, tables, page headers and footers and finally paragraphs and lists. Furthermore, other heuristics allowed them to extract clean segments in paragraphs and lists and exclude unwanted text from tables, page headers and footers. Their work possibly suggests that SBD of a document will only be solved once PDF structuring is. In FinSBD-2020, annotated boundaries excluded tables, page headers and footers and table of content.

For future work, it would be interesting to confirm if some of the submitted systems, *Subtl.ai* [21] and *Publish-InCovid19* [18], experimented only in English, would perform as well on the French data where list items reaches up to depth level 4 (only 3 in English). Finally, *PublishInCovid19* expressed interest in exploring the idea of multi-modality by exploiting text, its position and its appearance equally in an end-to-end trainable system. In submitted systems, visual and positional features were only used in heuristics or as features complementing word-level representation during supervised training.

7 Conclusions

This paper presents the setup and results for the FinSBD-2020 Shared Task on Sentence Boundary Detection in Unstructured text in the Financial Domain, organized as part of The Second Workshop on Financial Technology and Natural Language Processing (FinNLP) of the conference IJCAI-2020. A total of 18 teams from 8 countries registered of which 4 teams participated and submitted papers in the shared task with a wide variety of techniques.

All supervised approaches were based on LSTM. The most successful method was based on a BiLSTM-CRF applied in a sequence labeling setting. The best average F1 scores on the FinSBD English subtasks were 0.937 for subtask 1 and 0.844 for subtask 2. And the best average F1 scores on the FinSBD French subtasks were 0.471 for subtask 1 and 0.35 for subtask 2. Despite high performance, especially for English, SBD is far from being completely resolved, particularly for list segmentation.

The diversity of both public and private institutions that participated in FinSBD-2020 illustrates that the issue of SBD remains an area that requires further research and development especially concerning analysis of documents of unstructured formats. Achieving higher accuracy in sentence extraction that builds better NLP-based solutions proves to be a shared interest among a wide variety of fields.

Acknowledgments

We would like to thank our dedicated data and language analysts who contributed to building the French and English corpora used in this Shared Task: Sandra Bellato, Marion Cargill, Virginie Mouilleron and Aouataf Djillani.

References

[1] Mitchell P Marcus, Mary Ann Marcinkiewicz, and Beatrice Santorini. Building a large annotated corpus of english: The penn treebank. *Computational linguistics*, 19(2):313–330, 1993.

[2] Dan Gillick. Sentence boundary detection and the problem with the us. In *Proceedings of Human Language Technologies: The 2009 Annual Conference of the North American Chapter of the Association for Computational Linguistics, Companion Volume: Short Papers*, pages 241–244. Association for Computational Linguistics, 2009.

[3] Abderrahim Ait Azzi, Houda Bouamor, and Sira Ferradans. The finsbd-2019 shared task: Sentence boundary detection in pdf noisy text in the financial domain. In *Proceedings of the First Workshop on Financial Technology and Natural Language Processing*, pages 74–80, August 2019.

[4] Christopher Manning, Mihai Surdeanu, John Bauer, Jenny Finkel, Steven Bethard, and David McClosky. The stanford corenlp natural language processing toolkit. In *Proceedings of 52nd annual meeting of the association for computational linguistics: system demonstrations*, pages 55–60, 2014.

[5] Matthew Honnibal and Ines Montani. spacy 2: Natural language understanding with bloom embeddings, convolutional neural networks and incremental parsing. 2017.

[6] Edward Loper and Steven Bird. Nltk: the natural language toolkit. In *ETMTNLP '02: Proceedings of the ACL-02 Workshop on Effective tools and methodologies for teaching natural language processing and computational*, pages 63–70, 2002.

[7] Jonathon Read, Rebecca Dridan, Stephan Oepen, and Lars Jørgen Solberg. Sentence boundary detection: A long solved problem? In *Proceedings of COLING 2012: Posters*, pages 985–994, Mumbai, India, December 2012. The COLING 2012 Organizing Committee.

[8] Gregory Grefenstette and Pasi Tapanainen. What is a word, what is a sentence?: problems of tokenisation. 1994.

[9] Michael D Riley. Some applications of tree-based modelling to speech and language. In *Proceedings of the workshop on Speech and Natural Language*, pages 339–352. Association for Computational Linguistics, 1989.

[10] Tibor Kiss and Jan Strunk. Unsupervised multilingual sentence boundary detection. *Computational Linguistics*, 32(4):485–525, 2006.

[11] Marcos V Treviso, Christopher D Shulby, and Sandra M Aluisio. Evaluating word embeddings for sentence boundary detection in speech transcripts. *arXiv preprint arXiv:1708.04704*, 2017.

[12] Denis Griffis, Chaitanya Shivade, Eric Fosler-Lussier, and Albert M Lai. A quantitative and qualitative evaluation of sentence boundary detection for the clinical domain. *AMIA Summits on Translational Science Proceedings*, 2016:88, 2016.

[13] Roque López and Thiago AS Pardo. Experiments on sentence boundary detection in user-generated web content. In *International Conference on Intelligent Text Processing and Computational Linguistics*, pages 227–237. Springer, 2015.

[14] Dwijen Rudrapal, Anupam Jamatia, Kunal Chakma, Amitava Das, and Björn Gambäck. Sentence boundary detection for social media text. In *Proceedings of the 12th International Conference on Natural Language Processing*, pages 254–260, 2015.

[15] Carlos-Emiliano Gonzalez-Gallardo and Juan-Manuel Torres-Moreno. Sentence boundary detection for french with subword-level information vectors and convolutional neural networks. 02 2018.

[16] Jaromír Savelka, Vern R. Walker, Matthias Grabmair, and Kevin D. Ashley. Sentence boundary detection in adjudicatory decisions in the united states. 2017.

[17] George Sanchez. Sentence boundary detection in legal text. In *Proceedings of the Natural Legal Language Processing Workshop 2019*, pages 31–38, Minneapolis, Minnesota, June 2019. Association for Computational Linguistics.

[18] Janvijay Singh. Publishincovid19 at the finsbd-2 task: Sentence and list extraction in noisypdf text using a hybrid deep learning and rule-based approach. In *The Second Workshop on Financial Technology and Natural Language Processing of IJCAI 2020*, 2020.

[19] Ke Tian, Hua Chen, and Jie Yang. aiai at the finsbd-2 task: Sentence, list, and itemsboundary detection and items classification of financial textsusing data augmentation and attentionmodel. In *The Second Workshop on Financial Technology and Natural Language Processing of IJCAI 2020*, 2020.

[20] Emmanuel Giguet and Gaël Lejeune. Daniel at the finsbd-2 task: Extracting lists and sentences from pdf documents, a model-driven approach to pdf document analysis. In *The Second Workshop on Financial Technology and Natural Language Processing of IJCAI 2020*, 2020.

[21] Aman Khullar, Abhishek Arora, Sarath Chandra Pakala, Vishnu Ramesh, and Manish Shrivastava. Subtl.ai at the finsbd-2 task: Document structure identification by paying attention. In *The Second Workshop on Financial*

Technology and Natural Language Processing of IJCAI 2020, 2020.

PublishInCovid19 at the FinSBD-2 Task: Sentence and List Extraction in Noisy PDF Text Using a Hybrid Deep Learning and Rule-Based Approach

Janvijay Singh
Flipkart Private Limited
janvijay.singh@flipkart.com

Abstract

This paper describes the approach that we employed to tackle the FinSBD-2 shared task in IJCAI-2020. FinSBD-2 comprises of two subtasks: 1) extraction of boundaries of sentences, lists and items from noisy PDF (financial documents) text and 2) organisation of lists and items in a visual hierarchy. We solve these subtasks in two phases. In the first phase, we pre-process the data to embed relevant visual cues and form non-recursive and non-hierarchical tags. We then formulate the boundary prediction problem as a sequence labelling task and evaluate two neural architectures, namely BiLSTM-CRF and BERT. In the second phase, we identify the recursive relation among different items as well as their hierarchical visual layout. A rule-based method is used to achieve desired recursiveness and hierarchy in tags predicted from the first phase. The rules are based on visual cues like left-indentation and bullet-style of items. Our combined final approach achieved an F1-score of 0.937 on subtask-1 and 0.844 on subtask-2 for the English test set. We were ranked first overall in terms of MEAN F1-score.

1 Introduction

Sentence Boundary Detection (SBD) involves identification of boundaries (begin/from-end/to token indices) of sentences within a text. Sentences are the foundational units of most of the Natural Language Processing (NLP) applications including Part of Speech Tagging, Discourse Parsing [Polanyi *et al.*, 2004], Machine Translation, Sentiment Analysis and Information Retrieval [Read *et al.*, 2012]. Hence, errors introduced during the extraction of sentences can propagate further and degrade the performance of the complete NLP pipeline. Despite its fundamental importance in building NLP-based solutions, SBD has so far not received enough attention. Most of the previous research work in this area has focussed on formal texts [Agarwal *et al.*, 2005; Kiss and Strunk, 2006; Akita *et al.*, 2006; Gillick, 2009; Kreuzthaler and Schulz, 2015], such as news and European parliament proceedings, where existing rule-based and machine learning methods are highly accurate due to the perfectly clean data. SBD remains a challenging task when the input text is noisy or unstructured.

Documents encoded in machine-readable formats (such as Adobe PDF format) have the exact layout of human-readable documents. However, the text extracted from such documents loses these formatting features and is highly noisy or unstructured. Financial documents or prospectus are also encoded in such machine-readable formats. Apart from the textual paragraphs, financial documents contain tabular data, titles, sub-titles, keywords, lists, headers and footers, which further increases the complexity of SBD by making the extracted text noisier. At IJCAI-2019, the FinSBD shared task [Azzi *et al.*, 2019] was proposed to address the SBD research focussing on noisy text extracted from financial documents. In specific, FinSBD was concerned with the identification of begin and end token indices for sentences present in such noisy text.

The first step to extract information from financial documents is to transform the noisy or unstructured text into the semi-structured (with well-marked boundaries for information elements) text. Apart from the sentences, lists are the other most commonly occurring element in financial documents. Contrary to sentences, lists include multiple sentences and a visible hierarchy of information. Therefore, identifying the intra-list hierarchy and distinction in sentences and lists can make information extraction much more accurate. Building on this idea, FinSBD-2 shared task was proposed at IJCAI-2020. It comprises of following two subtasks: 1) identification of boundaries for sentences, items and lists and 2) identification of the hierarchy of items contained in the lists. We tackle these sub-tasks in two phases, using a hybrid rule-based and deep learning approach.

In the first phase, we pre-process the data to embed relevant visual cues and form non-recursive and non-hierarchical list/item tags. We then formulate the boundary prediction problem as a sequence labelling task and evaluate two neural architectures, namely BiLSTM-CRF and BERT. In the second phase, we employ a rule-based approach to identify the recursive and hierarchical relation in the items predicted from the first phase. The rules are based on visual cues like left-indentation and bullet-style of items.

The rest of the paper is structured as follows: Section 2 states the task definition. Section 3 describes the specifics of our methodology. Section 4 explains the experimental setup and the results, and Section 5 concludes the paper.

Proceedings of the Second Workshop on Financial Technology and Natural Language Processing

2   Task Definition

In the literature, SBD has been attempted using several approaches. These approaches fall into three major categories: (a) rule-based approaches, which rely on hand-crafted heuristics (e.g. Stanford Core NLP[1], SpaCy[2] etc); (b) supervised machine learning based approaches, which utilise annotated training data to predict boundaries ([Reynar and Ratnaparkhi, 1997; Gillick, 2009; Du and Huang, 2019]); and (c) unsupervised machine learning approaches, where the training data is unlabelled ([Read *et al.*, 2012]). Rule-based methods are widely used for SBD since they provide ease of usage and decent performance for most of the NLP tasks. In presence of data with annotated boundaries, supervised machine learning approaches tend to provide the best performance.

Training dataset provided with FinSBD-2 shared task comprises of following:

1. String of text extracted from financial documents;

2. Bounding box coordinates corresponding to each character in the text; and

3. Set of pairwise (begin/from-end/to) character indices for some classes, *namely sentences, lists, items, item1, item2, item3 and item4.*

Set *sentences* and *lists* have non-overlapping elements; this implies that a character cannot be a part of both sentence and list segment. Each element of set *items* overlaps with exactly one element in set *lists*, this implies that a list can contain multiple items. Similar to lists, an item can contain multiple items inside it. Hence, items and lists are recursive in nature. Sets *item1, item2, item3 and item4* provide the hierarchical structure of the list. Set *item1* comprises of items which are one-level inside the containing list. Set *item2* comprises of items which are one-level inside containing *item1*, and two-level inside containing *list*. The hierarchical structure for items in set *item3* and *item4* is defined similarly. Set *items* is a union of sets *item1, item2, item3 and item4*.

Modelling this task as a sequence-labelling problem is not trivial because of a few reasons. Firstly, due to the recursiveness in lists and items, the end boundary of multiple list and item segments can share the same indices. This will require us to classify a few token indices into multiple classes. Secondly, recursiveness causes list and item segments to span over up to 1500 tokens (words). Since most of the sequence labelling models learn far smaller contextual dependencies, it becomes essential to deal with this recursiveness at pre-processing stage only. Thirdly, items at different hierarchical levels are indistinguishable from one another if the context is constrained to a small length. Therefore, determining hierarchy based on visual cues such as bullet-style and left indentation should be carried out once the boundaries of lists and items are precisely known. To formulate this task as a sequence labelling problem, we pre-process the dataset to remove the recursiveness and hierarchy among lists and items.

With non-recursive and non-hierarchical boundaries for lists and items, we formulate the boundary prediction problem as a sequence labelling task. In sequence labelling,

each token in the sequence is classified to one among certain classes (classes are commonly represented using IOB tagging scheme [Evang *et al.*, 2013]). For our task, we define the following seven classes:

- S-SEN: begin and end of a sentence with a single token;

- B-SEN: begin of a sentence segment;

- E-SEN: end of a sentence segment;

- S-IT: begin and end of list/item with a single token;

- B-IT: begin of a list/item segment;

- E-IT: end of a list/item segment;

- O: other, neither of the classes mentioned above.

We utilise this sequence labelling model to predict boundaries for sentences and non-hierarchical lists/items. We then employ a rule-based method to identify the recursiveness and hierarchy in the previously predicted list/item segments. The rules for this method are based on left-indentation (determined from bounding-box coordinates) and bullet-style. Specifics of the different phases mentioned here are described in subsequent sections.

3   Methodology

Our approach is composed of two phases. In the first phase, we learn to predict the non-hierarchical and non-recursive sentence, list and item boundaries. Details of the first phase are included in sub-section 4.1 and 4.2. In the second phase, we identify the recursiveness and hierarchy in segments predicted from the first phase using a rule-based approach. Section 4.3 and 4.4 describe the details of the second phase.

3.1   Pre-Processing Dataset

The dataset provided with FinSBD-2 shared task cannot be used directly to train our sequence labelling model because of a couple of reasons. Firstly, the dataset contains the text extracted from financial documents as a large string of characters. Moreover, the segment labels are also provided at the character level. In contrast, our sequence labelling models operate at word level and on a smaller input sequence length. Secondly, as described in the previous section, non-hierarchical and non-recursive list/item labels are more suited to the task of sequence labelling. Therefore, we recreate the training set using the following pre-processing strategy:

1. We create a *unified set* of all the segments in set *lists* and *items*. We call a segment X as a child of segment Y, if begin index of $Y \leq$ begin index of X and end index of $X \leq$ end index of Y. For each segment X in the *unified set* if X has atleast one child segment, we change the end index of X to the minimum begin index of all its child segments. With these steps, the final *unified set* contains non-hierarchical and non-recursive list/item boundaries.

2. We tokenize the string of characters extracted from financial documents using word_tokenizer [3] from NLTK. In addition to tokenization this removes extra whitespace characters (such as \n) from the text. We then

[1]https://stanfordnlp.github.io/CoreNLP/ssplit.html
[2]https://spacy.io/usage/linguistic-features/#sbd
[3]https://www.nltk.org/api/nltk.tokenize.html

assign a tag (one from S-SEN, B-SEN, E-SEN, S-IT, B-IT, E-IT and O) to each tokenized word, utilizing the character based indices for sentence and list/item (from *unified set*) segments. Hence, we achieve the word/tag sequence for each financial document.

3. The x-coordinates provided with the dataset increases from left to right on a page in PDF, whereas y-coordinates increases from top to bottom. We define a *visual line* as a contiguous sub-sequence of words which have overlapping y-coordinate bounds. Left-indentation for a *visual line* is the minimum x-coordinate of a character present in it. To embed visual cues, we embed dummy tokens $\langle tabopenX \rangle$ and $\langle tabcloseX \rangle$ at the beginning and ending of *visual line* respectively. Here X is equal to left-indentation of visual line divided (integer division) by five units. These cues help us achieve slightly better metrics at sequence labelling task.

4. We use a sliding window (parameterised by the window and hop length) upon word/tag sequence to achieve sequences of smaller length. We use a hop length of 20 words, to ensure that the sequence labelling model is provided with varied contexts.

3.2 Deep Learning Models for Sequence Labelling

Deep Learning (DL) models have achieved state-of-the-art performance in most of the NLP tasks. In the domains of sequence labelling tasks (such as Named Entity Recognition[4] and Part of Speech Tagging[5]), recurrent neural network [Peters *et al.*, 2018; Straková *et al.*, 2019] and multi-headed self-attention based DL models [Devlin *et al.*, 2019] have surpassed performance of all other methods. In our work, we evaluate two neural architectures, namely, BiLSTM-CRF and BERT, which are described below.

BiLSTM-CRF

Recurrent Neural Networks (RNNs) are suited to sequential input data since they execute the same function at each time-step and allow the model to share parameters across input sequence. In order to predict at a time-step, RNNs utilise a hidden vector which captures the useful information from past time-steps. In case of longer input sequences, RNNs suffer from the problem of vanishing gradients. Long short-term memory (LSTM) [Hochreiter and Schmidhuber, 1997] was introduced to alleviate the problem of vanishing gradients. LSTM employ a gating mechanism to capture long-range dependencies in the input sequence. In contrast to uni-directional LSTM, bidirectional LSTM (BiLSTM) [Schuster and Paliwal, 1997] makes prediction by utilising hidden state vector from past as well as future time-steps.

Our BiLSTM-CRF model is composed of: 1) a character-level BiLSTM layer; 2) a dropout layer [Srivastava *et al.*, 2014]; 3) a word-level BiLSTM layer; and 4) a linear-chain Conditional Random Field (CRF) [Sutton and McCallum, 2012]. The character-level BiLSTM operates on words and is employed to learn morphological features from them. We concatenate the output vectors of character-level BiLSTM

---

[4]http://nlpprogress.com/english/named_entity_recognition.html
[5]http://nlpprogress.com/english/part-of-speech_tagging.html

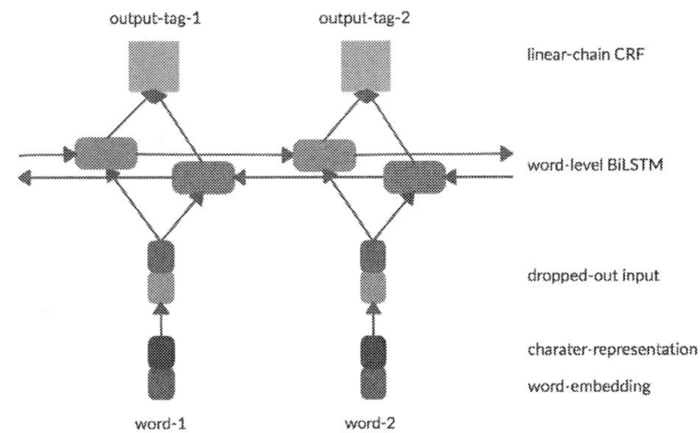

Figure 1: The architechture of our BiLSTM-CRF model.

(character representation) with pretrained word embeddings (GloVe [Pennington *et al.*, 2014]) to provide our model with more powerful word representations. In order to prevent the model from depending on one representation or the other too strongly, we pass this concatenated vector through a dropout layer. The output of the dropout layer is then passed to the word-level BiLSTM layer, which outputs a vector corresponding to each word in the input sequence. For our task, output labels share dependencies among themselves, such as an end-tag is followed by a begin-tag. In order to model these dependencies, we use a linear-chain CRF at the end, instead of the commonly used softmax layer. A linear-chain CRF is parameterised by a transition matrix (transitions within output labels), and consequently is capable of learning dependencies in the output sequence. The complete architecture of our BiLSTM-CRF model for this task is shown in Fig. 1.

BERT

Transformer [Vaswani *et al.*, 2017] based neural models have shown promising results in most of the NLP tasks. Its architecture is composed of feed-forward layers and self-attention blocks. The fundamental difference in RNN based models and transformer is that transformer does not rely on recurrence mechanism to learn the dependencies in the input sequence. Instead, on each input time step, they employ self-attention. Attention can be thought of as a mechanism to map a query and a set of key-value pair to an output, where query, keys, values and output are all vectors. In the case of self-attention, for each vector in the input sequence, a separate feed-forward layer is used to compute query, key and value vectors. Attention-score for a input vector, is determined as the output of a compatibility function, which operates on input's key and the some query vector. The output of self attention mechanism is weighted sum of value vectors, where weight is determined by the attention-score. In case of multi-headed attention, multiple blocks of such self-attention modules operate on the input sequence.

Transformer's encoder is composed of 6 identical layers, where each layer is composed of two sublayers. These two layers are multi-head self-attention and a position-wise fully

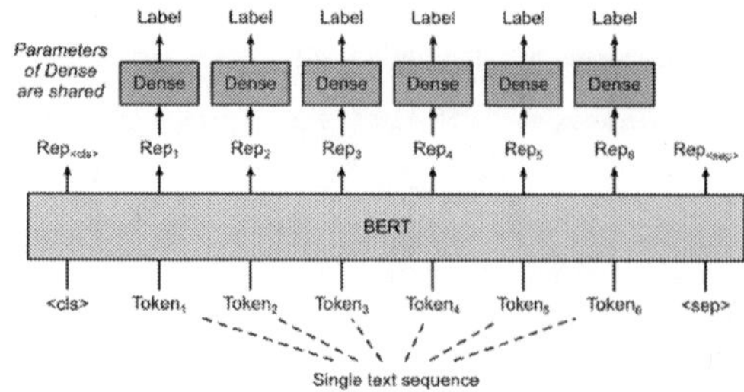

Figure 2: The token-tagging architecture for fine-tuning BERT.

connected feed-forward network. A residual connection is used around each sublayer, followed by layer normalisation. BERT [Devlin *et al.*, 2019] utilises a multi-layer Transformer encoder to pre-train deep bidirectional representations by jointly conditioning on both left and right context across all layers. As a result, pre-trained BERT representations can be fine-tuned conveniently using only one additional output layer.

For a given token, BERT's input representation is constructed by summing the corresponding token, segment, and position embeddings. BERT is trained using two unsupervised prediction tasks, Masked Language Model and Next Sentence Prediction. In order to fine-tune BERT on a sequence labelling task, BERT representation of every token of the input text is fed into the same extra fully-connected layers to output the label of the token. The predictions are not conditioned on the surrounding predictions. Since we view our task as a sequence labelling problem, we configure BERT to instantiate the token tagging architecture which is shown in Fig 2.

3.3 Post-Processing Predicted Tags

To extract a sentence or list/item segment, both begin and end tags need to be predicted accurately. From predictions on the validation dataset, we realise that many unretrieved segments have a single missing begin or end tag. In order to recover as many as possible missing/erroneous tags, we employ (in the order as described) the following post-processing strategy on the predicted tags:

1. If E-IT tag is missing for a B-IT tag, then E-IT occurs at the end of a *visual line* (one with B-IT tag or the following ones) if:
   - first tag in next *visual line* is B-IT or B-SEN.
   - last tag in the current *visual line* is E-SEN.
   - vertical-spacing between current *visual line* and next *visual line* is greater than most frequent inter *visual line* spacing (specific to a document).

2. If B-IT tag is missing for a E-IT tag, then B-IT occurs at:
   - the word next to the just (all the tags in between are O) previously occurring E-IT or E-SEN tag.
   - the just previously occurring B-SEN.

3. If B-SEN tag is missing for a E-SEN tag, then B-SEN occurs at the word next to the just previously occurring E-SEN tag.

4. If E-SEN tag is missing for a B-SEN tag, then E-SEN occurs at the word previous to the just next occurring B-SEN tag.

3.4 Identification of Recursiveness and Hierarchy

After the prediction of non-hierarchical items, we identify the recursiveness and hierarchy among them using a rule-based method. The rules of this method rely on two pieces of information, namely, left-indentation and bullet of the item segment. Bullet of an item segment can be a roman number, an English letter or a special symbol present at its start. Left-indentation for an item segment is the minimum x-coordinate of its first word (excluding bullet). We define a bullet's *predecessor* as the bullet that will occur just before it in the list of ordered bullets of corresponding bullet-style. e.g. predecessor of bullet (c) will be (b), predecessor for bullet 5. will be 4., predecessor for • will be •. We call a bullet to be of *start type* if it occurs first in the list of ordered bullets of corresponding bullet-style. e.g. (a), 1. and • are of *start type*. With these pieces of information we employ the *algorithm* described below. We maintain a set called *candidate lists* which stores the final *lists* and recursiveness/hierarchy among its item segments.

1. Sort all the items extracted from a financial document on the basis of their occurrence in the original text string. Jump to 2.

2. If *last-item* has been assigned call *last-item* as *first-item*, else choose the first item from the list of sorted item segments and call it *first-item*. Create a list with just *first-item* and call it *candidate list*. Jump to 3.

3. If no new items are left in sorted list of item segments exit the algorithm. Call the next new item in sorted list of item segments as *current-item*. If *candidate list* has just one element then jump to 4, else jump to 5.

4. If *current-item* has a bullet of *start type* mark it as child of *first-item* and jump to 3, else store *candidate list* in *candidate lists* and jump to 2. Before jumping, assign *current-item* to *last-item*.

5. If left-indentation of *current-item* and *last-item* are equal, jump to 6. If left-indentation of *current-item* is greater than that of *last-item* jump to 7. If left-indentation of *current-item* is less than that of *last-item* jump to 8.

6. If *last-item*'s bullet is *predecessor* of *current-item*'s bullet then mark *current-item* as child of *last-item*'s parent; store *current-item* in *candidate list* and jump to 3, else store *candidate list* in *candidate lists* and jump to 2. Before jumping, assign *current-item* to *last-item*.

7. If *current-item* has a bullet of *start type* mark it as child of *last-item*; store *current-item* in *candidate list* and jump to 3, else store *candidate list* in *candidate lists* and jump to 2. Before jumping, assign *current-item* to *last-item*.

8. Assign parent of *last-item* to *candidate-sibling*. Jump to 9.

9. If *candidate-sibling* has greater left-indentation than the *current-item*, assign parent of *candidate-sibling* to *candidate-sibling* and jump to 9, else jump to 10.

10. If *candidate-sibling*'s left-indentation is equal to that of *current-item* and *candidate-sibling*'s bullet is *predecessor* of *current-item*'s bullet then mark the parent of *current-item* with parent of *candidate-sibling*; store *current-item* in *candidate list* and jump to 3, otherwise store *candidate list* in *candidate lists* and jump to 2. Before jumping, assign *current-item* to *last-item*.

With above mentioned algorithm we achieve a set called *candidate lists* which captures parent-child relationships in initial item segments. If an item in the *candidate lists* has atleast one child, we change its end boundary to maximum of end boundaries of its children. The items at highest level (with no parents) correspond to *lists*. Items at one level lower correspond to *item1* and so on.

4 Experiments

We evaluated two neural architectures followed by rule-based post-processing. In this section, we describe the dataset, system settings, evaluation metrics, results and a brief erroranalysis for our system.

4.1 Dataset

The dataset for FinSBD-2 shared task (English track) was provided in the form of JSON files. Each of the JSON files contained text and character-based coordinates extracted from a different financial document. The train and test set contained six and two files, respectively. Segment boundaries were provided in the form of character-based index pairs. Segment boundaries for the test dataset were provided after submission of our system's predictions. Table 1 summarises the statistics for the official FinSBD-2 dataset.

In Table 1, columns *Min.*, *Max.* and *Avg* correspond to minimum, maximum and average length (in number of words) of segments of a particular type. The column *#Count* denotes the number of occurrences of a certain segment-type in the dataset. The row *items (modified)* corresponds to the non-hierarchical and non-recursive list/item segments (corresponding to tags S-IT, B-IT and E-IT). Since the average length of any segment-type lies far away from the mean of its range, we can deduce that the length distribution of all segment-types is highly unbalanced. Additionally, the distribution of segment length for train and test dataset is quite different. On average, segments in the test dataset are longer as compared to the train dataset. This difference implies that the test set may be more complicated (more recursive lists/items and more complex sentences).

We define *coverage* as the percentage of unique words from the test set, which appear in the training set. *Coverage* gives us a fair idea of the number of unseen words/tokens, which the model sees at the testing stage. For FinSBD-2 shared task, the training dataset contains 7173 unique words in total. Whereas, the test dataset contains 4894 unique words in total. The vocabulary *coverage* for test set turns out to be 70.55%, implying that around 30% of the words in test set didn't appear in train set.

Train Dataset				
Segment-Type	Min.	Max.	Avg.	#Count
sentences	1	270	24.4	8070
lists	21	1520	149.88	249
items	1	456	32.9	1111
items (modified)	1	236	26.75	1360
Test Dataset				
Segment-Type	Min.	Max.	Avg.	#Count
sentences	1	391	29	2450
lists	15	1150	213.144	69
items	2	622	45.68	322
items (modified)	2	249	36.10	401

Table 1: Dataset (English) statistics for FinSBD-2020 shared task.

Hyper-parameter	BiLSTM-CRF	BERT
Max sequence length	300 (words)	500 (sub-words)
Lower case	False	False
Epochs	25 (max)	5
Batch-size	20	32
Learning rate	0.001	5e-5
Optimizer	Adam	Adam
Pre-trained model	-	bert-base-cased
Char-LSTM size	50	-
Word-LSTM size	200	-
Embedding dropout	0.3	-
Pre-trained embedding	GloVe	-

Table 2: Hyper-parameters employed in training neural models.

4.2 System Settings

In the first phase of our approach, we train two deep neural models, namely, BiLSTM-CRF and BERT. We train the BiLSTM-CRF model to a maximum of 25 epochs, along with an early-stopping strategy. With this strategy, we stop the training if the model does not show any improvements in F1-score on validation split for 500 continuous iterations. In addition to this, we also employ exponential moving averages of the trained parameters to achieve slightly better F1-scores on the validation split. For the pretrained word embeddings, we use GloVE[6] which are trained on large Common Crawl dataset and can effectively represent 84 billion cased tokens.

To train the BERT for our task, we fine-tune a pre-trained model, namely *bert-base-cased*. We have utilised *huggingface*'s BERT APIs[7] to train our model. Since the pre-trained BERT model was trained of a maximum input sequence length of 512 (including special tokens), we could not experiment with larger context window. We ran our experiments on single NVIDIA V100 GPU. It took around 20 and 30 minutes to train BERT and BiLSTM-CRF model, respectively. Table 2 summarises the hyper-parameters which we employed to

---

[6]http://nlp.stanford.edu/data/glove.840B.300d.zip
[7]https://huggingface.co/transformers/model_doc/bert.html

Class	BiLSTM–CRF			BERT		
	P	R	F1	P	R	F1
S-SEN	0.308	0.500	0.381	0.143	0.5	0.222
B-SEN	0.923	0.942	0.932	0.921	0.952	0.936
E-SEN	0.946	0.954	0.950	0.922	0.962	0.941
S-IT	-	-	-	-	-	-
B-IT	0.919	0.875	0.897	0.882	0.88	0.881
E-IT	0.877	0.873	0.875	0.88	0.875	0.878

Table 3: Scores on predictions from deep neural models on test set.

Segment-Type	P	R	F1
sentences	0.923	0.938	0.931
lists	0.968	0.895	0.929
items	0.991	0.916	0.951
item1	0.907	0.905	0.906
item2	1.000	0.697	0.783
item3	-	-	-
item4	-	-	-
Subtask-1 (Macro F1) :	0.937		
Subtask-2 (Macro F1) :	0.844		

Table 4: Scores after final rule-based approach on test set.

train both the models.

4.3 Evaluation Metrics

To extract a segment from the text, both begin and end boundaries should be predicted accurately. Hence, the evaluation metric should penalise the predictions in which either of the boundaries is incorrect. Consider that P and T represent the set of predicted and ground-truth boundary pairs (begin and end index pairs) for certain segment-type. Then, pairwise precision, recall and F1-score for the boundary prediction of the considered segment-type is defined as follows:

$$Precision = \frac{|P \bigcap T|}{|P|}$$

$$Recall = \frac{|P \bigcap T|}{|T|}$$

$$F1 = \frac{2 * Precision * Recall}{Precision + Recall}$$

FinSBD-2 is composed of two subtasks. Subtask-1 aims at evaluating the system's ability to predict and differentiate between sentences, lists and items accurately. Therefore, its official evaluation metric is mean of pairwise F1-score of sets *sentences*, *items* and *lists*. Whereas, subtask-2 aims at the prediction of the hierarchical layout of items, and hence its official evaluation metric is mean of pairwise F1-score of sets *item1*, *item2*, *item3* and *item4*.

4.4 Results and Error Analysis

FinSBD-2 shared task dataset had no separate validation split. In order to tune the hyper-parameters of our models, we chose one among the six financial documents in the train set for the validation purpose. Utilising this validation data, we tuned parameters such as input sequence length and hop-length for our final models. Table 3 and Table 4 summarise the results of our final models on the official test set.

In the first phase, we defined the problem as a sequence labelling task with seven output clases. Table 3 states the precision, recall and F1-score of our BiLSTM-CRF and BERT models in the first phase on our approach. Using the results table 3, we can conclude following points:

- Both the models predicted SEN tags more accurately than IT tags, presumably because sentences are more homogeneous and have little intra-class variations as compared to items.

- Both the models achieve better F1-score for the B-IT tag than the E-IT tag. This can be attributed to the fact that the beginning of item has more distinctive features, such as bullets/numbers, as compared to the ending of items.

- Similarly, models achieve better F1-score for E-SEN compared to B-SEN due to more reliable punctuation characters at the ending of the sentence.

- Class S-SEN has too few examples both in train and test set, and thus the numbers for this class do not convey much about models' performance.

For these two models, we also computed the weighted mean of F1-score of all the classes. BiLSTM-CRF and BERT achieved the final F1-score of 0.959 and 0.956. Thus, we conclude that both the models gave an almost similar performance on the task.

In the second phase, we utilised the outputs of first phase to identify the recursiveness and hierarchy. Table 4 states the precision, recall and F1-score of our rule-based approach. Our rule-based approach is susceptible to prediction errors, if the phase-1 fails to recall even a single item in some list. The falling F1-scores with the increased hierarchy (*lists > item1 > item2*) further reflect on this fact. The Macro-F1 scores for subtask-1 and subtask-2 were ranked first among all the submissions.

5 Conclusion and Future Work

In this paper, we described our approach to tackle the FinSBD-2 shared task. Our approach was composed of two phases. In the first phase, we formulated the modified version of the task as a sequence labelling problem. We experimented with two neural models, namely, BiLSTM-CRF and BERT. In the second phase, we employed a rule-based approach to identify recursiveness and hierarchy among item segments from the first phase. We experimented with different hyper-parameter settings to tune our model. We submitted a system based on BiLSTM-CRF with an input length 300 as our final entry to the shared task. Our final system achieved the highest MEAN F1-score in the shared task. Our approach in this shared task should motivate research into the usage of visual information for sentence/list extraction from noisy PDF documents. In the future, we wish to explore the idea of multi-modality and end-to-end trainable deep neural models for this task.

References

[Agarwal *et al.*, 2005] Nishant Agarwal, K. Ford, and Mickhail N Shneider. Sentence boundary detection using a maxent classifier. 2005.

[Akita *et al.*, 2006] Yuya Akita, Masahiro Saikou, Hiroaki Nanjo, and Tatsuya Kawahara. Sentence boundary detection of spontaneous japanese using statistical language model and support vector machines. 01 2006.

[Azzi *et al.*, 2019] Abderrahim Ait Azzi, Houda Bouamor, and Sira Ferradans. The FinSBD-2019 shared task: Sentence boundary detection in PDF noisy text in the financial domain. In *Proceedings of the First Workshop on Financial Technology and Natural Language Processing*, pages 74–80, Macao, China, August 2019.

[Devlin *et al.*, 2019] Jacob Devlin, Ming-Wei Chang, Kenton Lee, and Kristina Toutanova. BERT: Pre-training of deep bidirectional transformers for language understanding. In *Proceedings of the 2019 Conference of the North American Chapter of the Association for Computational Linguistics: Human Language Technologies, Volume 1 (Long and Short Papers)*, pages 4171–4186, Minneapolis, Minnesota, June 2019. Association for Computational Linguistics.

[Du and Huang, 2019] Jinhua Du and Yan Huang. Aig investments.ai at the finsbd task: Sentence boundary detection through sequence labelling and bert fine-tuning. 2019.

[Evang *et al.*, 2013] Kilian Evang, Valerio Basile, G. Chrupała, and Johan Bos. Elephant: Sequence labeling for word and sentence segmentation. pages 1422–1426, 01 2013.

[Gillick, 2009] Dan Gillick. Sentence boundary detection and the problem with the U.S. In *Proceedings of Human Language Technologies: The 2009 Annual Conference of the North American Chapter of the Association for Computational Linguistics, Companion Volume: Short Papers*, pages 241–244, Boulder, Colorado, June 2009. Association for Computational Linguistics.

[Hochreiter and Schmidhuber, 1997] Sepp Hochreiter and Jürgen Schmidhuber. Long short-term memory. volume 9, page 1735–1780, Cambridge, MA, USA, November 1997. MIT Press.

[Kiss and Strunk, 2006] Tibor Kiss and Jan Strunk. Unsupervised multilingual sentence boundary detection. volume 32, page 485–525, Cambridge, MA, USA, December 2006. MIT Press.

[Kreuzthaler and Schulz, 2015] Markus Kreuzthaler and Stefan Schulz. Detection of sentence boundaries and abbreviations in clinical narratives. volume 15 Suppl 2, page S4, 06 2015.

[Pennington *et al.*, 2014] Jeffrey Pennington, Richard Socher, and Christopher Manning. GloVe: Global vectors for word representation. In *Proceedings of the 2014 Conference on Empirical Methods in Natural Language Processing (EMNLP)*, pages 1532–1543, Doha, Qatar, October 2014. Association for Computational Linguistics.

[Peters *et al.*, 2018] Matthew Peters, Mark Neumann, Mohit Iyyer, Matt Gardner, Christopher Clark, Kenton Lee, and Luke Zettlemoyer. Deep contextualized word representations. In *Proceedings of the 2018 Conference of the North American Chapter of the Association for Computational Linguistics: Human Language Technologies, Volume 1 (Long Papers)*, pages 2227–2237, New Orleans, Louisiana, June 2018. Association for Computational Linguistics.

[Polanyi *et al.*, 2004] Livia Polanyi, Chris Culy, Martin van den Berg, Gian Lorenzo Thione, and David Ahn. A rule based approach to discourse parsing. In *Proceedings of the 5th SIGdial Workshop on Discourse and Dialogue at HLT-NAACL 2004*, pages 108–117, Cambridge, Massachusetts, USA, April 30 - May 1 2004. Association for Computational Linguistics.

[Read *et al.*, 2012] Jonathon Read, Rebecca Dridan, Stephan Oepen, and Lars Jørgen Solberg. Sentence boundary detection: A long solved problem? In *Proceedings of COLING 2012: Posters*, pages 985–994, Mumbai, India, December 2012. The COLING 2012 Organizing Committee.

[Reynar and Ratnaparkhi, 1997] Jeffrey C. Reynar and Adwait Ratnaparkhi. A maximum entropy approach to identifying sentence boundaries. In *Proceedings of the Fifth Conference on Applied Natural Language Processing*, ANLC '97, page 16–19, USA, 1997. Association for Computational Linguistics.

[Schuster and Paliwal, 1997] M. Schuster and K. K. Paliwal. Bidirectional recurrent neural networks. volume 45, pages 2673–2681, 1997.

[Srivastava *et al.*, 2014] Nitish Srivastava, Geoffrey Hinton, Alex Krizhevsky, Ilya Sutskever, and Ruslan Salakhutdinov. Dropout: A simple way to prevent neural networks from overfitting. volume 15, page 1929–1958. JMLR.org, January 2014.

[Straková *et al.*, 2019] Jana Straková, Milan Straka, and Jan Hajic. Neural architectures for nested NER through linearization. In *Proceedings of the 57th Annual Meeting of the Association for Computational Linguistics*, pages 5326–5331, Florence, Italy, July 2019. Association for Computational Linguistics.

[Sutton and McCallum, 2012] Charles Sutton and Andrew McCallum. An introduction to conditional random fields. *Found. Trends Mach. Learn.*, 4(4):267–373, April 2012.

[Vaswani *et al.*, 2017] Ashish Vaswani, Noam Shazeer, Niki Parmar, Jakob Uszkoreit, Llion Jones, Aidan N Gomez, Ł ukasz Kaiser, and Illia Polosukhin. Attention is all you need. In I. Guyon, U. V. Luxburg, S. Bengio, H. Wallach, R. Fergus, S. Vishwanathan, and R. Garnett, editors, *Advances in Neural Information Processing Systems 30*, pages 5998–6008. Curran Associates, Inc., 2017.

aiai at the FinSBD-2 task: Sentence, List, and Item Boundary Detection and Items Classification of Noisy Financial Texts Using Data Augmentation and Attention Model

Ke Tian, Hua Chen & Jie Yang

Rakuten Inc, Japan

Jiangxi Normal University, China

South China University of Technology University, China

tianke0711@gmail.com, hua.chen@kyudai.jp, 1661075801@qq.com

Abstract

This paper describes the method that we submitted to the FinSBD2-shared task in IJCAI-2020 to detect the sentence, list, and item boundaries and classify the items from noisy unstructured English and French financial texts. We used the spatial and semantic information of text to augment each tokenized word of text as a fixed-length sentence, and we labeled each word sentence as different boundary types. Then, we proposed the deep attention model based on word embedding to detect the sentence, list, and items boundaries in noisy English and French texts extracted from the financial documents and classified the item sentences into different item types. The experiment shows that the proposed method could be an effective solution to deal with the FinSBD2-shared task.

1 Introduction

The sentence is the fundamental unit in the written language. Thus, using sentence boundary detection (SBD), which detects the beginning and end of the sentence, is the first step of many language tasks, for example Part-of-speech (POS) tagging, discourse parsing, and machine translation. Until now, research about SBD has been confined to formal texts, such as news and European parliament proceedings, which have high accuracy using rule-based machine learning and deep learning methods due to the perfectly clean text data [Tian et al., 2019b]. However, there is almost no SBD research to address the problem in noisy texts, which are extracted automatically from machine-readable files, such as the financial PDF file format. One type of financial file is prospectus documents. Financial prospectuses are official PDF documents in which investment funds precisely describe their characteristics and investment information. The most critical step of extracting any information from these PDF files is to first analyze the information to get noisy unstructured text data, clean the text to format the information, and finally, transform it into semi-structured text so that sentence and list boundaries are well organized [FinNLP-2020, 2020]. Therefore, using SBD is an essential step to process the noisy financial text. The FinNLP work-

shop in IJCAI-2019 is the first proposal of FinSBD-2019 shared tasks that detect sentence boundaries in the noisy text of finance documents [Ait Azzi et al., 2019]. However, these financial prospectuses documents also contain many visual demarcations that indicate a hierarchy of sections, including bullets and numbered texts. There are many sentence fragments and titles—and not just complete sentences; some are lists or item texts. The prospectuses often contain punctuation errors. To organize the dense information into a more easily read format, lists are often utilized. Therefore, detection of the list, item boundary, and items classification is also crucial in the processing of the noisy text of finance documents. The task of FinSBD2 in the second FinNLP-2020 extended last year's task to include the detection of the list, items boundary detection, and items classification of the noisy text of finance documents.

There are English and French datasets in the FinSBD2 task. Our proposed method used the deep attention model and data augmentation method to approach the English and French tasks. According to the final leader board, the result is that our method could be a possible solution to deal with the English and French tasks, respectively.

Section 2 explains the details of the FinNLP-2020 task. Section 3 describes our method. Section 4 shows experimental configurations and discusses the results. Then, Section 5 concludes this paper.

2 Task Description

The FinSBD2 tasks included two sub-tasks. One is to detect the start and end char index of the sentence, list, and items part in noisy English and French text of finance documents. Another task is to classify the text of the item into four items: item1, item2, item3, and item4. We take one of the English task JSON files as an example to describe the task data.

J1: {"text": " \nCredit Suisse Fund I (Lux) \nInvestment Company with Variable Capital established \nunder...." "sentence": [{"start": 2, "end": 28,"coordinates": {"lines": [{ "x0": 216.42, "x1": 425.83,"y0": 441.44, "y1": 452.16, "page": 1}],"start": {"text": "C","x0": 216.42,"x1": 228.75, "y0": 441.44, "y1": 452.16, "page": 1}, "end": {

"text": ")", "x0": 419.49, "x1": 425.83, "y0": 441.44, "y1": 452.16, "page": 1}}}, "list": [..], "Item":[..], "Item1":[…], "Item2":[], "Item3":[…], Item4:[…].

As shown in the English JSON file J1, "text" is the text from the English financial PDF document. "Sentence" is the sentence text. Moreover, the start and end char index of sentence text is provided. In addition, the rectangle coordinate (xmin: the left upper x coordinate, ymin: the left upper y coordinate, xmax: the right bottom x coordinate, ymax: the right bottom y coordinate) data of each character of text is provided for text spatial visualization. The list and item texts label data are the same as sentence text information. As submitted prediction JSON data, the start and end char index of the sentence, list, and items should be predicted respectively, and items include four item types: item1, item2, item3, and item4. There are 29 labeled JSON (6 English and 23 French) in the training data. The test data is composed of 2 English and 10 French prediction JSON data.

3   Method

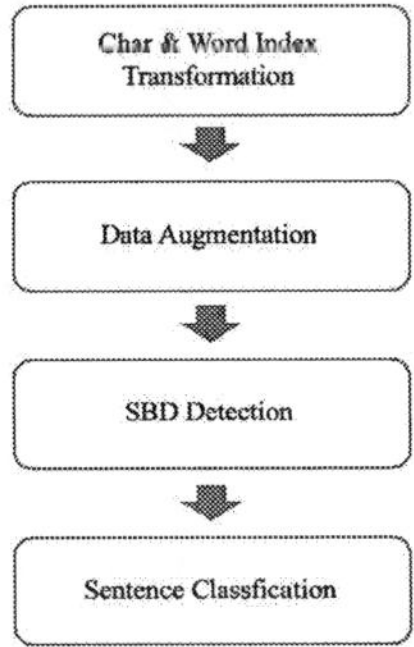

Figure 1: Procedure of proposed method

The whole processing procedure of the proposed method to deal with these two tasks is shown in Figure 1. Firstly, we transform the begin and end char index of the sentence, list, and items to the begin and end word token index in the word token text. Secondly, the spatial coordinate of the begin index of each word, the previous n word tokens, and the next n word tokens of each work token are used to augment each tokenized word to be a fixed sentence. After the fixed sentences are created, the fixed sentence could be labeled as four classes: begin word, end word, independent word, and other words. Then, the deep attention model is used to detect each fixed sentence. Thirdly, after the boundary label of each tokenized word in the text is detected, the begin and end char indexes of the sentence are detected. Then, the deep attention model is used to classify the predicted sentences into six types: sentence, list, item1, item2, item3, item4.

The details about char and word index transformation and data augmentation are described in Section 2.1. The sentence boundary detection and sentence classification are described in Section 2.2, and the ensemble result is presented in Section 2.3.

3.1   Data Augmentation

In the training JSON data, the begin and end char index of the sentence, list, and items are provided. We found that just char index information is not enough to predict the sentence boundary since the number of chars in training text is limited. In order to get more information for prediction boundary detection, it is better to obtain the begin and end word index of sentences. However, the char and word index transformation are not provided by the task. We have tried the spaCy library to do the word tokenization of English and French text. The spaCy library [spaCy, 2020] provides a function to obtain the begin char index of each word token in the text.

We observed that the end part of a sentence does not just use punctuation like '.' and ';' It includes some words like ')' and ':', which caused the ending part to be complicated. Like the ending part, the beginning part of the sentence also is not just words beginning with upper letters like 'The' and 'This.' It also includes symbol characters like '(' and '1.' Therefore, using only the rule to detect the beginning and ending of a sentence may not be effective. Besides, there are some words that also sentence that the beginning word and end word is the word itself.

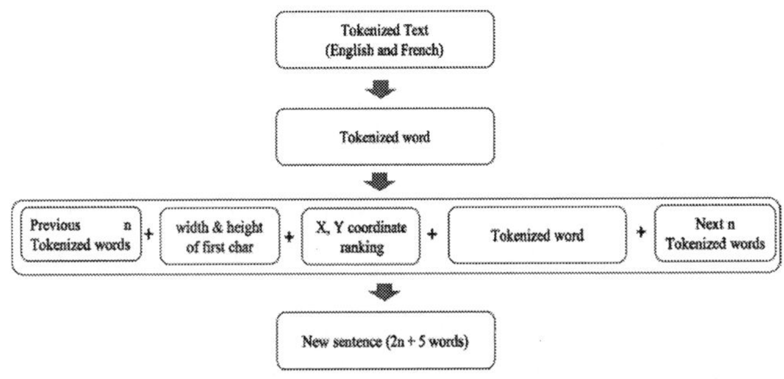

Figure 2: Procedure of data augmentation for boundary detection

We found that unusual beginnings and endings are identifiable by context. The surrounding words around beginning and ending words could help to identify the sentence boundary. Moreover, the size of the begin char is different from other chars. Most of the begin chars are upper letters, so the widths and heights are longer than that of lower letters. Moreover, the position of the beginning index is often located in the left part of the whole page. Based on these observations, the spatial coordinate, width, and height ranking of the begin char index of each word, the previous n word tokens, and the next n word tokens of each work token are used to augment each work token to be a fixed tokenized sentence. The procedure of data augmentation for sentence boundary detection training and test data is shown in Figure 2.

We take the J1 sentence as an example to describe how to augment each word to be a fixed sentence. After using the spaCy library to token the text, we found that the J1 token text is as follows: [""\n"", 'Credit', Suisse', 'Fund', 'I', '(', 'Lux', ')', '\n', 'Investment', 'Company',......]

As each tokenized word, the previous n tokenized words following n tokenized words of each tokenized word, x and y coordinate ranking, width and height ranking of first char are taken to be concatenated into a new sentence. For example, take the "n is 5" as an example. As the first word is "/n" in the J1, there were no previous 5 words, so we added 5 "pre" words at the beginning of the sentence, and X, Y coordinate ranking, width, and height ranking are null. Therefore, the new sentence for "/n " is the T1 sentence. With the beginning word " Credit ," the new sentence is T2. As the end word ""')", the new sentence is T3. At the end of the J1 text, there were no next 5 words, so we added 5 "EOS" words at the end of the sentence. The labels of T1, T2, and T3 are "OS", "BS", and "ES," respectively, which are the same as the labels of the tokenized words "\n,'" "Credit," and "')," respectively. Besides, there are some sentences in which the begin and end char is located in the same word. So the label of such a kind of word is labeled as "IS." The train and test data in English and French use the same method to augment words for a fixed sentence. There are four labels (OS, BS, ES, IS) for the train and test data. Therefore, the goal of sentence boundary detection is converted to classify the labels of the new augmented sentence.

T1: ['pre', 'pre', 'pre', 'pre', 'pre', 'coor_x_null, 'coor_y_null', ' width_null',' height_null', ' \n', 'Credit', 'Suisse', 'Fund', 'I', '(]

T2: ['pre', 'pre', 'pre', 'pre', ' \n', 'coor_x_164', 'coor_y_364', ' width_11', 'height_6', 'Credit', 'Suisse', 'Fund', 'I', '(', 'Lux']

T3: ['Suisse', 'Fund', 'I', '(', 'Lux', 'coor_x_367', 'coor_y_364' , 'width_5', 'height_6', ')', '\n', 'Investment', 'Company', 'with', 'Variable']

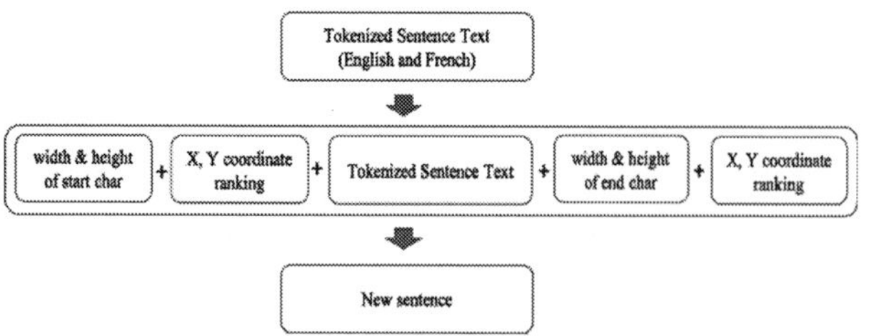

Figure 3: Procedure of data augmentation for sentence classification

Regarding the sentence classification data, the start and end char index of sentences, lists, and items are provided. Based on the char and word transformation, the tokenized word

sentence text of the sentences, lists, and items could be inferred. The spatial information and width and height rankings of start char and end char are added to augment the training and test sentence texts. The procedure of data augmentation for sentence classification training and test data is shown in Figure 3.

We take one of the J1 sentence texts as an example to describe how to augment the J1 sentence to be a new sentence. As T4 sentence text. X & Y coordinate ranking, width & height ranking of first char and end char are taken to be concatenated into a new sentence named T5. The train and test data in English and French use the same method to augment the text of the sentences, lists, and items.

T4: ['Suisse', 'Fund', 'I', '(', 'Lux', ')']

T5: ['coor_x_164','coor_y_364','width_11','height_6','Credit' ,'Suisse','Fund','I','(','Lux',')','coor_x_374','coor_y_364','width_4','height_6']

Now the goal of the FinSBD2 task has changed to text classification. Word embedding is the foundation of deep learning for natural language processing. We use the new train, test text data to train the word embedding as the first SBD classification. In the recreated English text data, there are 329,908 recreated sentences with 9,894 unique token words from the training and test data. In the French text, there are 698,612 recreated sentences with 12,374 unique token words from the training and test data. Regarding sentence classification, there are 11,931 and 20,858 sentence texts of the sentences, lists, and items in English and French train and test data, respectively. The CBOW model [Tomas Mikolov, 2013] is taken to train word vectors for the English and French text data, and the word2vec dimension is set to 100.

3.2 Sentence Boundary Detection and Sentence Classification

To complete the task goal and get the submission data, we first classify the tokenized words into four classes: BS, ES, OS, and IS with augmented sentence classification. The start and end char index are based on the word index using spaCy. After we obtain the word label of text, the sentence text can be extracted based on boundary labels. Secondly, the extracted sentence texts are predicted to be sentence, list, and item labels. Finally, the submission data with sentence label and char index is complete.

Through the task train data, we observe that some keywords can help determine the category of a sentence. For example, "." and ")" indicate the ending part of the sentence. Thus, some keywords in the sentence have more importance in predicting the label of sentence text. Since the attention mechanism can enable the neural model to focus on the relevant part of your input, such as the words of the input text, the attention mechanism is used to solve the task [Ke Tian et al., 2019a]. In this paper, we mainly use the feed-forward attention mechanism [Colin Raffel et al., 2015]. We put in the attention layer in the long short-term memory (LSTM) [Sepp Hochreiter et al., 1997] model, which has been provided adequately in the sentence boundary detection [Ke Tian et al., 2019b], as shown in Figure 4. In this paper, the attention-based LSTM is utilized for sentence boundary detection and sentence classification.

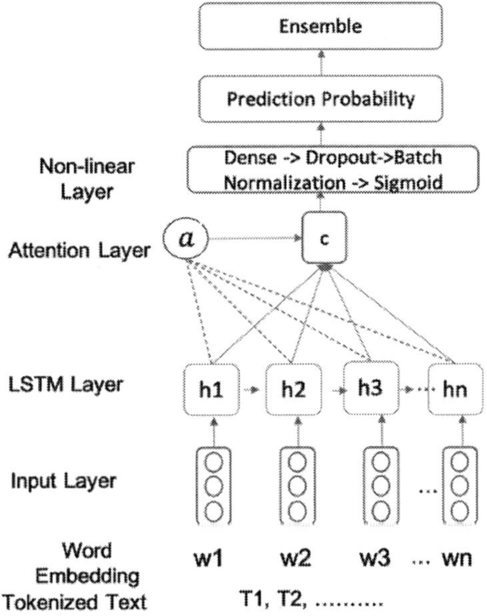

Figure 4: Attention-based LSTM model

Regarding the structure of the proposed model, as the LSTM layer, the embedding dimension and max word length of word embedding are set at 100 and 2n+1 (n is the number of words surrounding the tokenized word), respectively, for English and French boundary detection. As the sentence classification, embedding dimension is 100 for both English and French tasks. For max word length, the French text is 400, and the English text is 700. The embedding layer of the word embedding matrix as an input layer of LSTM, and the size of the output dimension is 300. We used the feed-forward attention mechanism as the attention layer. As the non-linear layer, the activation function is to dense the output of the attention layer to be 256 dimensions, and by using the dropout rate of 0.25, the output result after the dropout rate will be batch normalization. Finally, the sigmoid activation function is to dense the dimension of batch normalization input to be the length of the label as the final output layer for boundary detection and sentence classification.

3.3 Ensemble Result

As the model training stage, the 5-fold cross-validation is used to train the deep attention model for predicting the test data for boundary detection and sentence classification. We sum 5 folds of predicted probability and get the mean value of 5 folds for the final predicted probability result.

4 Experiment

4.1 Experiment Design and Implementation

In the experiment stage, the spaCy-based method and the proposed method were implemented to complete the boundary detection and sentence classification goals. Moreover, in the data processing stage, we have kept the upper letter of words to train the word embedding in the English and French text. In addition, we tested the different numbers of words surrounding each tokenized word. The numbers 10 are used to complete these tasks. The deep attention model in our paper was implemented using Keras deep learning libarary [Keras, 2019].

Based on the evaluation requirements of the FinSBD2 Task, the F-scores were taken to evaluate the performance of predicted sentence, list, and item boundaries, which are pairs of character indexes ("start" and "end"), using the proposed model in the paper.

4.2 Experiment Result and Discussion

Based on the result, the results of the deep attention model are shown in Table 1. As seen in Table 1, as the English task, the score of the spaCy based is worse than the proposed method score. Moreover, the final score of the aiai team in the final leader board is shown in Table 2.

Method	Lang	Subtask 1	Subtask 2
spaCy	French	0.199	0
	English	0.208	0
Proposed method	French	0.471	0.35
	English	0.413	0.203

Table 1: Experiment result

	English		French		
Team name	Subtask1	Subtask2	Subtask1	Subtask2	mean
PublishCovid19	0.937	0.844	0	0	0.445
aiai	0.413	0.203	0.471	0.35	0.359
Daniel	0.317	0	0.262	0	0.145
Subtl.ai	0.217	0	0	0	0.054
Anuj	0.126	0	0.025	0	0.038

Table 2: Final leader board ranking

The above result shows that the proposed method could be a possible solution to predict the beginning and end char index of the sentences, lists, and items in English and French text.

However, the score of the proposed method still needs to be improved compared with the ideal score. We surmised that the following reasons may cause the score to be low. Firstly, the preprocessing of text is not done enough for boundary detection and sentence classification. Secondly, the parameter tuning (such as n words tuning and other parameters) is not often done due to busy schedules. Thirdly, we have only used the deep attention model—other models such as the Bidirectional Encoder Representations from Transformers (BERT) [Devlin et al., 2018] and the Named Entity Recognition (NER) methods have not been tried in the current tasks. Fourthly, the limited amount of task training data may influence the performance of the proposed method. Finally, in the English word and char transformation, there are some words that do not match the relative char index.

5 Conclusions and Future Work

This paper primarily informs the aiai team how to tackle the FinSBD2-2020 shared tasks. There are two tasks—one is to predict the start and end char index of the sentences, lists, and items part in noisy English and French text of finance documents. Another one is to classify the items' text into four items: item1, item2, item3, and item4. We approach these two tasks as text classification problems using data augmentation and the deep attention model. The experimented result showed that the proposed model might effectively solve the goal of the task.

However, our method still needs to be improved to achieve better performance in the following directions. Firstly, it is better to do more parameter tuning in the current model to improve the accuracy of boundary detection and sentence classification. Moreover, we will explore different methods and models, such as the BERT model, to improve the boundary detection accuracy.

Acknowledgments

This work is financially supported by the Scientific Research Foundation of Jiangxi Normal University for the PhD (No. 0901/12019572).

References

[Ait Azzi et al., 2019] Abderrahim Ait Azzi, Houda Bouamor, and Sira Ferradans. The finsbd-2019 shared task: Sentence boundary detection in pdf noisy text in the financial domain. *In The First Workshop on Financial Technology and Natural Language Processing (FinNLP 2019)*, Macao, China, 2019.

[Colin Raffel et al., 2015] Colin Raffel and Daniel P. W. Ellis. Feed-forward networks with attention can solve some long term memory problems. https://arxiv.org/abs/1512.08756, 2015.

[FinNLP-2020 2020] FinNLP-2020. https://sites.google.com/nlg.csie.ntu.edu.tw/finnlp2020/shared-task-finsbd-2. Accessed: May 2020.

[Ke Tian a et al., 2019a] Ke Tian and Zi Jun Peng. aiai at FinNum task: Financial numeral tweets fine-grained classification using deep word and character embedding-based attention model. The 14th NTCIR Conference, Tokyo, Japan, June 2019.

[Ke Tian et al., 2019b] Ke Tian and Zi Jun Peng. aiai at FinSBD task: Sentence Boundary Detection in Noisy Texts From Financial Documents Using Deep Attention Model. aiai at FinSBD task: Sentence Boundary Detection

[Keras, 2019] Keras. The python deep learning library. https://keras.io. Accessed: May 2019

[Sepp Hochreiter et al., 1997] Sepp Hochreiter and Jürgen Schmid- huber. Long short-term memory. Neural Computation, 9(8):1735-1780, 1997.

[spaCy 2020] spaCy. https://spacy.io. Accessed: May 2020

[Tomas Mikolov, 2013] Tomas Mikolov, Ilya Sutskever, Kai Chen, Greg Corrado and Jeffrey Dean. Distributed represen- tations of words and phrases and their compositionality. https://arxiv.org/abs/1310.4546, 2013.

Daniel at the FinSBD-2 task :
Extracting Lists and Sentences from PDF Documents:
a model-driven end-to-end approach to PDF document analysis

Emmanuel Giguet[1]* and **Gaël Lejeune**[2]

[1]Normandie Univ, UNICAEN, ENSICAEN, CNRS, GREYC
14000 Caen, France
[2]STIH, Sorbonne University
75005 Paris, France
emmanuel.giguet@unicaen.fr, gael.lejeune@sorbonne-universite.fr

Abstract

In this paper, we present the method we have designed and implemented for identifying lists and sentences in PDF documents while participating to FinSBD-2 Financial Document Analysis Shared Task. We propose a model-driven approach for the French and English datasets. It relies on a top-down process from the PDF itself in order to keep control of the workflow. Our objective is to use PDF structure extraction to improve text segment boundaries detection in an end-to-end fashion.

1 Introduction

Our team participated to the FinSBD-2 Shared Task dedicated to Sentence Boundary Detection in Financial Prospectuses. The task aims at identifying sentences, ordered lists, unordered lists, and list items in PDF Documents. It also aims at recovering the hierarchical structure of embedded lists. It was our first participation to this shared task. Our motivation is to improve our model-driven approach to multilingual document analysis.

Our approach was illustrated in FinTOC'2019 Shared Task [Rémi Juge, 2019]. It was dedicated to Table Of Content structure extraction from PDF Financial Documents. The task aimed at identifying and organizing the headers of the document according to its hierarchical structure. Since our approach gave good results on this task [Giguet and Lejeune, 2019], we took advantage of the second edition of FinTOC, called FinTOC-2020, to improve the implementation of our model driven approach. We seized the opportunity of the second edition of FinSBD [Ait Azzi et al., 2019], to promote our overall model-driven approach and to enrich our document model with smaller units, i.e paragraphs, sentences and lists.

The paper is organized as follows. Section 2 discusses the rationale behind the interest for sentences in NLP. Section 3 provides the state of the art approaches to tackle the problem. Section 4 presents the preprocessing applied to the PDF documents. The next sections are dedicated to our document model-based approach: section 5 presents how to handle page layout at document scope; section 6 describes the detection and Structure Induction of various Document Objects including headers and footers, tables, lists, paragraphs. Section 7 presents the results we obtained on the task. Section 8 concludes and gives some perspectives about this work.

2 The importance of sentences in NLP Architectures

One way to present NLP tasks is to describe them as a series of transformation from an input format (e.g., a PDF file, a HTML file, a set of character strings) to an output format suitable for downstream components (e.g., an XML or JSON enriched file) or for end-users (e.g., a HTML file). NLP Components piped together form an NLP pipeline.

The rationale behind the NLP pipeline is to favor factorization and reuse of existing NLP components. In that way, tackling a new task may consist in preprocessing a new input format in order to feed an existing NLP pipeline (e.g., converting PDF binary file to machine-readable text) or to compose a pipeline by choosing the appropriate components for a given task. In NLP, the two main input and output formats are inherited from traditional grammar: words and sentences. The text representation is usually reconstructed from these units (see for instance DOC2VEC [Le and Mikolov, 2014]).

For many NLP components, the word (approximated by the concept of "token") is the core analysis grain and the sentence is the parsing frame. In that perspective, solving the tokenization task is considered to be a prerequisite to the proper application of NLP techniques. In some languages the task will be considered to be solved, in particular for English [Smith, 2020], while in under resourced languages like dialects [Bernhard et al., 2017] or ancient language variants [Gabay et al., 2019] the task requires intensive care from the research community. Tokens and sentences can be produced from any character string but it is common to tokenize from small text blocks (e.g., paragraphs, headers) rather than complete documents. Text blocks are search spaces in which token boundaries and sentence boundaries are computed. To this end, text blocks are expected to be large enough to contain at least one sentence. It should not be too large to limit memory consumption and computational costs.

---

*Contact Author

While many algorithms can handle long text blocks the same way they process short blocks, some NLP approaches are very sensitive to the input length. Some tasks can be performed by linear time algorithms, other ones involve a higher computational cost, with a time complexity sometimes higher than quadratic in some cases [Corro, 2020]. Another example is word embeddings models where the input length is a key feature. For instance, the CAMEMBERT model (BERT for French) can not process inputs longer than five hundred twelve tokens [Martin *et al.*, 2020]. Obviously, whatever the time complexity, the space complexity also has to be controlled in order to limit the amount of space and memory taken by the underlying algorithms.

Processing long documents such as financial prospectuses with an NLP pipeline requires the proper definition of text blocks and sentences. While small text blocks such as paragraphs or headers are expected to be easily computed, the NLP architect has to guarantee that the computed blocks and sentences always fit the requirement of the different NLP components, in terms of time and space complexity. The task is not trivial when the pipeline is made of NLP components designed by various contributors.

Assuming that paragraphs and headers are always relevant text blocks leads to failure. It does not guarantee that paragraphs will never exceed the expected maximum length. Similarly, assuming that sentence tokenization guarantees a certain maximum length fails when confronted to text without any punctuation.

3 Sentence Segmentation in Practice

3.1 State of the art on Sentence Boundary Detection

Sentence boundary detection plays a crucial role in Natural Language Processing. For a long time, sentences have been considered as given input. Things changed with the rise of robust parsing in the 90's. What is a sentence and how to detect them automatically in raw texts becomes crucial. The concept of sentence is questioned by [Grefenstette and Tapanainen, 1994]. [Giguet, 1995] adresses the problem in the context of multilingual sentence tokenization in raw texts.

[Ait Azzi *et al.*, 2019] retraces the milestones and achievements in Sentence Boundary Detection, from the first rule-based approaches to the recent deep-learning approaches. They open a new challenge related to the identification of sentences in noisy unstructured PDF documents from the finance sector. Obviously the issue is much broader and impacts all the works concerning PDF document analysis.

[Dale *et al.*, 2000] highlights the fact that there are four challenges for sentence segmentation: (I) Language Dependence, (II) Character-Set Dependence, (III) Application Dependence and (IV) Corpus Dependence. Except for "Application Dependence", all of these challenges are linked to variations in the input data. Therefore, the techniques that have been developed by the community tend to focus on handling the variability of the data to be processed. One of the main questions regarding SBD is whether the sentence boundaries are explicitly marked or not. It relies to both language dependence and corpus dependence since all languages will not

mark explicitly depending on the text genre for instance. In an experiment on multilingual SBD [Kiss and Strunk, 2006] it has been shown that the main issue is that the period can serve multiple purposes and that handling this "polysemy" allows to get rid of most of boundary errors. In other application domains there has been more focus on the detection of sentence starters, obviously the best example would be speech processing [Bachenko *et al.*, 1995].

3.2 State of the art on Lists and Enumerations

Research on lists and enumerations as text objects playing an important role in the text architecture has been conducted by [Virbel, 1999; Pascual and Virbel, 1996] in Toulouse, France. [Luc, 2001] studied the representation of the internal structure of enumerations with two text structure models: the Rhetorical Structure Theory (RST) and the model of text architecture, dedicated to the study and representation of visuo-spatial structures of texts. [Maurel, 2004; Maurel *et al.*, 2006] studied visuo-spatial structures of texts, in particular enumerations. This work, related to Natural Language Processing, concerns the oral transposition of these structures by Text-To-Speech systems. Regarding list detection, [Déjean, 2010] introduced a method for detecting numbered sequence in documents.

4 Preprocessing PDF Documents

In previous INEX Book Structure Extraction Competitions, we used to consider the whole document to extract the structure [Giguet and Lucas, 2010a; Giguet and Lucas, 2010b; Giguet *et al.*, 2009]. In our participation to this FinSBD shared task; we wanted to start over from this approach in order to get an end-to-end pipeline from the PDF file itself to sentence segmentation[1]. The experiment is conducted from PDF documents to ensure the control of the entire process. The document content is extracted using the `pdf2xml` command [Déjean, 2007]. It allow us to extract text content with its structural information via vectorial shapes.

4.1 Dealing with Text Content : tokens, lines and blocks

There is no concept of "word" or "number" or "token" in a PDF file. Therefore, these units have to be inferred. In order to ease the processing, `pdf2xml` defines a "token" as a computational unit based on character spacing. In practice, most output tokens correspond to words or numbers but they can also correspond to a composition of several interpretable unit (e.g., "Introduction . . . . . . 5" or a breakdown of an interpretable unit (e.g., "C" "O" "N" "T" "E" "N" "T").

We assume that the PDF financial prospectuses are automatically generated by the PDF converter of a word processor. Thus, we do not check if the document is a scanned document or if it is the output of an OCR application.

Consequently, we do not consider possible trapezoid or parallelogram distortion, page rotation or curved lines. This assumption simplifies the initial stages: baselines and line-spacing are inferred from the coordinates on the y-axis; left,

---

[1]Code : https://github.com/rundimeco/daniel_fintoc2019/FINSBD2/

right and centered alignments are inferred from the coordinates on the x-axis.

For `pdf2xml`, tokens are linked to two other units that we do not use in our experimentation:

line : a sequence of tokens which may correspond to a coherent visual text line (relatively to token-spacing)

block : a sequence of lines which may correspond to a coherent visual text block (relatively to line-spacing).

We only rely on the `pdf2xml` "token" unit. We redefine our own "line" unit in order to better control the coherence of our hierarchy of graphical units.

4.2 Dealing with Vectorial Shapes

One of the main advantages of using `pdf2xml` is to enable our approach to rely on vectorial information during document analysis. Text background, framed content, underline text, table grid are crucial information that contributes to sense making: we have no reason to ignore them. They simplify the reader's task of sense-making [Sorin, 2015], so that they may contribute in a positive way to automatic document analysis.

Most vectorial shapes are basic closed path, mostly rectangles. Graphical lines or graphical points do not exist: lines as well as points are rectangles interpreted by the cognitive skills of the reader as lines or points.

In order to use vectorial information in document analysis, we implemented a preprocessing stage that enables to build composite vectorial shapes and to interpret them as text backgrounds, cell borders, underlines. This preprocessing component returns results that are used to detect framed content and table grids.

As an example of vectorial preprocessing, more than thirteen rectangles may have to be processed to identify a single table cell with background and borders:

- eight adjacent rectangles for the borders : two horizontal borders, two vertical borders and four square corners;

- at least five rectangles for paving the cell background: four rectangles for cell paddings, and at least one rectangle for text background.

In the context of FinSBD, dealing with vectorial information allows to detect tables and ignore them. Since no sentence boundaries has to be searched in tables, table exclusion contributes to avoid the generation of potentially numerous false positive since tables are long and frequent in financial prospectuses.

5 Handling Page Layout at Document Scope

5.1 Dealing with Content Areas

We assume that PDF converters serialize the content of a page area by area, depending on the page layout. A *content area* corresponds to a page subdivision such as a column, a header, a footer, or a floating table or figure. However, content areas are represented neither in the PDF structure nor in the `pdf2xml` output. Content areas are implicitly inferred and interpreted by the cognitive skills of the reader.

As an example, the repetition of a content located at the bottom of contiguous pages (i.e., positional information), with identical style properties (i.e., morphological information), visually detached from the above content and smaller than the above content (i.e., contrastive information), leads the reader to perceive a content area and to interpret it as a footer. In the PDF document, it is only a series of characters with style properties in the 2D coordinate system of sequential pages.

When a content area is processed by the PDF converter, we assume that characters and lines are serialized in reading order, so that there is no ordering problem to consider inside a content area. However, when parsing a page, we cannot always expect to find the content serialized in reading order: PDF converters can serialize content areas in several ways. For instance, the header and footer areas can be serialized before the page's main content. Indeed, the boundary delimitation of content areas inside a page is one of the main challenges.

Bounding the content areas over pages is not immediate due to the absence of marks that separate them from other adjacent areas. In our process, positional information, morphological information and contrastive information are inferred from the document structure in order to help the boundary delimitation of content areas.

5.2 From Page Layout to Page Layout Models

Page Layout Analysis (PLA) aims at recognizing and labeling content areas in a page (e.g., text regions, tables, figures, lists). It is the subject of abundant research and articles. ICDAR challenges show the efforts of a large international community interested in Document Analysis and Recognition [Antonacopoulos *et al.*, 2009].

While PLA is often achieved at page scope and aims at bounding content regions, we have taken a model-driven approach at document scope. We try to directly infer Page Layout Models from the whole document and we then try to instantiate them on pages. This strategy has been used earlier, in the Resurgence Project [Giguet, 2008; Giguet, 2011].

Our Page Layout Model (PLM) is hierarchical and contains 2 positions at top-level: the *margin area* and the *main content area*.

The margin area contains two particular position, the *header area* located at the top, and the *footer area* located at the bottom. *Aside areas* may receive particular content such as vertically-oriented text.

The main content area contains *column areas* containing text, figures or tables. *Floating areas* are defined to receive content external to column area, such as large figures, tables or framed texts.

The positions that we try to fill at document scope are header, footer and main columns. First, pages are grouped depending on their size and orientation (i.e., portrait or landscape). Then header area and footer area are detected. Column areas are in the model but due to time constraints, the detection module is not fully implemented in this prototype yet.

5.3 Detecting Header and Footer Areas

Header area boundaries and footer area boundaries are computed from the repetition of similar tokens located at similar positions at the top and at the bottom of contiguous pages [Déjean and Meunier, 2006]. We take into account possible odd and even page layouts. The detection is done on the first twenty pages of the document. While this number is arbitrary, we consider it is enough to make reliable decisions in case of odd and even layouts.

A special process detects page numbering and computes the shift between the PDF page numbering and the document page numbering. Page numbering is computed from the repetition of tokens containing decimals and located at similar positions at the top or at the bottom of contiguous pages. These tokens are taken into account when computing header and footer boundaries.

Considering FinSBD Task, identifying header and footer allows to build the main content flow over pages. Hence, it avoids to get paragraphs, sentences or list items merged with header and footer content when they overlap two pages.

6 Parsing with a Document Model

In INEX Book Structure Extraction Competition, we introduced a relevant strategy to divide a document in main parts and chapters [Giguet *et al.*, 2009].

As we participated at FinTOC Shared Task [Giguet and Lejeune, 2019], we used a fallback strategy to divide the document in parts: the Table of Content (TOC) if detected is used to separate preliminaries from the main content of the document. The underlying idea is to rely on the main part's internal regularities when making decisions. This is useful for inferring paragraph models or list item models.

Contrary to our model-based approach, this fallback does not allow to separate the document body from its appendices or annexes. That is unfortunate since appendices and annexes may have their own regularities that should not be mixed with the document body regularities in the inference engine.

6.1 Detecting the Table of Contents

The TOC is located in the first pages of the document. It can spread over a limited number of contiguous pages. One formal property is common to all TOCs: the page numbers are right-aligned and form an increasing sequence of integers.

These characteristics are fully exploited in the core of our TOC identification process: we consider the pages of the first third of the document as a search space. Then, we select the first right-aligned sequence of lines ending by an integer and that may spread over contiguous pages.

Linking TOC Entries and Headers

Linking Table of Content Entries to main content is one of the most important process when structuring a document [Déjean and Meunier, 2010]. Computing successfully such relations demonstrates the reliability of header detection and permits to set hyperlinks from toc entries to document headers.

Once TOC is detected, each TOC Entry is linked to its corresponding page number in the document. This page number is converted to the PDF page number thanks to the page shift (see section 5.3). Then header is searched in the related PDF page. When found, the corresponding line is categorized as header.

6.2 Detection and Structure Induction of Document Objects in PDF Documents

In the main content area of our model, column areas and floating areas are both planned to contain information. While column areas are planned to contain the main text stream, floating areas are planned to contain spotlight contents that are relatively independent from the main content. Floating areas contains information that are not part of the main stream of text. Figures, tables, framed text may be such autonomous document components.

6.3 Table Detection and Table Structure Induction in PDF Documents

Table detection and table structure induction are beyond the scope of this article. However table detection is important for FinSBD in order to exclude table content from the main text stream. This way, we are able to exclude table rows when searching for list items or sentences. Table structure induction does not affect list or sentence boundary detection modules.

The table detection module analyzes the PDF vectorial shapes. Our algorithm builds table grids from adjacent framed table cells. The framed table cells are built from vectorial shapes that may represent cell borders. The table grid is defined by the graph of adjacent framed table cells.

The table structure is inferred from the vectorial grid, the vectorial cell backgrounds, and the inner text spacing. This way we handle table cells that span over multiple columns. Due to lack of time, table cells that span over multiple rows is not implemented yet.

Table detection and table structure induction have been designed and implemented outside FinSBD and reused as is for convenience.

6.4 Unordered List Structure Induction in PDF Documents

Unordered lists are also called *bulleted lists* since the list items are supposed to be marked with bullets. Unordered list may spread over multiple pages.

Unordered list items are searched at page scope. The typographical symbols (i.e., glyph) used to introduce items are not predefined. We infer the symbol by identifying multiple left-aligned lines introduced by the same single-character token. This strategy allows the algorithm to capture various bullet symbols such as squares, white bullets... Alphabetical or decimal characters are rejected as possible bullet style type.

The aim of the algorithm is to identify PDF lines which corresponds to new bulleted list item (i.e., list item leading lines). The objective is not to bound list items which cover multiple lines. Indeed, the end of list items are computed while computing paragraph structures: a list item ends when the next list item starts (i.e., same bullet symbol, same indentation) or when less indented text objects starts.

Share Class	ISIN Code	Swiss Securities Number (Telekurs)	German Security Identification Number	Accumulative or Income	Denomination Currency	Status	Listed? Yes/No	Minimum Subscription Amount	Minimum Additional Subscription Amount	Minimum Redemption Amount	Management Fee	Sales commission	Initial Issue Price
Class MU$ D1 Man Convertibles Far East – EUR Shares	LU0061927850	051.117	936 576	Accumulative	Euro (EUR)	Active	Yes	EUR 1'000	EUR 1'000	1 share	1.50%	up to 5% of net asset value	EUR 100
Class MU$ I168 Man Convertibles Far East – EUR Shares	LU0686792739			Accumulative	Euro (EUR)	Dormant	n/a	EUR 100'000	EUR 1'000	1 share	0.75%	up to 5% of net asset value	EUR 100
Class MU$ D157 Man Convertibles Far East – EUR Shares	LU0871786606			Accumulative	Euro (EUR)	Dormant	n/a	EUR 100'000	EUR 1'000	1 share	0.75%	up to 5% of net asset value	EUR 100
Class MU$ D2 Man Convertibles Far East - CHF Shares	LU0424369766	10109862	A0RNJ5	Accumulative	Swiss franc (CHF)	Active	No	CHF 1'000	CHF 1'000	1 share	1.50%	up to 5% of net asset value	CHF 100
Class MU$ I169 Man Convertibles Far East – CHF Shares	LU0686792812			Accumulative	Swiss franc (CHF)	Active	No	CHF 100'000	CHF 1'000	1 share	0.75%	up to 5% of net asset value	CHF 100
Class MU$ D198 Man Convertibles Far East – CHF Shares	LU0871786789			Accumulative	Swiss franc (CHF)	Dormant	n/a	CHF 100'000	CHF 1'000	1 share	0.75%	up to 5% of net asset value	CHF 100

Figure 1: Illustration of a PDF table rendered as a HTML/CSS table thanks to vectorial shape analysis

6.5 Ordered List Structure Induction in PDF Documents

Ordered list items are searched at document scope. We first select numbered lines thanks to a set of regular expressions and we analyze each numbering prefix as a tuple $\langle P, S, I, C \rangle$ where :

P refers to the numbering pattern (string);

S : numbering style type (single character, see below);

I : numbering count written in numbering style type (single character);

C : decimal value of the numbering count (integer).

The numbering style types are defined as follows :

- Unambiguous style types:
    - D: Decimal
    - L: Lower-Latin
    - M: Upper-Latin
    - G: Lower-Greek
    - H: Upper-Greek
    - R: Lower-Roman
    - S: Upper-Roman
- Ambiguous style types:
    - ?: Lower-Latin OR Lower-Roman
    - !: Upper-Latin OR Upper-Roman

To illustrate, the line "A.2.c) My Header" is analyzed as $\langle$ A.2.L), L, c, 3 $\rangle$.

Then, lines are grouped in clusters sharing the same numbering pattern, for instance:

- 2.a and 2.b → cluster 2.L (Lower-Latin)
- A.2.c) and A.2.f) → cluster A.2.L (Lower-latin)
- A.2.i) and A.2.v) → cluster A.2.? (ambiguous, Lower-Latin or Lower-Roman)

The disambiguation process separates ambiguous line clusters from unambiguous line clusters. Ambiguous patterns are mapped to their corresponding unambiguous patterns. For instance, A.2.?) is mapped to A.2.L) and A.2.R) if patterns exist.

The disambiguation process assigns an unambiguous style type to ambiguous lines. The process relies on compatible unambiguous clusters as disambiguation contexts.

Two cases are considered:

1. Ambiguous lines that are mapped to a single unambiguous patterns are directly disambiguated. For instance, A.2.?) is directly mapped to A.2.L) if no cluster A.2.R) exists.

2. Ambiguous lines that can be mapped to multiple unambiguous patterns are analyzed to identify a compatible unambiguous cluster. For instance, line A.2.v) is compatible with the cluster A.2.R) if A.2.v) is missing in the cluster and if line numbering A.2.iv) exists and both line numbers and/or left-alignments are compatibles.

Once the disambiguation stage is achieved, we split every cluster in order to build ordered series. For instance, the cluster containing lines 2.a, 2.b, 2.c, 2.a, 2.b is split in two ordered series 2.a, 2.b, 2.c and 2.a, 2.b.

Finally, we detect and resolve missing or unexpected items. For instance, first item of a numbered list may be missing when the numbering item is located on the same line of its parent item (the missing item is the second token): list item (a) is not detected when line starts with (2) (a). For instance, (X) is an unexpected item which must be removed from the cluster: (A), (B), (C), (X), (D), (E).

The aim of the algorithm is to identify PDF lines which corresponds to new ordered list item (i.e., list item leading lines). The objective is not to bound list items which cover multiple lines. The end of list items are computed in a second stage, while computing paragraph structures: a list item ends when the next list item starts (i.e., same numbering pattern and same indentation) or when less indented text objects starts.

6.6 Paragraph Structure Induction in PDF Documents

The aim of paragraph structure induction is to infer paragraph models that are later used to detect paragraph instances. A paragraph model can be seen as a paragraph style defined in any word processor (see figure 2).

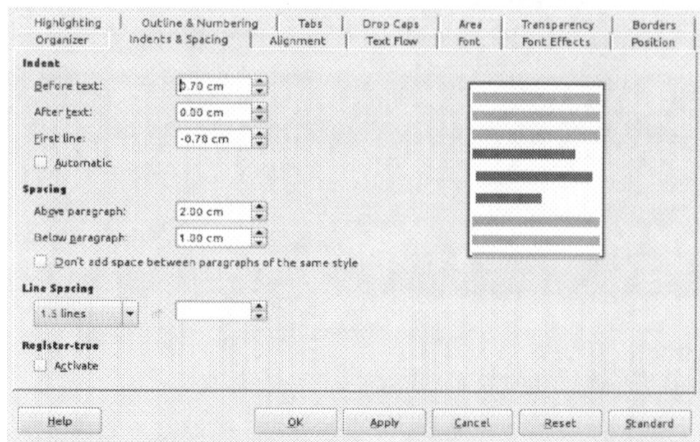

Figure 2: Settings in paragraph style of LibreOffice word processor

In other words, the aim of the process is to automatically infer the settings of paragraph styles.

Paragraphs are complex objects: a canonical paragraph is made of a leading line, multiple body lines and a trailing line. The leading line can have no positive or negative indentation. In context, paragraphs may be visually separated from other objects thanks to above spacing and below spacing.

In order to build paragraph models, we first identify reliable paragraph bodies. Paragraph bodies are sequences of three or more lines with same line spacing and compatible left and right coordinates. Then, leading lines and trailing lines are identified considering same line spacing, compatible left and/or right coordinates (to detect left and right alignments), same style.

Reliable paragraph lines are categorized as follows: L for leading line, B for body lines, T for trailing line. Header lines are categorized H (see section 6.1). Other lines are categorized as ? for undefined.

In order to fill paragraph models, paragraph settings are derived from the reliable paragraphs that are detected. When derived, leading lines of unordered and ordered list items are considered to create list item models (see sections 6.4 and 6.5 above).

Once paragraph models and list item models are built, the models are used to detect less reliable paragraphs and list items (i.e., containing less than three body lines). Compatible models are applied and lines are categorized L, B (if exists) or T (if exists). Remaining undefined lines are categorized considering line-spacing.

7 Evaluation of the Sentence Boundary Detection

While the shared task is dedicated to Sentence Boundary Detection, we focused on designing our top-down pipeline for the PDF itself. Therefore, we did not have enough time to fine tune the output. The main difficulty we encountered was to align our internal representation to the expected FinSBD representation since both representations are very different.

A complex ad-hoc module had to be implemented to try to map our structure to the expected character-based structure.

Our algorithm consists in splitting the text blocks extracted by our top-down pipeline using a single regular expression based on the presence of an end of sentence punctuation mark followed by a space separator or a line separator. In the following tables we show the detailed results of an improved version of our system in which the beginning and end of paragraphs are correctly detected. We only kept the subtask1 result of our original submission to ease comparisons. We removed the results on lists and numbered items since our system does not give these units yet.

In Table 1 and table 2 are shown the results obtained on the train set, respectively in English and in French. We focused on the sentence and the items for the system we submitted. Our system has much better results in terms of Precision but seems to miss many sentences.

Document	sent			item		
	f1	prec.	recall	f1	prec.	recall
Invesco-Fu	37.8	44.2	33.0	0	0.0	0
EdR-Privat	43.7	34.8	58.9	11.1	78.6	6.0
CANDRIAM-G	63.8	83.7	51.5	78.5	73.9	83.6
Dexia-Equi	65.9	80.5	55.8	46.1	67.3	35.0
Credit-Sui	78.5	89.9	69.8	48.0	69.1	36.7
Macro	57.9	66.6	53.8	36.7	57.8	32.3

Table 1: Results on the English train set, 32.6 F-measure on subtask1 (VS 23.6 for our official submission) sorted by F-measure on sentences

Our results on the test set are shown in Table 3 and table 4. One can see that the results are high in English as compared to the train set but the dataset is too small to draw any conclusion from that. The fact that the same pattern in French maybe show that our rule based system does not suffer too much from over-fitting.

8 Conclusion

Our team participated to the FinSBD-2 Shared Task dedicated to Sentence Boundary Detection in Financial Prospectuses. It was our first participation to this shared task. Our motivation was to improve our model driven approach to multilingual document analysis.

The work we have achieved is very promising. We had the opportunity to handle the full workflow and to define, control and implement each NLP component.

Concerning FinSBD shared task, we lack time to finalize the creation of list objects, unordered list objects and sentences. We chose to control the whole workflow and it was a bit too ambitious regarding time constraints since aligning our internal representations to the offsets of the groundtruth.

In a near future, we intend to enhance the implementation of our page layout model in order to be compliant with the page layout model described in [Giguet, 2008]. We would also like to implement the document model we introduced in INEX Book Structure Extraction Competition in order to divide a document in main parts and chapters [Giguet et al., 2009]. This strategy applied at document scope could have

Document	sent			item		
	f1	prec.	recall	f1	prec.	recall
LCL-OBLIGA	28.8	36.3	23.8	2.9	3.4	2.6
LCL-DOUBLE	33.4	36.8	30.7	3.7	5.3	2.9
LCL-INVEST	34.6	43.6	28.7	1.1	2.6	0.7
AMUNDI-VIE	34.9	44.3	28.8	2.5	6.5	1.6
FUNDQUEST-	38.1	51.9	30.1	43.0	44.4	41.7
BNP-PARIBA	44.8	70.8	32.8	45.0	39.1	52.9
QUILVEST-C	51.0	62.1	43.3	34.6	51.9	25.9
GROUPAMA-O	53.1	60.5	47.3	39.7	40.0	39.5
AVIVA-INTE	53.3	66.1	44.6	32.0	29.1	35.6
CREDIT-MUT	53.7	83.5	39.6	33.8	26.1	47.9
GUTENBERG-	54.2	58.4	50.5	34.5	37.0	32.3
Fondo-BNP-	57.2	59.2	55.3	66.7	73.7	60.9
CM-CIC-EUR	57.3	56.8	57.8	44.8	41.4	48.8
FCPI-IDINV	59.8	78.4	48.3	88.9	88.9	88.9
GASPAL-CON	61.5	73.4	52.9	35.8	70.7	24.0
Le-PALÉ-FR	62.0	76.8	51.9	60.1	48.8	78.2
NORDEN-SMA	62.1	74.0	53.4	49.7	40.4	64.7
ORCHIDEE-I	62.3	64.8	60.1	54.5	70.6	44.4
SÉLECT-OBL	65.6	90.9	51.3	32.9	28.6	38.7
Sécuri-Tau	68.1	84.3	57.1	28.6	19.0	57.1
QUADRIGE-M	69.2	85.6	58.1	82.8	89.1	77.4
FCPI-Innov	72.8	84.6	63.9	50.2	52.6	48.1
INNOVEN-EU	77.7	89.7	68.5	8.5	11.8	6.7
Macro	54.6	66.6	46.9	38.1	40.0	40.1

Table 2: Results on the French train set 31.9 F-measure on subtask1 (VS 33.5% for our original submission) sorted by F-measure on sentences

Document	sent			item		
	f1	prec.	recall	f1	prec.	recall
Arabesque-	71.8	88.4	60.5	55.3	88.7	40.1
MAGALLANES	76.9	92.1	66.0	23.8	88.9	13.7
Macro	74.3	90.2	63.2	39.5	88.8	26.9

Table 3: Results on the English test set : 37.9 F-measure on subtask1 (VS 31.7 for our original submission) sorted by F-measure on sentences

made more accurate decisions at lower level of the hierarchy (i.e., divide-and-conquer strategy).

References

[Ait Azzi *et al.*, 2019] Abderrahim Ait Azzi, Houda Bouamor, and Sira Ferra. The finsbd-2019 shared task:sentence boundary detection in pdf noisy text in the financial domain. In Chung-Chi Chen, Hen-Hsen Huang, Hiroya Takamura, and Hsin-Hsi Chen, editors, *Proceedings of the First Workshop on Financial Technology and Natural Language Processing*, pages 74–80, Macao, China, August 2019.

[Antonacopoulos *et al.*, 2009] Apostolos Antonacopoulos, David Bridson, Christos Papadopoulos, and Stefan Pletschacher. A realistic dataset for performance evaluation of document layout analysis. In *Proceedings of the International Conference on Document Analysis and Recognition, ICDAR*, pages 296–300, 01 2009.

[Bachenko *et al.*, 1995] Joan Bachenko, Eileen Fitzpatrick, and Jeffrey Daugherty. A rule-based phrase parser for real-time text-to-speech synthesis. *Natural Language Engineering*, 1(2):191–212, 1995.

[Bernhard *et al.*, 2017] Delphine Bernhard, Amalia Todirascu, Fanny MARTIN, Pascale Erhart, Lucie Steible, Dominique Huck, and Christophe Rey. Problèmes de tokénisation pour deux langues régionales de France, l'alsacien et le picard. In *DiLiTAL 2017*, Actes de l'atelier " Diversité Linguistique et TAL ", pages 14–23, Orléans, France, June 2017.

[Corro, 2020] Caio Corro. Span-based discontinuous constituency parsing: a family of exact chart-based algorithms with time complexities from $o(n^6)$ down to $o(n^3)$, 2020.

[Dale *et al.*, 2000] Robert Dale, H. L. Somers, and Hermann Moisl. *Handbook of Natural Language Processing*. Marcel Dekker, Inc., USA, 2000.

[Déjean and Meunier, 2006] Hervé Déjean and Jean-Luc Meunier. A system for converting pdf documents into structured xml format. In Horst Bunke and A. Lawrence Spitz, editors, *Document Analysis Systems VII*, pages 129–140, Berlin, Heidelberg, 2006. Springer Berlin Heidelberg.

[Déjean and Meunier, 2010] Hervé Déjean and Jean-Luc Meunier. Reflections on the inex structure extraction competition. In *Proceedings of the 9th IAPR International Workshop on Document Analysis Systems*, DAS '10, page 301–308, New York, NY, USA, 2010. Association for Computing Machinery.

[Déjean, 2007] Hervé Déjean. *pdf2xml open source software*, 2007. Last access on July 31, 2019.

[Déjean, 2010] Hervé Déjean. Numbered sequence detection in documents. In Laurence Likforman-Sulem and Gady Agam, editors, *Document Recognition and Retrieval XVII*, volume 7534, pages 41 – 52. International Society for Optics and Photonics, SPIE, 2010.

[Gabay *et al.*, 2019] Simon Gabay, Marine Riguet, and Loïc Barrault. A Workflow For On The Fly Normalisation Of 17th c. French. In *DH2019*, Utrecht, Netherlands, July 2019. ADHO.

Document	sent			item		
	f1	prec.	recall	f1	prec.	recall
CM-CIC-OBL	32.3	27.7	38.8	40.0	36.2	44.7
LCL-MULTI-	35.3	34.5	36.2	0	0.0	0.0
HEXASTEP-H	40.6	71.5	28.3	11.1	33.3	6.7
AMUNDI-IND	50.0	51.5	48.6	0	0	0.0
LAZARD-ACT	57.1	69.8	48.2	39.1	29.3	58.6
FIP-IXO-DE	58.7	71.1	50.0	50.0	100.0	33.3
BNP-Pariba	59.0	54.1	64.9	31.6	24.5	44.4
GREEN-BOND	59.5	67.1	53.6	27.6	52.2	18.8
KLE-EONIA-	60.4	70.3	53.0	63.5	61.4	65.9
ECUREUIL-P	67.8	73.0	63.4	55.7	53.1	58.6
Macro	52.1	59.1	48.5	31.9	39.0	33.1

Table 4: Results on the French test set, 27.98 F-measure on subtask1 (VS 26.2 for our original submission) sorted by F-measure on sentences

[Giguet and Lejeune, 2019] Emmanuel Giguet and Gaël Lejeune. Daniel@FinTOC-2019 shared task : TOC extraction and title detection. In *Proceedings of the Second Financial Narrative Processing Workshop (FNP 2019)*, pages 63–68, Turku, Finland, September 2019. Linköping University Electronic Press.

[Giguet and Lucas, 2010a] Emmanuel Giguet and Nadine Lucas. The book structure extraction competition with the resurgence software at caen university. In Shlomo Geva, Jaap Kamps, and Andrew Trotman, editors, *Focused Retrieval and Evaluation*, pages 170–178, Berlin, Heidelberg, 2010. Springer Berlin Heidelberg.

[Giguet and Lucas, 2010b] Emmanuel Giguet and Nadine Lucas. The book structure extraction competition with the resurgence software for part and chapter detection at caen university. In Shlomo Geva, Jaap Kamps, Ralf Schenkel, and Andrew Trotman, editors, *Comparative Evaluation of Focused Retrieval - 9th International Workshop of the Initiative for the Evaluation of XML Retrieval, INEX 2010, Vugh, The Netherlands, December 13-15, 2010, Revised Selected Papers*, volume 6932 of *Lecture Notes in Computer Science*, pages 128–139. Springer, 2010.

[Giguet et al., 2009] Emmanuel Giguet, Alexandre Baudrillart, and Nadine Lucas. Resurgence for the book structure extraction competition. In Shlomo Geva, Jaap Kamps, and Andrew Trotman, editors, *INEX 2009 Workshop Pre-Proceedings*, pages 136–142, 2009.

[Giguet, 1995] Emmanuel Giguet. Multilingual sentence categorization according to language. In *Proceedings of the European Chapter of the Association for Computational Linguistics (EACL) SIGDAT Workshop "From text to tags : Issues in Multilingual Language Analysis*, pages 73–76, March 1995.

[Giguet, 2008] Emmanuel Giguet. Rapport scientifique du projet résurgence. Technical report, Université de Caen Basse-Normandie, November 2008.

[Giguet, 2011] Emmanuel Giguet. *De l'analyse syntaxique automatique à l'analyse automatique du discours dans les collections multilingues de documents numériques composites*. Mémoire d'habilitation à diriger des recherches, Université de Caen Basse-Normandie, September 2011.

[Grefenstette and Tapanainen, 1994] Gregory Grefenstette and Pasi Tapanainen. What is a word, what is a sentence? problems of tokenization. In *Proceedings of the 3rd Conference on Computational Lexicography and TextResearch*, pages 79–87, 1994.

[Kiss and Strunk, 2006] Tibor Kiss and Jan Strunk. Unsupervised multilingual sentence boundary detection. *Computational Linguistics*, 32(4):485–525, 2006.

[Le and Mikolov, 2014] Quoc V. Le and Tomas Mikolov. Distributed representations of sentences and documents. *CoRR*, abs/1405.4053, 2014.

[Luc, 2001] Christophe Luc. Une typologie des énumérations basée sur les structures rhétoriques et architecturales du texte. In *TALN2001, Université de Tours, 05/07/2001-07/07/2001*, pages 263–272. ., juillet 2001.

[Martin et al., 2020] Louis Martin, Benjamin Muller, Pedro Javier Ortiz Suárez, Yoann Dupont, Laurent Romary, Éric Villemonte de la Clergerie, Djamé Seddah, and Benoît Sagot. Camembert: a tasty french language model. In *Proceedings of the 58th Annual Meeting of the Association for Computational Linguistics*, 2020.

[Maurel et al., 2006] Fabrice Maurel, Mustapha Mojahid, Nadine Vigouroux, and Jacques Virbel. Documents numériques et transmodalité. transposition automatique à l'oral des structures visuelles de texte. *Document numérique*, 9, 09 2006.

[Maurel, 2004] Fabrice Maurel. *Transmodalité et multimodalité écrit/oral : modélisation, traitement automatique et évaluation de stratégies de présentation des structures "visuo-architecturale" des textes*. PhD thesis, Université de Toulouse 3, 2004.

[Pascual and Virbel, 1996] Elsa Pascual and Jacques Virbel. Semantic and Layout Properties of Text punctuation. 34th Annual meeting of the Association for Computational Linguistics. In *International Workshop on Punctuation in Computational Linguistics, Santa Cruz, USA, ,* Santa Cruz, USA, juin 1996. Univ. of California. Dates de conférence : juin 1996 1996. Pages de la publication : ?.

[Rémi Juge, 2019] Sira Ferradans Rémi Juge, Najah-Imane Bentabet. The fintoc-2019 shared task: Financial document structure extraction. In *The Second Workshop on Financial Narrative Processing of NoDalida 2019*, 2019.

[Smith, 2020] Noah A. Smith. Contextual word representations: Putting words into computers. *Commun. ACM*, 63(6):66–74, May 2020.

[Sorin, 2015] Laurent Sorin. *Contributions of textual architectures to the non-visual accessibility of digital documents*. Theses, Université Toulouse le Mirail - Toulouse II, December 2015.

[Virbel, 1999] Jacques Virbel. Structures textuelles. Planches. Fasciccule I : Enumérations. Rapport de recherche -, IRIT, Université Paul Sabatier, Toulouse, février 1999.

Subtl.ai at the FinSBD-2 task: Document Structure Identification by Paying Attention

Aman Khullar[1*], **Abhishek Arora**[1*], **Sarath Chandra Pakala**[1*], **Vishnu Ramesh**[1*] and **Manish Shrivastava** [1†]

[1]Subtl.ai, CIE, IIIT Hyderabad

aman.khullar@iiit.ac.in, abhishek.arora@iiit.ac.in, sarath@subtl.ai, vishnu@subtl.ai, manish@subtl.ai

Abstract

This paper presents a methodology submitted to the FinSBD-2 shared task to extract well formed sentences, lists and items from noisy unstructured financial PDF documents in English language. The proposed architecture for document structure identification, is a combination of deep learning and heuristic based approaches. We use two unidirectional Long Short-Term Memory(LSTM) encoders to get the sentence split tokens from the set of all the possible split points. Further, the outputs are passed on to an attention based LSTM network to select only the well formed sentences from all the possible sentences. These outputs are merged to ultimately produce all possible well formed sentences. Apart from the sentences, lists and items are identified using a combination of heuristics which identify patterns in the data. The final F1 score, 0.217 on this task, is obtained by comparing the start and end indices of sentences, lists and items. We have presented another parameter, which is used to evaluate the class coverage by checking the overlap between the predicted and ground truth sentences and obtained an average 40% class coverage score. This metric is more useful for industry researchers who require coverage of the content rather than character level precision. The proposed approach will empower both academia and industry researchers in their effort to handle noisy documents for various NLP tasks by providing a simple, fast and robust approach to identify structure in their documents.

Keywords:

Sentence Boundary Detection, NLP, Deep Learning, LSTM, Sentence overlap, Token classifier, Document structure identification, Attention mechanism

1 Introduction

A sentence forms the basic unit of text documents which are used for a wide variety of tasks in Natural Language Processing (NLP) like Named Entity recognition (NER), translation, speech recognition, topic segmentation etc. By definition, "A sentence is a set of words that is complete in itself, typically containing a subject and predicate, conveying a statement, question, exclamation, or command, and consisting of a main clause and sometimes one or more subordinate clauses."[1]. It can be clearly realised that it is imperative to clearly demarcate sentence boundaries from noisy text PDF documents so that those sentences in the text can be processed to be used in tasks similar to those mentioned above. Inaccuracy in determination of clear sentence boundaries can lead to misrepresentation of sentence units which can affect the information learnt by networks trained on such noisy data which in turn would affect NLP applications. It is also equally important to demarcate boundaries of list and items to understand the structural and hierarchical features of the document. This disambiguation increments the number of features for the network to learn which drives more accuracy for NLP applications such as identifying procedure and steps.

A sentence boundary is defined from the first character index of the start token of the sentence to the the last character index of the end token of the sentence. Similarly an item is defined in a similar way excluding any unicode bullets, alphanumerics etc. at the starting or ending. A list majorly comprise of a series of items under the same category clubbed together which may include a header sentence.

In the past, this problem in the NLP domain has not gained much importance to disambiguate sentences, list and item boundaries. Heuristics have been long used to identify sentence boundaries which are easy to setup, gives high speed performance but the way each document is setup and formatted without any strict standard rule of formatting, the accuracy of identification takes a hit, therefore, it becomes imperative to develop a robust way to identify such boundaries and have a reliable and clear disambiguation of sentences, items, lists as input data which is used for a wide variety of NLP tasks like sentiment analysis, NER, translation, speech recognition etc. This brings in the need for deep learning models which have gained importance recently which can learn a wide variety of patterns, semantic, contextual, positional information etc.

To solve this challenging task of sentence, list and item boundary detection, we have developed a deep learning model supported by task specific rules. Through this paper,

---

*Equal Contribution. Listing order is random.

†Contact Author

Proceedings of the Second Workshop on Financial Technology and Natural Language Processing

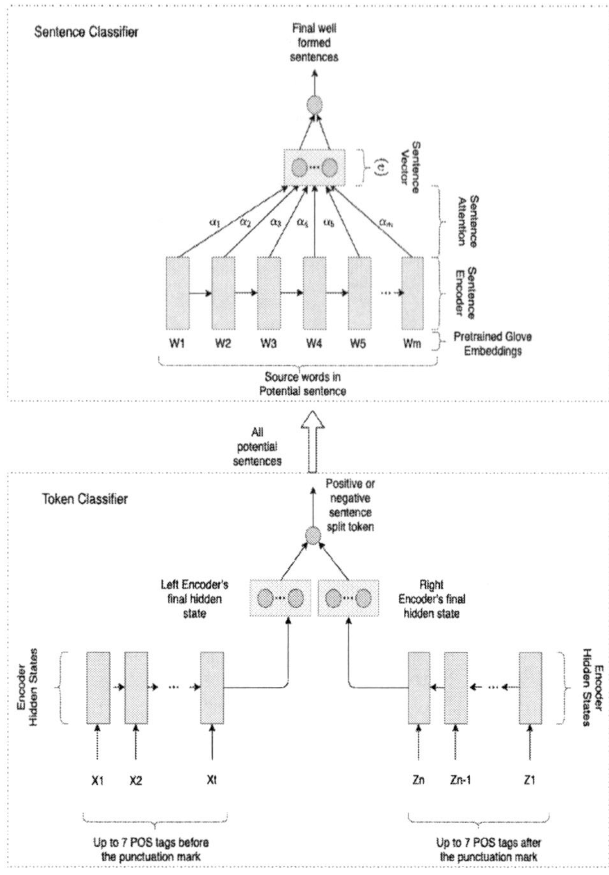

Figure 1: Sentence boundary identification architecture

our main contributions are as follows:

- We present a novel sentence boundary detection architecture which is able to give a competitive performance on noisy PDF documents.

- We propose heuristics to identify lists and items in the noisy PDF document.

- We propose content coverage evaluation metric which evaluates content overlap rather than precise character match.

The paper is structured as follows :- 1) Introduction section presents the problem and the need to disambiguate sentence boundaries while section 2 presents the research findings and development in this field. Section 3 describes the particular task for which the dataset description is given in section 4 and section 5 describes the proposed model to solve this task. The results are presented and discussed in section 6 and section 7 concludes the work which is followed by references.

2 Related Work

Traditionally the task of SBD has been solved using heuristics and rules based on the regular grammar. One of the popular approaches presented by Alembic information extraction [2] built an extensive regular-expression-based approach to solve

this problem. There have been other rule-based approaches by [3], [4] and [5]. Palmer et al.[6], however, recognized the shortcomings of the rule based approaches which were problem statement specific and required large manual effort. Hence they developed the Satz system which predicted if any punctuation mark was a sentence split point or not. They were among the first to develop machine learning based approach for solving this problem and since then many machine learning based approaches by [7], [8], [9], [10] and [11] approaches. Recently deep learning tools [12] have been used to solve this problem which have been able to produce state of the art results. Many of these approaches have however been confined to clean texts and have tested their results on WSJ corpus [13] and the Brown Corpus [7]. Azzi et al. [14] presented their solution for detecting sentence boundaries in Noisy text in the financial domain but their solution was limited to detecting sentences and not the lists and items contained within these documents. Our work improves upon this shortcoming to identify the lists and list items inside the noisy PDF documents along with the identification of sentences which can be used by any NLP system in their preprocessing step to get state of the art performance.

3 Task Definition

The goal for the FinSBD-2 2020 Shared Task [15] is to extract well segmented sentences identifying them by their start and end indices along with lists and items in English and French. This task is mainly split into two sub tasks :

1. Extraction of sentences, lists and items depicted by their starting and ending indices.

2. Arranging the lists and items in a hierarchical manner.

This task is provided with financial PDF documents as the training data along with a JSON corresponding to each PDF document. Each JSON consists of raw text extracted from the PDF and disambiguated clearly under each class such as sentence, list, item, item1, item2, item3 and item4 which is represented by their start and end index. Co-ordinates of these boundaries are provided as well for spatial and visual cues.

In this paper we focus on the first subtask which includes to disambugate text into sentence, list and item class in English language

There are two other PDF documents provided with their raw text exracted in a JSON file along with the spatial coordinates. This acts as a testing set on which the final models developed by all participating teams is evaluated. F1 scores are calculated for each class and the average is taken for the three classes (sentence, lists and items) for this subtask.

4 Dataset

The data that has been used was provided as part of the FinSBD-2 2020 challenge which contained 6 noisy financial PDF documents for training and 2 documents used for testing. The data consisted json files for each document with the start and end indices of each class namely - sentences, lists and items, along with the complete document text available as a single string. The coordinates of the starting and the ending characters for each of the elements in the class were also

	Train data	Val data	Test data
#Docs	5	1	2
#Characters	1,322,767	169,546	558,611
#Tokens	290,092	39,816	141,138
#Sentences	7,282	788	2,450
#Lists	207	42	69
#Items	843	268	332
#OOV Tokens	1,079	248	443

Table 1: Corpus statistics. The number of characters, tokens, sentences, lists, items and OOV words have been identified for each document.

provided. From these 6 PDF documents, 5 have been used for training our models while 1 was used for validation and 2 were used for testing. The data statistics for the documents in each of these train, val and test splits have been provided in Table 1. Data preprocessing involved cleaning the leading space characters from sentences and then tokenizing the sentence using Spacy's tokenizer [16]. The data was later processed to get a list of all ':', '\n' and '.' tokens along with a label to identify if the token was a positive split token (if it led to sentence, list or item split) or a negative split token (if it did not lead to sentence, list or item split).

5 Our Models

In this section we describe (1) our token classifier (2) sentence classifier (3) sentence boundary detection algorithm and (4) heuristics to identify sentences, lists and items from the text.

5.1 Token Classifier

Through our examination of the training data we identified that the potential tokens which could act as sentence split tokens were three characters namely - '\n', '.', and ':', which we call as potential sentence split tokens. Each sentence would end with a potential split token, even those sentences which do not have a visible punctuation mark, because in that case, the sentence ends with '\n' token. The token classifier model as depicted in Figure 1 illustrates how our model helps us identify the potential sentence split tokens among all the occurrences of these three tokens.

For every occurrence of any of these potential split tokens, we do the following steps:

(a) Convert the previous 7 tokens and the next 7 tokens into their corresponding POS tags.

(b) Convert these POS tags into their one hot vectors.

(c) Pass the previous 7 one hot POS encodings into a forward directional LSTM [17] with the last timestep corresponding to the token just before the potential split token being classified.

(d) Pass the next 7 one hot POS encodings into a backward directional LSTM with the last timestep corresponding to the token just after the potential split token being classified.

(e) Concatenate the final hidden states of these two LSTM encoders and pass a linear layer over it to classify if the potential split token is a positive sentence split token or not.

Domain specific documents contain several words which are not present in the pretrained open-domain word embeddings. As a result, the POS embeddings helped us overcome the ambiguity caused due to the out of vocabulary words while keeping the model computationally less expensive. The hyperparameter value of 7 has been taken as a large enough value to allow the encoder to understand the flow of the POS sequences, while being small enough to train the model efficiently. If on either sides of the point under consideration, we find another potential split token before the span of 7 tokens then this smaller set of tokens are passed to the encoder. This helps ensuring the independence of potential split tokens from each other and does not allow error to propagate in the case of incorrect prediction. The two unidirectional LSTMs complement each other as the final state of the forward directional LSTM maps the flow of POS encodings from the previous sentence and the backward directional LSTMs final hidden state maps the reverse flow of the POS encodings from the next sentence. These hidden states are then concatenated which helps the model to understand how the flow of POS tags, from both the previous as well as the next sentence, determines the split of a sentence.

5.2 Sentence Classifier

Drawing inspiration from previous work in well formed natural language queries [18], the sentence classifier model identifies if any given sentence is well formed or not. We were able to achieve good results for this sub-task by using an attention based LSTM model [19] as depicted in Figure 1.

This model tokenizes the sentences and then we use the pretrained Glove embeddings to get the embedding of each token present in the vocabulary. At each timestep (t), a word (W_t) is embedded using these pretrained embeddings. An LSTM encoder layer passes over these embeddings. At each timestep, we get a hidden state (h_t) which is followed by an attention layer on top of it:

$$x_t = W_e w_t, t \in [1, m] \tag{1}$$

$$\vec{h_t} = \overrightarrow{LSTM}(x_t), t \in [1, m] \tag{2}$$

$$u_t = \tanh\left(W_w h_t + b_w\right) \tag{3}$$

$$\alpha_t = \frac{\exp\left(u_t^{T} u_w\right)}{\Sigma_t \alpha_t h_t} \tag{4}$$

$$v = \Sigma_t \alpha_t h_t. \tag{5}$$

Here W_e represents the embedding matrix, x_t represents the embedded word, h_t represents the hidden state of the LSTM encoder at each timestep t, u_t is a word level context vector, α_t is the attention weight to given to each word in the input sentence and v is the final sentence [20] vector which captures the information for that sentence. This is followed by a linear layer to classify if the input sentence is a well formed sentence or not.

This sentence classifier has been used by us in two ways, namely :

(1) Overcome the shortcomings of the token classifier.

(2) Identify the end points for lists.

This helps us facilitate in improving our identification of the sentences, lists and items which has been explained in the next section.

5.3 Sentence Boundary Identification

Through the output of the sentence classifier, it becomes known if the sentence identified by the token classifier is a well formed sentence or not. In case it is a well formed sentence then we keep it, as it is. Otherwise, in case it is not well formed sentence, we merge this sentence with the previous identified sentence and then pass the concatenated sentences to the sentence classifier. In case these concatenated sentences turn out to be well formed, we consider both of these sentences as a single sentence. In case the concatenation with the previous sentence is also not able to form a well formed sentence then we try the same approach with the next sentence from the token classifier. If that also does not yield a well formed sentence, we skip this sentence. The result from this merge algorithm gives us the final set of well formed sentences.

5.4 Lists and Items Boundary Identification

The approach to detect items and thus the aggregated lists was focused around patterns specific to lists. From the training data, it was observed that 90% of items are either an alphanumeric pattern ("1.", "a.") or a Unicode pattern which start with a non-ASCII character to represent bullet points. After using these heuristics to find the start indices of every item, the list were aggregated by identifying:

(a) Co-occurrences of alphanumeric or Unicode class items within a window of 7 sentences.

(b) Incremental co-occurrences of alphanumeric pattern-based items("1." followed by "2.", or "a." followed by "b.")

Post this aggregation, the end index of the last item was identified using the sentence classifier. Based on the potential sentence split tokens, text blocks were added one at a time to the last item until the sentence classifier categorised the last item as well-formed. To account for inaccuracies in the sentence classifier, a window limit of 4 was set up, meaning not more than the next 4 text blocks were added to identify the end of the last item, and thus the end of the list.

6 Results and Analysis

6.1 Evaluation Metrics

The official evaluation metric is based on matching the start indices and end indices of sentences generated through the proposed methodology which are matched with the ground truth. finSBD 2020 has provided the start and end indices ground truth of each PDF document. The final F1 score takes an average F1 scores of all documents present in the test set. Another metric which is the sentence coverage is evaluated to illustrate the percentage overlap of the detected sentences with the ground truth sentences. Both the metrics are described below.

Document	Class	Precision	Recall	F1
	Sentence	0.67	0.62	0.64
Document 1	List	0.00	0.00	0.00
	Items	0.00	0.00	0.00
	Average	**0.22**	**0.20**	**0.213**
	Sentence	0.71	0.62	0.66
Document 2	List	0.00	0.00	0.00
	Item	0.00	0.00	0.00
	Average	**0.24**	**0.21**	**0.22**

Table 2: F1 score on 2 test documents

6.1.1 F1 scores

F1 score which is the geometric mean of precision and recall which are defined in eq. (6) and (7). F1 scores depicted in eq. (8) is calculated for each class i.e sentence, list and items is evaluated for each document and a simple average is taken. Predicted list, sentence or item is considered as a true positive if the start and end index generated with the help of the proposed methodology matches exactly with that present in the ground truth else it is treated as a false positive.

$$Precision\ (P) = \frac{True\ Positives}{True\ Positives + False\ Positives} \tag{6}$$

$$Recall\ (R) = \frac{True\ Positives}{True\ Positives + False\ Negatives} \tag{7}$$

$$F1\ Score = 2 \cdot \frac{P \times R}{P + R} \tag{8}$$

The results on the 2 test documents provided are shown in table 2.

6.1.2 Sentence Coverage

Sentences coverage is calculated by finding the percentage overlap of the predicted sentence with the sentence present in the ground truth. The formula to find this metric is presented below in eq. (9).

$$SentenceOverlap\ \% = \frac{Len(Common\ substring)}{Len(Ground\ truth\ sentence)} \tag{9}$$

For ex. if the ground truth sentence is "It is a good day." and the predicted sentence is "good day", the common substring will be "is good day" which has a length of 11 characters. Length of the ground truth sentence in this case will be 16. The corresponding sentence overlap wll thus be 68.75%.

The percentage overlap is calculated for each predicted sentence and is average over the number of predicted sentences. This is depicted in eq. (10)

$$Avg.\ Overlap\ \% = \frac{\sum Sentence\ Overlap}{Total\ no.\ of\ predicted\ sentences} \tag{10}$$

Using this formula, average overlap for each class including sentence, list and item is calculated. The results are presented in the table 3 for the 2 given test documents.

Document	Class	Overlap *100 (%)
	Sentence	0.82
	List	0.20
Document 1	Items	0.16
	Average	**0.39**
	Sentence	0.91
	List	0.16
Document 2	Item	0.15
	Average	**0.41**

Table 3: Sentence Coverage on 2 documents

6.2 Analysis

The analysis on the 2 test documents on both the evaluation metrics, gives a clear idea that deep learning model as proposed in this paper, outperformed rule-based approaches. The detection of sentences which used deep learning model was able to learn more patterns as compared to the heuristics built to identify lists and items. For industry applications, which is more concerned with accuracy rather than precision, F1 score becomes too strict metric in cases where just start and ending indices are compared to classify a sentence, list or an item as true positive, false positive or false negatives. Average F1 score on the 2 test documents for sentences is 0.65 with precision almost equal to recall indicating the number of false negative and false positives equal showing the dataset had comparable number of positive and negative sentences. The F1 scores does not give an idea for the list and items identified by the proposed methodology as the predicted items and list did not match exactly with the ground truth.

To get a better idea of the accuracy of the predicted list and items, sentence coverage metric is evaluated to show the overlap of the predicted sentences with those present in the ground truth. Sentences show an encouraging metric of an average score of 86.5% on the given set of 2 documents. The list have a average of 18% and items 15.5%. The main difference in the way of identification of sentenced and list or items is the usage of deep learning models in the former and logical heuristics for the latter. This is also due to the reason that each document does not follow a set of standard/universal rule for setting up of list and items which makes their identification tedious.

7 Conclusion and Future Work

This paper proposes a deep learning model which consists of primarily two stages to detect a sentence. In the first stage, positive split points to split the raw text string are found using a two uni-directional LSTMs. The sentences are split at these points and passed through a sentence classifier based on attention LSTMs, which classifies a sentence as well formed or not. Not well formed sentences are passed through a merge algorithm to finally get well formed sentences as output. The F1 metric when tested 2 test documents presents 0.65 as the average F1 whereas the sentence coverage gives an average overlap of 86.5%. This paper also proposes a set of heuristics to identify list and items in an unstructured document. F1 score to evaluate the accuracy of the prediction does not give a holistic picture as it simply matches the start and end index to evaluate. Hence, sentence coverage is used which gives an average of 18% for list and 15.5% on item on 2 doc-

uments. This shows the amount of overlap in the prediction when compared with the ground truth.

A lot of work has been done in the domain of NLP to detect sentences in unstructured documents and the accuracy of detection in the proposed model in this paper is encouraging. There is clear scope of improvement in the accuracy of detection of list and items in an unstructured PDF document. A deep learning model can be used to train a model to learn a wide variety of features which can be helpful in detecting list and item which will eventually increase the performance of a wide variety of NLP applications which depend upon this data processing step as input.

8 Acknowledgment

We would like to thank Product Lab and the Language Technologies Research Center (LTRC) at IIIT Hyderabad for providing us with the servers and the necessary compute used to train the models.

References

[1] Grammar-Monster, "Definition of sentence." https://www.grammar-monster.com/glossary/sentences.htm.

[2] J. Aberdeen, J. Burger, D. Day, L. Hirschman, P. Robinson, and M. Vilain, "Mitre: description of the alembic system used for muc-6," in *Proceedings of the 6th conference on Message understanding*, pp. 141–155, Association for Computational Linguistics, 1995.

[3] C. Hoffmann, "Automatische disambiguierung von satzgrenzen in einem maschinenlesbaren deutschen korpus," *Manuscript, University of Trier, Germany*, 1994.

[4] G. Grefenstette and P. Tapanainen, "What is a word, what is a sentence?: problems of tokenisation," 1994.

[5] A. Mikheev, "Periods, capitalized words, etc.," *Computational Linguistics*, vol. 28, no. 3, pp. 289–318, 2002.

[6] D. D. Palmer and M. A. Hearst, "Adaptive multilingual sentence boundary disambiguation," *Computational linguistics*, vol. 23, no. 2, pp. 241–267, 1997.

[7] D. Gillick, "Sentence boundary detection and the problem with the us," in *Proceedings of Human Language Technologies: The 2009 Annual Conference of the North American Chapter of the Association for Computational Linguistics, Companion Volume: Short Papers*, pp. 241–244, 2009.

[8] T. Kiss and J. Strunk, "Unsupervised multilingual sentence boundary detection," *Computational linguistics*, vol. 32, no. 4, pp. 485–525, 2006.

[9] F. Wong and S. Chao, "isentenizer: An incremental sentence boundary classifier," in *Proceedings of the 6th International Conference on Natural Language Processing and Knowledge Engineering (NLPKE-2010)*, pp. 1–7, IEEE, 2010.

[10] D. F. Wong, L. S. Chao, and X. Zeng, "isentenizer-: Multilingual sentence boundary detection model," *The Scientific World Journal*, vol. 2014, 2014.

[11] D. Rudrapal, A. Jamatia, K. Chakma, A. Das, and B. Gambäck, "Sentence boundary detection for social media text," 2015.

[12] C. Xu, L. Xie, and X. Xiao, "A bidirectional lstm approach with word embeddings for sentence boundary detection," *Journal of Signal Processing Systems*, vol. 90, no. 7, pp. 1063–1075, 2018.

[13] A. Taylor, M. Marcus, and B. Santorini, "The penn treebank: an overview," in *Treebanks*, pp. 5–22, Springer, 2003.

[14] A. A. Azzi, H. Bouamor, and S. Ferradans, "The finsbd-2019 shared task: Sentence boundary detection in pdf noisy text in the financial domain," in *Proceedings of the First Workshop on Financial Technology and Natural Language Processing*, pp. 74–80, 2019.

[15] finSBD 2, "finsbd-2 shared task definition." https://sites.google.com/nlg.csie.ntu.edu.tw/finnlp2020/shared-task-finsbd-2?authuser=0.

[16] E. AI, "Spacy library." https://spacy.io/.

[17] S. Hochreiter and J. Schmidhuber, "Long short-term memory," *Neural computation*, vol. 9, no. 8, pp. 1735–1780, 1997.

[18] B. Syed, V. Indurthi, M. Gupta, M. Shrivastava, and V. Varma, "Inductive transfer learning for detection of well-formed natural language search queries," in *European Conference on Information Retrieval*, pp. 45–52, Springer, 2019.

[19] D. Bahdanau, K. Cho, and Y. Bengio, "Neural machine translation by jointly learning to align and translate," *arXiv preprint arXiv:1409.0473*, 2014.

[20] Z. Yang, D. Yang, C. Dyer, X. He, A. Smola, and E. Hovy, "Hierarchical attention networks for document classification," in *Proceedings of the 2016 conference of the North American chapter of the association for computational linguistics: human language technologies*, pp. 1480–1489, 2016.

[21] H. Abelson, G. J. Sussman, and J. Sussman, *Structure and Interpretation of Computer Programs*. Cambridge, Massachusetts: MIT Press, 1985.

[22] R. Baumgartner, G. Gottlob, and S. Flesca, "Visual information extraction with Lixto," in *Proceedings of the 27th International Conference on Very Large Databases*, (Rome, Italy), pp. 119–128, Morgan Kaufmann, September 2001.

[23] M. Ostendorf, M. Collins, S. Narayanan, D. W. Oard, and L. Vanderwende, "Proceedings of human language technologies: The 2009 annual conference of the north american chapter of the association for computational linguistics," in *Proceedings of Human Language Technologies: The 2009 Annual Conference of the North American Chapter of the Association for Computational Linguistics*, 2009.

[24] R. J. Brachman and J. G. Schmolze, "An overview of the KL-ONE knowledge representation system," *Cognitive Science*, vol. 9, pp. 171–216, April–June 1985.

[25] G. Gottlob, "Complexity results for nonmonotonic logics," *Journal of Logic and Computation*, vol. 2, pp. 397–425, June 1992.

[26] G. Gottlob, N. Leone, and F. Scarcello, "Hypertree decompositions and tractable queries," *Journal of Computer and System Sciences*, vol. 64, pp. 579–627, May 2002.

[27] H. J. Levesque, "Foundations of a functional approach to knowledge representation," *Artificial Intelligence*, vol. 23, pp. 155–212, July 1984.

[28] H. J. Levesque, "A logic of implicit and explicit belief," in *Proceedings of the Fourth National Conference on Artificial Intelligence*, (Austin, Texas), pp. 198–202, American Association for Artificial Intelligence, August 1984.

[29] B. Nebel, "On the compilability and expressive power of propositional planning formalisms," *Journal of Artificial Intelligence Research*, vol. 12, pp. 271–315, 2000.

[30] IJCAI Proceedings, "IJCAI camera ready submission." https://proceedings.ijcai.org/info.

The FinSim 2020 Shared Task: Learning Semantic Representations for the Financial Domain

Ismaïl El Maarouf, **Youness Mansar**, **Virginie Mouilleron**, **Dialekti Valsamou-Stanislawski**
Fortia Financial Solutions
{ismail.elmaarouf, youness.mansar, virginie.mouilleron, dialekti.valsamou}@fortia.fr

Abstract

The FinSim 2020 shared task, colocated with the FinNLP workshop, offered the challenge to automatically learn effective and precise semantic models for the financial domain.

Going beyond the mere representation of words is a key step to industrial applications that make use of Natural Language Processing (NLP). This is typically addressed using either unsupervised corpus-derived representations like word embeddings, which are typically opaque to human understanding but very useful in NLP applications or manually created resources such as taxonomies and ontologies, which typically have low coverage and contain inconsistencies, but provide a deeper understanding of the target domain.

Finsim is inspired from previous endeavours in the Semeval community, which organized several competitions on semantic/lexical relation extraction between concepts/words. To the best of our knowledge, FINSIM 2020 was the first time such a task was proposed for the Financial domain.

The shared task attracted 6 participants and systems were ranked according to 2 metrics, Accuracy and Mean rank. The best system beat the baselines by over 20 points in accuracy.

1 Introduction

The FinSim 2020 shared task, organized by Fortia Financial Solutions[1], an AI startup with expertise in Financial Natural Language Processing (NLP), was part of the second edition of the 2nd Workshop on Financial Technology and Natural Language Processing (FinNLP [2]). It focused on automatically learning effective and precise semantic models adapted to the financial domain. More specifically it addressed the task of automatic categorization of financial instrument terms. The range of financial instrument is vast and the category encompasses all sorts of tradable contracts. Financial instruments can be challenging as, while traditional instruments such as *Bonds* or *Stocks* are straightforward, other instruments such as *Futures* pose a number of difficulties as they may apply to various underlying instrument types (e.g. bond futures, equities futures). Similarly, while the a feature is key to the definition of some instruments such as future contracts, its presence is not critical to the definition others. Thus, the challenge of automatic classification of financial instruments, is coupled with a challenge of semantic analysis.

Going beyond the mere representation of words is a key step to industrial applications that make use of Natural Language Processing (NLP). The semantic models those applications rely on is critical to their success in addressing traditional semantic tasks such as Named Entity Recognition, Relation Extraction, or Semantic parsing.

NLP applications can rely on annotated datasets, but there are also approaches which leverage manual resources like taxonomies, ontologies, and knowledge bases, for their source of knowledge. Indeed, creating annotated dataset is a costly endeavour and it is challenging to design an annotation dataset that can be exploited for other tasks than the ones it was initially designed for. Thus, on one end of the spectrum, there are approaches which typically rely on grammar or regular expressions and heavily rely on the quality of a manually created resource.

On the other end of the spectrum, there are Machine Learning (ML) approaches which attempt to automatically build semantic resources from raw text, like word embeddings, that are typically opaque to human understanding. In the literature, and e.g. in competitions, such unsupervised approaches have been more successful in building effective NLP applications. In industrial applications, both approaches have met success and it is true that in some contexts, approaches relying on manually crafted are often preferred to pure ML approaches because the former provide more control and are more predictable.

Finally there are approaches which attempt to automatically make use of manual resources but also rely on automatically derived word representations in order to build hybrid models. This is to these approaches that the task is addressed.

The FinSim task provided a raw corpus of financial prospectuses, from which to derive automatic representations, a train set of financial instrument terms classified by types of financial instruments, as well as mappings to an ontology of the financial domain, namely FIBO (The Financial Industry

---

[1] https://www.fortia.fr/

[2] https://sites.google.com/nlg.csie.ntu.edu.tw/finnlp2020/home

Proceedings of the Second Workshop on Financial Technology and Natural Language Processing

Business Ontology[3]). There are also resources available on the internet such as the Investopedia dictionary of financial terms [4], and classifications such as the CFI [5].

The paper is structured as follows: section 2 will introduce previous work related to the shared task, and section 3 will describe it in detail. Section 4 will introduce participants and section 5 will present the results.

2 Related work

The task proposed at FinSim 2020 is a task of hypernym categorization: given a training set of terms and a fixed set of labels, participants are asked to learn to categorize new terms to their most likely hypernym. Two words are said to be in a hypernymy (or ISA) relation if one of them can be conceived as a more generic term (e.g. "seagull" and "bird").

2.1 Literature on hypernymy extraction

Semantic relation extraction is a topic largely discussed in the literature and has been addressed from a variety of angles. Seminal work include the creation and use of hyperonym lexical patterns [Hearst, 1992] to extract hyponym-hypernym pairs. Substantive work draws from automatic thesaurus construction (see [Grefenstette, 1994]) which led to work on distributional analysis, which is the basis for a lot of data-driven work including [Lin, 1998] or [Baroni and Lenci, 2009].

More recently, neural networks have been used to learn word representations from text and proved very effective in a variety of NLP tasks ([Mikolov et al., 2013a], [Devlin et al., 2019], [Radford et al., 2019]). Such data-driven approaches capture a lot of similarities between terms in context, however it is not clear how those similarities relate to handcrafted relations such as hypernymy.

Finally, another strand of research to which we cannot do justice here, makes use of knowledge bases to operate relation extraction such as hypernymy relations. This domain tends to focus on names rather than nouns and in general, systems are not relation-specific but tend to cover multiple relation types. Work include [Mintz et al., 2009], or [Zeng et al., 2015]. A number of approaches proposed to create knowledge base embeddings, in which the similarity between terms or names is automatically derived from the structure of the knowledge base (see e.g. [Wang et al., 2014]).

2.2 Hypernymy relation extraction shared tasks

In terms of shared tasks, Taxonomy Extraction Evaluation (TExEval, [Bordea et al., 2015]) was the first shared task on taxonomy induction by focusing on the last step of organizing the taxonomy into hypernym-hyponym relations between (pre-detected) terms in four different domains (chemicals, equipment, foods, science). Because they did not provide a corpus, participants were limited in the data they could use and had to structure a list of terms into a taxonomy (with the possibility of adding intermediate concepts).

The second edition of Tex-Eval ([Bordea et al., 2016]) proposed the same challenge but focusing on multilinguality (English, Dutch, Italian and French) and 3 target domains (Environment, Food and Science). This time, the organizers provided a script to build a corpus from Wikipedia[6].

[Jurgens and Pilehvar, 2016] addressed the problem of classifying new terms against an existing taxonomy, a task they called taxonomy enrichment. This task relied on Wordnet[7] and asked participants to attach a given word to, or merge it with, an existing WordNet synset. For each word, participants were provided a definition in natural language. The construction of the dataset (1,000 words) proved difficult, particularly in the identification of the appropriate synsets to associate a given term with, for reasons listed in their paper and mainly related to the structure of Wordnet.

[Camacho-Collados et al., 2018] proposed a multilingual (English, Spanish, and Italian), multi-domain (Medical and Music)) task for hypernym discovery. The task put forward the necessity of providing a corpus to limit the search space for hypernyms; as opposed to [Bordea et al., 2016] which used an Encyclopaedic corpus, [Camacho-Collados et al., 2018] provided a web-base corpus (3-billion word UMBC corpus[8]) as well as data from Pubmed[9]. The task provided participants with a list of hyponym-hypernym pairs, and, despite the fact that both terms occurred in the corpus, there was no guarantee that there were hypernymy contexts.

Finally, there are also a large number of datasets and challenges that specifically look at how to automatically extract relations in order to populate knowledge bases such as DBpedia or Wikidata. The Knowledge Base Population track (KBP) at the NIST Text Analaysis Conference[10] is a popular series which focus on relations involving Named entities rather than words of the language (see [Shen et al., 2014] for more details).

To the best of our knowledge, FINSIM 2020 was the first time a task of Hypernymy categorization was proposed for the Financial domain.

3 Task description

3.1 Overview

At FinSim, participants were given a list of carefully selected terms from the financial domain such as "European depositary receipt", "Interest rate swap" and were asked to design a system which can automatically classify them to the most relevant hypernym (or top-level) concept in an external ontology. For example, given the set of concepts "Bonds", "Unclassified", "Share", "Loan", the most relevant hypernym of "European depositary receipt" is "Share". FinSim focused on the category of Financial instruments. A financial instrument is a general category for any contract that can be traded by investors.

---

[3]https://spec.edmcouncil.org/fibo/

[4]https://www.investopedia.com/financial-term-dictionary-4769738

[5]https://www.quotemedia.com/apifeeds/cfi_code

[6]http://wikipedia.org

[7]https://wordnet.princeton.edu/

[8]http://ebiquity.umbc.edu/blogger/2013/05/01/umbc-webbase-corpus-of-3b-english-words/

[9]9https://www.nlm.nih.gov/databases/download/pubmed_medline.html

[10]https://tac.nist.gov/tracks/index.html

3.2 Description of the dataset and labels

We provided participants with (i) a raw corpus from which the participants could extract financial word representations, (ii) an ontology that structures and associate the financial terms with their labels from a carefully designed tagset and (iii) a list of term category pairs that instantiate the ontology concepts.

3.3 The Prospectus corpus

We provided a set of financial prospectuses in English to be used for training embeddings for this task [11]. Financial prospectuses provide key information for investors and detail investment rules linked to particular financial instruments. The files had been downloaded from various websites and it was forbidden to re-distribute them. The corpus size is estimated to about 10 million tokens. More precisely, the corpus is made of 156 prospectuses in PDF format. Their individual size varies between a dozen pages to several hundreds.

3.4 The FIBO ontology

FIBO is an interesting and pioneering effort (still in progress) to formalize the semantics of the financial domain using a large number of ontologies. More detail can be found on their website[12]. Participants were encouraged to use this resource (as well as others) in designing their system and this is why we provided a number of scripts to facilitate its processing.

We also provided a mapping from each of the categories used in FinSim to a concept in the FIBO ontology (in the file *data/outputs/fibo_mapping.json*). In creating this mapping, we chose to map FinSim labels to the most relevant concepts rather than to "instruments" concepts from the instruments ontology. Indeed some instruments, like *Swaps*, have an ontology of their own. Finally, it is worth noting that there is a development version of FIBO which may contain useful content yet not finally released or validated for production.

3.5 The FinSim dataset

Tagset

The first stage for building the dataset involved building the tagset. FinSim focuses on 8 categories of financial instruments (`Bonds`, `Forwards`, `Funds`, `Future`, `MMIs`, `Option`, `Stocks`, `Swap`).

These labels refer to the most important and most frequently used types of financial instruments (except for cash deposits). As previously noted, there are multiple classifications available for financial instruments, such as CFI codes. Many organizations design their own classifications or adjust existing ones according to their needs. Categorisation of financial instruments can be approached from two angles:

- a featured-based approach will classify instruments according to their properties (such as whether it contains a maturity condition)
- a kind-based approach will classify them according to their prototypical kind in a list of available kinds (even if they share properties with other kinds of instruments).

[11] Available under *data/English_prospectuses* in our data

[12] https://spec.edmcouncil.org/fibo/

- Currencies
  - Cash
    - Deposits
- Securities
  - Equities
    - **Stocks**
  - Debt
    - **Bonds**
    - **MMIs**
      - Certificate of deposit
      - Commercial papers
      - Treasury notes
  - **Funds**
    - Standard Funds
    - Alternative Funds
    - ETFs
- Contracts
  - Derivatives
    - **Options**
    - Warrants
    - **Swaps**
    - **Forwards**
    - **Futures**
  - Non-derivatives
    - SFTs
      - Repos
      - Rev-repos
      - SLB
    - Loans

Figure 1: FinSim Asset tree

Termset

The next stage involved selecting appropriate terms of financial instruments and categorizing them. We iteratively and manually built up the lexicon by looking up keywords on the internet and in the prospectus corpus.

Because we wanted to test models' capacity to generalize from unseen data, we included a set of terms not present in the Prospectus corpus, however the majority of terms had at least one mention. We also selected different types of linguistic expressions. For example, funds are often designated:

- elliptically by naming them by their type, e.g. *SICAV*, *Unit trust*,
- via an acronym, which are known to be very ambiguous forms ,e.g. *AIF*,
- by their role, e.g. *feeder* or *master*
- by selecting larger noun groups including the hypernym, e.g. *hedge* ***fund***, *closed end* ***fund***
- the term itself *fund* or a compound variant, e.g. *subfund*

The dataset was built by two annotators and all were reviewed by a second annotator, expert in the finance domain, who built the asset tree depicted in Figure 1 .

As in [Camacho-Collados *et al.*, 2018] the train and the test sets were of equal size (see Table 1). Careful attention was

Corpus	train	test
Number of terms	100	99

Table 1: Dataset of terms for FinSim 2020

taken to use the same class distribution between train and test datasets. The format of the data was a JSON file containing the terms and their associated hypernym, as {*"label": "Option", "term": "Over-the-counter option"*}.

3.6 Metrics

As metrics we used Average Accuracy and Mean Rank. For each term x_i with a label y_i from the n samples in the test set, the expected prediction is a top 3 list of labels ranked from most to least likely to be equal to the ground truth by the predictive system $\hat{y}_i^l$. We note by $rank_i$ the rank of the correct label in the top-3 prediction list, if the ground truth does not appear in the top-3 then $rank_i$ is equal to 4.

Given those notation the accuracy can be expressed as:

$$Accuracy = \frac{1}{n} * \sum_{i=1}^{n} I(y_i = \hat{y}_i^l[0])$$

And the Mean Rank as:

$$Mean\_Rank = \frac{1}{n} * \sum_{i=1}^{n} rank_i$$

A lower value of the Mean Rank is better. This metric is useful because it does not treat all the errors the same way, if the correct label is ranked fourth in the prediction list then its evaluation is penalized more heavily than if it is ranked second. Mean Rank was used by [Camacho-Collados *et al.*, 2018] in their shared task.

3.7 Baselines

Two baselines were provided to help participants design their systems.

The first baseline used pretrained embeddings to compute a representation for the labels and computed the distance between this vector and the vector of each candidate term.

The second baseline split the term into words and using their pretrained embedddings, learnt a Logistic Regression model in a supervised manner from the trainset.

4 Participants and systems

Team	Affiliation
IITK	IITK, India
Anuj	Publicis Sapient, USA
ProsperaMnet	University of Szeged - Hungary
FINSIM20	IIIT & VIT , India
Ferryman	Complex lab, UESTC
AIAI	Rakuten

Table 2: List of the 6 participating teams in the FinSim Shared Task.

A total of 6 teams who participated from which 4 submitted a paper to describe their method. The shared task brought together private and public research institutions including Publicis Sapient, IITK, IIIT, VIT and University of Szeged (see Table 2 for more details).

Participating teams explored and implemented a wide variety of techniques and features. In this section, we give a short summary of the methods proposed by each participating team (for further details, all papers are published in the proceedings of the FinNLP 2020 Workshop).

IITK This team's system is based on a comparison between context-independent word embeddings in the form of Word2vec word vectors [Mikolov *et al.*, 2013b] that were trained on financial prospectuses and context-dependent word vectors using BERT [Devlin *et al.*, 2019]. Their system is a combination of two prediction strategies. The first strategy is a rule-based approach that is applied to test samples that have exactly one label mentioned in the entity that needs to be classified, in this case the top prediction simply the label that was mentioned. The second strategy is based on a Naive Bayes classifier applied to word embeddings. Their system achieved the overall rank 1 in the shared task when based on 100 dimension Word2vec vectors, over-performing larger dimension Word2vec vectors and BERT embeddings.

Anuj This team took advantage of an external data source (*Investopedia*) in order to supplement the terms with their in-domain definition. Their ML system is based on hand-crafted features and bi-gram TF-IDF features followed by a linear SVM model. This system scored 1st on the accuracy metric and second on the overall ranking of the shared task.

ProsperaMnet This team builds their system on sparse word embeddings and an algorithm proposed in [Balogh *et al.*, 2020] that tries to quantify the extent to which a specific dimension of the sparse word vector relates to certain common sense properties of concepts. They compare their approach to a dense-vector baseline and show that their approach works better than the baseline, especially when used with the best regularization hyper-parameter. This System scored second on the Average Rank metric and 3rd in the overall ranking.

FINSIM20 This team compared different types of algorithms under multiple configuration in order to solve the task. They first used either generic Glove word embeddings [Pennington *et al.*, 2014] or fine-tuned on financial prospectuses along with a cosine similarity metric in order to rank the labels that best fit an entity. They also run experiments using a KNN approach either based on the original training set or an extended version of the data-set that they generated using Hearst Patterns [Hearst, 1992]. They also explored graph-based methods where they built a graph in which each entity is a node and then leveraged the relations between nodes to detect hypernymy-hyponymy. Their best approach is based on Universal Sentence Encoder [Cer *et al.*, 2018] and cosine similarity, this approach scored third place overall on the shared task.

5 Results and discussion

5.1 Results

We ranked submissions using the metrics defined in 3.6 and we provided an overall ranking by combining them. IITK came first as it obtained he best performance according to both metrics. ProsperaMnet and Anuj were second depending on the metric. This variation is explained by the fact that the Anuj system was a single class model and only provided a single category as answer (as opposed to a ranked list of labels).

Rank	Team
1	IITK
2	Anuj
3	ProsperaMnet
3	FINSIM20
4	Ferryman
5	AIAI

Table 3: Overall results

Team	Mean rank
IITK	1.21
ProsperaMnet	1.34
Anuj	1.42
FINSIM20	1.43
Ferryman	1.59
AIAI	1.94

Table 4: Mean-Rank Ranking

Team	Accuracy
IITK	0.858
Anuj	0.858
FINSIM20	0.787
ProsperaMnet	0.777
Ferryman	0.757
AIAI	0.545

Table 5: Accuracy Ranking

5.2 Discussion

Most teams used some type of unsupervised word embeddings, either being context-independent like Word2vec [Mikolov *et al.*, 2013a] or Glove [Pennington *et al.*, 2014] or context-dependent like BERT [Devlin *et al.*, 2019] or Universal Sentence Encoder [Cer *et al.*, 2018] while one team built their system on TF-IDF of bi-gram words. The word embeddings are generally averaged and used as is for the subsequent steps in the predictive system.

Given the small size of the training data, some teams tried to extend the dataset either by using an external source of term definitions or by automatically extracting hypernym examples using Hearst Patterns [Hearst, 1992].

Baseline	Mean rank	Accuracy
Baseline 2	1,838	0,606
Baseline 1	2,111	0,505

Table 6: Baseline Performance

The most common unsupervised approach for this classification was using the cosine similarity between the term representation and the label representation in the embedding space, the labels are then ranked by decreasing order of similarity. Since the training sample is small, most teams based their approach on a model that learns linear boundaries between the target classes like a linear SVM or a logistic regression.

6 Conclusions and perspectives

This paper introduced FinSim, the first shared task in Hypernymy categorization to focus on the financial domain. This task attracted 6 teams across the world, although 20 teams initially expressed their interest. The challenge posed by FinSim is how to appropriately make use of corpus-derived representations, such as word embeddings, with existing manually designed taxonomies. In order to do that, it drew from previous similar shared tasks and proposed a train set of terms along with their categories, from a tagset of financial instruments.

The task was addressed by a variety of approaches, both supervised and unsupervised, and attempting to make use of external resources such as Investopedia or FIBO, and pretrained embeddings such as Glove or BERT, or using more traditional ngram counts as features for their models.

The best team reached 0.858 accuracy, which largely beats the baselines (0.5 and 0.6), which means that, despite the small size of the corpus, the effort put in modeling paid off.

The FinSim shared task made it easy for participants to access data by providing scripts for data processing and baseline models as guidance.

This task focused on financial instruments. Obviously one way this task could be extended, would be by selecting a larger number of financial instruments. One of the pieces of feedback from participants was that the size of the corpus was small, and powerful methods did not work. Another direction for future work is to look at different semantic categories, as provided in FIBO, e.g. types of business entities, types of rates and indicators. Another perspective would be to change the type of task and turn it into a Named Entity Recognition task, but that would involve a substantial dataset creation. Finally it is also envisaged to extend the task to other languages such as French or German.

Acknowledgments

This work was fully supported by Fortia Financial Solutions.

References

[Balogh *et al.*, 2020] Vanda Balogh, Gábor Berend, Dimitrios I. Diochnos, and György Turán. Understanding the semantic content of sparse word embeddings using a commonsense knowledge base. In *The Thirty-Fourth AAAI Conference on Artificial Intelligence, AAAI 2020,*

">

The Thirty-Second Innovative Applications of Artificial Intelligence Conference, IAAI 2020, The Tenth AAAI Symposium on Educational Advances in Artificial Intelligence, EAAI 2020, New York, NY, USA, February 7-12, 2020, pages 7399–7406. AAAI Press, 2020.

[Baroni and Lenci, 2009] Marco Baroni and Alessandro Lenci. One distributional memory, many semantic spaces. In *Proceedings of the Workshop on Geometrical Models of Natural Language Semantics*, pages 1–8, Athens, Greece, March 2009. Association for Computational Linguistics.

[Bordea *et al.*, 2015] Georgeta Bordea, Paul Buitelaar, Stefano Faralli, and Roberto Navigli. Semeval-2015 task 17: Taxonomy extraction evaluation (texeval). In *Proceedings of SemEval 2015, co-located with NAACL HLT 2015*, Denver, Col, USA, 2015.

[Bordea *et al.*, 2016] Georgeta Bordea, Els Lefever, and Paul Buitelaar. Semeval-2016 task 13: Taxonomy extraction evaluation (texeval-2). In *Proceedings of the 10th International Workshop on Semantic Evaluation*, San Diego, CA, USA, 2016.

[Camacho-Collados *et al.*, 2018] Jose Camacho-Collados, Claudio Delli Bovi, Luis Espinosa-Anke, Sergio Oramas, Tommaso Pasini, Enrico Santus, Vered Shwartz, Roberto Navigli, , and Horacio Saggion. Semeval-2018 task 9: Hypernym discovery. In *Proceedings of the 12th International Workshop on Semantic Evaluation (SemEval-2018)*, New Orleans, LA, United States, 2018.

[Cer *et al.*, 2018] Daniel Cer, Yinfei Yang, Sheng-yi Kong, Nan Hua, Nicole Limtiaco, Rhomni St. John, Noah Constant, Mario Guajardo-Cespedes, Steve Yuan, Chris Tar, Brian Strope, and Ray Kurzweil. Universal sentence encoder for English. In *Proceedings of the 2018 Conference on Empirical Methods in Natural Language Processing: System Demonstrations*, pages 169–174, Brussels, Belgium, November 2018. Association for Computational Linguistics.

[Devlin *et al.*, 2019] Jacob Devlin, Ming-Wei Chang, Kenton Lee, and Kristina Toutanova. BERT: Pre-training of deep bidirectional transformers for language understanding. In *Proceedings of the 2019 Conference of the North American Chapter of the Association for Computational Linguistics: Human Language Technologies, Volume 1 (Long and Short Papers)*, pages 4171–4186, Minneapolis, Minnesota, June 2019. Association for Computational Linguistics.

[Grefenstette, 1994] Gregory Grefenstette. *Explorations in Automatic Thesaurus Discovery*. Kluwer Academic Publishers, Boston, London, Dordrecht, 1994.

[Hearst, 1992] Marti A. Hearst. Automatic acquisition of hyponyms from large text corpora. In *COLING 1992 Volume 2: The 15th International Conference on Computational Linguistics*, 1992.

[Jurgens and Pilehvar, 2016] David Jurgens and Mohammad Taher Pilehvar. Semeval-2016 task 14: Semantic taxonomy enrichment. In *Proceedings of the 10th International Workshop on Semantic Evaluation*, San Diego, CA, USA, 2016.

[Lin, 1998] Dekang Lin. Automatic retrieval and clusteringof similar words. In *Proceedings of the 17th international conference on Computational linguistics (Coling)*, Montreal, Quebec, Canada, 1998.

[Mikolov *et al.*, 2013a] Tomas Mikolov, Ilya Sutskever, Kai Chen, Greg Corrado, and Jeffrey Dean. Distributed representations of words and phrases and their compositionality. In *Proceedings of the 26th International Conference on Neural Information Processing Systems - Volume 2*, NIPS'13, page 3111–3119, Red Hook, NY, USA, 2013. Curran Associates Inc.

[Mikolov *et al.*, 2013b] Tomas Mikolov, Ilya Sutskever, Kai Chen, Greg S Corrado, and Jeff Dean. Distributed representations of words and phrases and their compositionality. In C. J. C. Burges, L. Bottou, M. Welling, Z. Ghahramani, and K. Q. Weinberger, editors, *Advances in Neural Information Processing Systems 26*, pages 3111–3119. Curran Associates, Inc., 2013.

[Mintz *et al.*, 2009] Mike Mintz, Steven Bills, Rion Snow, and Daniel Jurafsky. Distant supervision for relation extraction without labeled data. In *Proceedings of the Joint Conference of the 47th Annual Meeting of the ACL and the 4th International Joint Conference on Natural Language Processing of the AFNLP*, pages 1003–1011, Suntec, Singapore, August 2009. Association for Computational Linguistics.

[Pennington *et al.*, 2014] Jeffrey Pennington, Richard Socher, and Christopher D Manning. Glove: Global vectors for word representation. In *EMNLP*, volume 14, pages 1532–1543, 2014.

[Radford *et al.*, 2019] Alec Radford, Jeffrey Wu, Rewon Child, David Luan, Dario Amodei, and Ilya Sutskever. Language models are unsupervised multitask learners. *OpenAI Blog*, 1(8):9, 2019.

[Shen *et al.*, 2014] Wei Shen, Jianyong Wang, and Jiawei Han. Entity linking with a knowledge base: Issues, techniques, and solutions. *IEEE Transactions on Knowledge and Data Engineering*, 27(2):443–460, 2014.

[Wang *et al.*, 2014] Zhen Wang, Jianwen Zhang, Jianlin Feng, and Zheng Chen. Knowledge graph embedding by translating on hyperplanes. In *Proceedings of the Twenty-Eighth AAAI Conference on Artificial Intelligence*, AAAI'14, page 1112–1119. AAAI Press, 2014.

[Zeng *et al.*, 2015] Daojian Zeng, Kang Liu, Yubo Chen, and Jun Zhao. Distant supervision for relation extraction via piecewise convolutional neural networks. In *Proceedings of the 2015 conference on empirical methods in natural language processing*, pages 1753–1762, 2015.

IITK at the FinSim Task: Hypernym Detection in Financial Domain via Context-Free and Contextualized Word Embeddings

Vishal Keswani[*] , **Sakshi Singh**[*] and **Ashutosh Modi**

Indian Institute of Technology Kanpur (IITK)

{vkeswani,sakshia}@iitk.ac.in, ashutoshm@cse.iitk.ac.in

Abstract

In this paper, we present our approaches for the FinSim 2020 shared task on "Learning Semantic Representations for the Financial Domain". The goal of this task is to classify financial terms into the most relevant hypernym (or top-level) concept in an external ontology. We leverage both context-dependent and context-independent word embeddings in our analysis. Our systems deploy Word2vec embeddings trained from scratch on the corpus (Financial Prospectus in English) along with pre-trained BERT embeddings. We divide the test dataset into two subsets based on a domain rule. For one subset, we use unsupervised distance measures to classify the term. For the second subset, we use simple supervised classifiers like Naive Bayes, on top of the embeddings, to arrive at a final prediction. Finally, we combine both the results. Our system ranks 1st based on both the metrics, i.e., mean rank and accuracy.

1   Introduction

Natural Language Processing has mainstream applications in a wide range of domains. In the Financial domain, sentiment analysis is vastly simplified, while applications like financial document processing remain relatively unexplored. According to the popular educational website Investopedia[1], "A prospectus is a formal document that is required by and filed with the Securities and Exchange Commission (SEC) that provides details about an investment offering to the public." The ease in availability of financial texts in the form of Financial Prospectus opens a broad area of domain-specific research for computational linguists and machine learning researchers.

A hypernym is simply a word (or concept) denoting a superordinate category to which words (or concepts) having more specific meaning belong. Hypernym detection is a relatively old problem studied in NLP for more than two decades [Shwartz *et al.*, 2016]. It finds applications in question answering [Yahya *et al.*, 2013], web retrieval, website naviga-

tion or records management [Bordea *et al.*, 2015] and taxonomy evaluation [Yu *et al.*, 2015]. In cognitive science, hypernyms are analogous to higher levels of abstraction in the hierarchy within which we innately organize concepts. Any concept at a lower level can be categorized as a hyponym while the corresponding higher-level concept is its hypernym. A hyponym can be associated with multiple hypernyms (Labrador: Dog, Animal; Revenue Bond: Bond, Security). Hence, hyponym-hypernym pairs are associated with a kind of 'is-a' relationship.

The problem of discovering suitable hypernyms has been formulated in different ways in the past. Previously, the SemEval community has organized similar tasks under the umbrella of taxonomy evaluation [Bordea *et al.*, 2015; Bordea *et al.*, 2016]. The problem can also be proposed as a binary verification task, i.e., given a pair of terms, find whether they form a hypernym-hyponym pair. Most recently in SemEval-2018, the problem was reformulated as given a hyponym, find candidate hypernyms in a domain-specific search space [Camacho-Collados and Navigli, 2017]. The FinSim task [Maarouf *et al.*, 2020] is perhaps the first hypernym detection task in the Financial domain. The problem is devised as a multi-class classification task. Each financial term (hyponym) is classified into one of the eight high-level classes (hypernym), which are mutually exclusive from each other.

In section 2, we provide a brief literature review of the work already done in this field. In section 3, we describe the techniques used in our systems including word-embeddings and classifiers. In section 4, we discuss the experimental setup. This includes the systems that we submitted along with post-submission analysis. Section 5 summarises the results of all the systems. Finally, we conclude the paper in section 6 and suggest future directions for research.

2   Related Work

The literature on modelling hypernymy can be classified into two broad categories: Pattern-based and Distributional. Pattern-based approaches rely on the co-occurrence of hyponym and hypernym [Grefenstette, 2015], substring matching, lexico-syntactic patterns [Lefever *et al.*, 2014] or organizing terms in a hierarchy or directed acyclic graph [Velardi *et al.*, 2013].

Distributional approaches are relatively recent. Distributional approaches capture far away relationships and, un-

---

[*] Authors equally contributed to this work.

[1] https://www.investopedia.com/terms/p/prospectus.asp

Proceedings of the Second Workshop on Financial Technology and Natural Language Processing

like the pattern based approaches, do not rely on the co-occurrence of hyponym and hypernym in text. A typical model uses a distributional representation of a word also called word-embedding, as input for a classification layer [Santus *et al.*, 2014; Fu *et al.*, 2014; Weeds *et al.*, 2014; Espinosa-Anke *et al.*, 2016; Nguyen *et al.*, 2017].

Shwartz et al. [2016] combined both pattern-based and distributional approaches in a neural network based model. Bernier-Colborne and Barriere [2018] use a combination of embeddings and Hearst-style patterns for hypernym detection. We leverage both the approaches in our analysis. We test for string inclusion to divide the dataset into two subsets. We then perform separate analysis on the subset of terms that include a class label and the subset of terms that exclude any class label or include multiple labels.

3 Methods

We employed a variety of methods that were essentially distributional. Figure 1 shows a typical system. It primarily consists of an embedding layer followed by a classification layer. We discuss both the layers below.

3.1 Word-embeddings

We employ two types of word-embeddings. One is based on the context-free Word2vec model [Mikolov *et al.*, 2013]. The second is the contextualized state-of-the-art language representation model, BERT [Devlin *et al.*, 2018].

Context-free embeddings: Word2vec

We use Word2vec embeddings [Mikolov *et al.*, 2013] for capturing semantic and syntactic properties of words. It is a dense low-dimensional representation of a word. We trained the embeddings on the whole corpus of Financial Prospectus. Word2Vec represents each word as a vector. We tried different dimensions ranging from 50 to 500. A term is represented by an average of word embeddings of each word contained in the term.

Contextualized embeddings: BERT

Bidirectional Encoder Representations from Transformers (BERT) [Devlin *et al.*, 2018] is the state-of-the-art language model, that has been found to be useful for numerous NLP tasks. It is deeply bidirectional (takes contextual information from both sides of the token) and learns a representation of text via self-supervised learning. BERT models pre-trained on large text corpora are available, and these can be trained for a specific NLP task or further fine-tuned on a specific corpus. We used BERT Base Uncased configuration[2], which has 12 layers (transformer blocks), 12 attention heads and 110 million parameters. We extract sentences from the corpus containing the terms in train and test datasets (maximum 5 for each term). We extracted the default pre-trained embeddings from the last hidden layer for each word in a sentence. We obtain term-embeddings by taking an average of embeddings of its constituent words. This way, we get multiple embeddings for the same term. They are again combined by taking an average. We have limited access to computational resources,

---

[2]https://github.com/google-research/bert

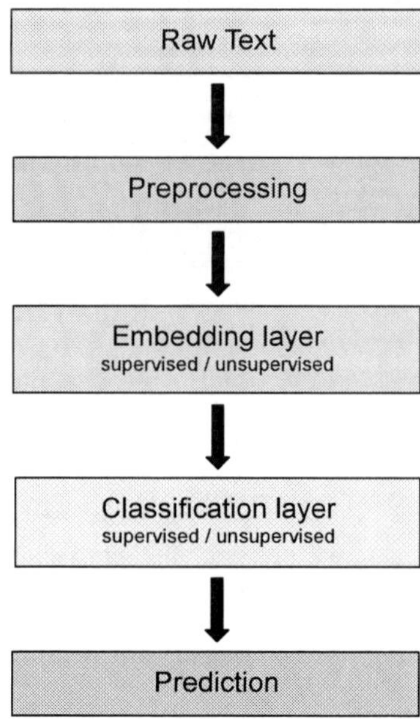

Figure 1: A typical system pipeline

however, with higher computational capability, BERT can be fine-tuned on the whole corpus before extracting embeddings.

3.2 Classifiers

We use simple classifiers on top of the embedding layer. This is due to the small size of the train and test datasets (roughly 100 terms each). We perform both supervised and unsupervised classification.

Unsupervised classification

We obtain embeddings both for the terms and the 8 class labels. We test three different measures of distance/similarity. First, we use cosine-similarity. It is a measure of similarity between two vectors. The more the cosine-similarity score, the closer are the embeddings of the term and the label. We rank the labels in descending order of similarity. We then employ two distance measures, L1 and L2, to find the distance between embeddings of the term and the class labels. The smaller the distance, the closer is the term to that class label. We rank the labels in the ascending order of distance for prediction. These measures do not depend on the size of the dataset as they do not involve further training in the classification layer.

Supervised classification

We test two simple supervised classifiers, namely Naïve Bayes and Logistic Regression. Naïve Bayes is a popular classical machine learning classifiers [Rish and others, 2001]. The primary assumption behind the model is that given the class labels. All features are conditionally independent of each other, hence the name Naïve Bayes. It is highly scalable, that is, takes less training time. It also works well on small datasets. We used the default Bernoulli Naïve Bayes

Train		Test		Example	
# hypernyms within term	**# terms**	**# hypernyms within term**	**# terms**	**Term**	**Hypernym**
0	41	0	29	Debenture	Bonds
1	53	1	66	Covered Bond	Bonds
2	6	2	4	Bond Future	Future
	100		99		

Table 1: Distribution of terms as per hypernym inclusion

classifier from sklearn library[3]. Since the embeddings used are continuous, we first tried Gaussian Naive Bayes. However, the results were unsatisfactory. We then tried Bernoulli Naive Bayes. It binarizes the continuous embeddings with a default threshold of 0. It performed best with the default threshold, far better than Gaussian Naïve Bayes. In the following paper, we address Bernoulli Naïve Bayes as simply Naïve Bayes.

Logistic regression [Kleinbaum *et al.*, 2002] uses logistic function as the representation, in a manner similar to linear regression, to model a binary dependent variable. The eight classes are treated as eight binary variables, which are assigned a probability between 0 and 1. Being a simple model, it works pretty well on small datasets. We use the default Logistic Regression classifier from the sklearn library.

4 Experimental Setup

In this section, we quantitatively describe the dataset provided by the organizers and the challenges accompanying it. We then mention the preprocessing steps briefly. Finally, we discuss the architecture and parameters of the systems in detail.

4.1 Data description

As a part of the task, we are provided with a training dataset of 100 terms with corresponding class labels (hypernyms). The test dataset comprised of 99 financial terms. As a common observation, the majority of the terms contained the label within them (Table 1). For instance, consider the term "Convertible Bonds". The corresponding label for this term is "Bonds". Hence, such terms can be separately dealt using a rule-based approach. The text corpus provided by the organizers consisted of 156 Financial Prospectuses in PDF.

The dataset (Table 1) comes with a lot of inherent challenges. Firstly, the dataset is too small for a supervised approach, especially neural network classifiers. Secondly, there were some terms in the training data, which were not present in the provided corpus. Also, the corpus was provided as PDFs and converting them to txt format added much noise and sentence boundary detection proved to be a challenge.

Another issue is related to acronyms. In both train and test datasets, there were multiple terms written as acronyms. For example, the term "CDS" stands for Credit Default Swap. If the full form was given, this term would have easily qualified for subset 1, and direct classification would have been possible. However, because of the acronym form, the correct classification is solely dependent on the presence of "CDS" in the corpus. The constituent terms Credit, Default and Swap also cannot be used to classify it.

4.2 Data preprocessing

Text preprocessing steps included removal of punctuation, stop words and special characters, followed by lower-casing, lemmatization and tokenization. We used the nltk library[4] [Loper and Bird, 2002] for the same. The tokens were then converted to vectors using Word2vec or BERT embeddings. Finally, the average of all the word vectors is taken to create final embedding for each term.

4.3 Systems

As mentioned in section 4.1, some of the terms contained the label within them. We split the test dataset into two subsets. Subset 1 consists of terms containing exactly one class label within them. Subset 2 has the remaining terms, those with no class label or more than one class label. Subset 1 and subset 2 comprise of 66 and 33 terms, respectively. We perform a separate analysis on both subsets. On observing the training dataset, the terms in subset 1 can be directly classified into the corresponding label since they contain the label within them. This rule-based approach, of directly classifying a term into the label, works very well for our dataset with 100% accuracy. But it does not provide a ranking of labels useful in potential exceptional cases for which the label contained in the term might not be the correct label. Though no such example is encountered in our dataset of 199 points in total, we do not have evidence to eliminate the possibility in which the ranking would be useful in evaluation according to mean rank. Hence, we run all the approaches used for subset 2 on subset 1 also.

A typical system is represented in Figure 1. The combination of the classification layer and the embedding layer used in subset 1 and subset 2 may vary for each system. We describe five such combinations for subset 1 and subset 2. Both are combined to obtain results on the complete test dataset. The results for these systems are discussed in section 5.

System 1

In this system, we use Word2vec word-embeddings of dimension 100 in the embedding layer. In the classification layer, we use L2 norm for subset 1 and Bernoulli Naive Bayes classifier for subset 2. This is the system that stood 1st in the FinSim task in terms of both Mean Rank and Accuracy.

---

[3]https://scikit-learn.org/stable/

[4]https://pythonspot.com/category/nltk/

Embedding	Dim	Unsupervised						Supervised					
		Cosine Sim.		L1		L2		Naïve Bayes			Logistic Regression		
		MR	ACC	MR	ACC	MR	ACC	#train	MR	ACC	#train	MR	ACC
Word2vec	50	1.06	0.95	1.04	0.95	1.06	0.95	100	1.47	0.73	100	1.26	0.85
	100	1.02	0.98	1.02	0.98	1.00	1.00	100	1.21	0.85	100	1.11	0.89
	300	1.00	1.00	1.00	1.00	1.00	1.00	100	1.04	0.97	100	1.03	0.97
BERT	768	1.21	0.95	1.21	0.95	1.21	0.95	100	1.04	0.98	100	1.00	1.00

Table 2: Performance on subset 1 (MR = mean rank, ACC = accuracy)

Embedding	Dim	Unsupervised						Supervised					
		Cosine		L1		L2		Naïve Bayes			Logistic Regression		
		MR	ACC	MR	ACC	MR	ACC	#train	MR	ACC	#train	MR	ACC
Word2vec	50	2.97	0.18	2.67	0.27	2.54	0.27	100	2.09	0.48	100	1.97	0.48
								166	2.18	0.48	166	1.97	0.52
	100	2.73	0.21	2.24	0.36	2.33	0.33	100	1.56	0.64	100	1.84	0.52
								166	1.51	0.61	166	1.76	0.54
	300	2.58	0.33	2.48	0.24	2.27	0.30	100	1.70	0.61	100	1.82	0.52
								166	1.70	0.64	166	1.76	0.54
BERT	768	2.61	0.33	2.45	0.39	2.5	0.36	100	2.06	0.52	100	1.97	0.48
								166	2.12	0.45	166	1.88	0.54

Table 3: Performance on subset 2 (MR = mean rank, ACC = accuracy)

System 2

In this system, we use Word2vec word-embeddings of dimension 300 in the embedding layer. In the classification layer, we use L2 norm for subset 1 and Bernoulli Naive Bayes classifier for subset 2.

System 3

In this system, we use word-embeddings obtained from BERT of dimension 768 in the embedding layer. In the classification layer, we use logistic regression for both the subsets.

5 Results

We discuss the performance of all the approaches and systems on the test dataset. Table 2 describes the results of different approaches on subset 1. It is clear from the table that unsupervised approaches (cosine similarity, L1 norm and L2 norm) prove to be better than supervised approaches (Naïve Bayes and Logistic Regression) for subset 1 with Word2vec word-embeddings. Among the unsupervised, L2 norm dominates. For BERT embeddings, logistic regression dominates.

Table 3 describes the results of different approaches on subset 2. Contrary to subset 1, supervised approaches perform better than unsupervised approaches on subset 2. Naïve Bayes dominates among the supervised classifiers for the Word2vec word-embeddings while logistic regression dominates for BERT embeddings. Since we obtain 100% accuracy for subset 1, as assumed based on the rule, and the training dataset is small, we add the terms in subset 1, with their predicted labels, in the training dataset. Hence, we present results for subset 2 on 100 training data points (original train dataset) as well as on 166 training data points (original train dataset + subset 1). In the following systems, we use results with 166 training data points on subset 2 for consistency.

Table 4 shows the results for the systems discussed in subsection 4.3. System 1 and 2 show the performance of Word2vec word-embeddings of dimensions 100 and 300, respectively. These systems are a combination of unsupervised and supervised approaches separately applied on subset 1 and 2, respectively. They outperform any of the approaches applied to the aggregate test data. For both the systems, the classification layers consist of L2 norm for subset 1 and Naïve Bayes classifier for subset 2 as they dominate in their respective categories. System 3, reveals the performance of BERT word-embeddings in the embedding layer. It uses the logistic regression classifier, for both subsets 1 and 2, in the classification layer as it performs the best with BERT word-embeddings.

System	Mean Rank	Accuracy
1	1.17	0.87
2	1.23	0.88
3	1.29	0.85

Table 4: Results of different systems on the whole test data

Although system 1 stood $1st$ in the task on both metrics, in post-submission analysis, system 2 outperforms system 1 in terms of accuracy. Overall, the Word2vec embeddings outperform BERT embeddings. This may be because BERT embeddings are context-dependent and do not produce a unique embedding for each word. On the contrary, Word2vec embeddings are unique for every word and are more suited for a task where proper nouns are being classified.

6 Conclusion

As part of FinSim 2020 shared task on Learning Semantic Representations in the Financial Domain, we attempt to solve the problem of hypernym detection minted for Financial texts. We employ static Word2vec and dynamic BERT embeddings under the top classification layers consisting of simple classifiers. Word2vec dominates for both dimensions (100 and 300). Though BERT embeddings come out to be equally accurate for terms containing the one hypernym within them, they lag behind for the other subset of terms. With higher computational resources, BERT could be pre-trained on the whole corpus, and the performance may improve. Unsupervised metrics are efficient and independent of data size, but they lag behind supervised classifiers for terms exclusive of class label.

For future research, the data size could be increased significantly to bring deep learning based classifiers into the picture, and the task could be enhanced from hypernym detection to hypernym discovery. Overall, the task advances the NLP community towards the broad area of Financial Document Processing and encourages collaboration between the fields of Finance and NLP.

References

[Bernier-Colborne and Barriere, 2018] Gabriel Bernier-Colborne and Caroline Barriere. Crim at semeval-2018 task 9: A hybrid approach to hypernym discovery. In *Proceedings of The 12th International Workshop on Semantic Evaluation*, pages 725–731, 2018.

[Bordea *et al.*, 2015] Georgeta Bordea, Paul Buitelaar, Stefano Faralli, and Roberto Navigli. Semeval-2015 task 17: Taxonomy extraction evaluation (texeval). In *SemEval@NAACL-HLT*, 2015.

[Bordea *et al.*, 2016] Georgeta Bordea, Els Lefever, and Paul Buitelaar. Semeval-2016 task 13: Taxonomy extraction evaluation (texeval-2). In *Proceedings of the 10th International Workshop on Semantic Evaluation (SemEval-2016)*, pages 1081–1091, 2016.

[Camacho-Collados and Navigli, 2017] Jose Camacho-Collados and Roberto Navigli. Babeldomains: Large-scale domain labeling of lexical resources. In *Proceedings of the 15th Conference of the European Chapter of the Association for Computational Linguistics: Volume 2, Short Papers*, pages 223–228, 2017.

[Devlin *et al.*, 2018] Jacob Devlin, Ming-Wei Chang, Kenton Lee, and Kristina Toutanova. Bert: Pre-training of deep bidirectional transformers for language understanding. *arXiv preprint arXiv:1810.04805*, 2018.

[Espinosa-Anke *et al.*, 2016] Luis Espinosa-Anke, Jose Camacho-Collados, Claudio Delli Bovi, and Horacio Saggion. Supervised distributional hypernym discovery via domain adaptation. In *Conference on Empirical Methods in Natural Language Processing; 2016 Nov 1-5; Austin, TX. Red Hook (NY): ACL; 2016. p. 424-35*. ACL (Association for Computational Linguistics), 2016.

[Fu *et al.*, 2014] Ruiji Fu, Jiang Guo, Bing Qin, Wanxiang Che, Haifeng Wang, and Ting Liu. Learning semantic hierarchies via word embeddings. In *Proceedings of the 52nd Annual Meeting of the Association for Computational Linguistics (Volume 1: Long Papers)*, pages 1199–1209, 2014.

[Grefenstette, 2015] Gregory Grefenstette. Inriasac: Simple hypernym extraction methods. *arXiv preprint arXiv:1502.01271*, 2015.

[Kleinbaum *et al.*, 2002] David G Kleinbaum, K Dietz, M Gail, Mitchel Klein, and Mitchell Klein. *Logistic regression*. Springer, 2002.

[Lefever *et al.*, 2014] Els Lefever, Marjan Van de Kauter, and Véronique Hoste. Hypoterm: Detection of hypernym relations between domain-specific terms in dutch and english. *Terminology. International Journal of Theoretical and Applied Issues in Specialized Communication*, 20(2):250–278, 2014.

[Loper and Bird, 2002] Edward Loper and Steven Bird. Nltk: the natural language toolkit. *arXiv preprint cs/0205028*, 2002.

[Maarouf *et al.*, 2020] Ismail El Maarouf, Youness Mansar, Virginie Mouilleron, and Dialekti Valsamou-Stanislawski. The finsim 2020 shared task: Learning semantic representations for the financial domain. In *Proceedings of IJCAI-PRICAI 2020*, Kyoto, Japan (or virtual event), 2020.

[Mikolov *et al.*, 2013] Tomas Mikolov, Kai Chen, Greg Corrado, and Jeffrey Dean. Efficient estimation of word representations in vector space. *arXiv preprint arXiv:1301.3781*, 2013.

[Nguyen *et al.*, 2017] Kim Anh Nguyen, Maximilian Köper, Sabine Schulte im Walde, and Ngoc Thang Vu. Hierarchical embeddings for hypernymy detection and directionality. *arXiv preprint arXiv:1707.07273*, 2017.

[Rish and others, 2001] Irina Rish et al. An empirical study of the naive bayes classifier. In *IJCAI 2001 workshop on empirical methods in artificial intelligence*, volume 3, pages 41–46, 2001.

[Santus *et al.*, 2014] Enrico Santus, Alessandro Lenci, Qin Lu, and Sabine Schulte Im Walde. Chasing hypernyms in vector spaces with entropy. In *Proceedings of the 14th Conference of the European Chapter of the Association for Computational Linguistics, volume 2: Short Papers*, pages 38–42, 2014.

[Shwartz *et al.*, 2016] Vered Shwartz, Yoav Goldberg, and Ido Dagan. Improving hypernymy detection with an integrated path-based and distributional method. *arXiv preprint arXiv:1603.06076*, 2016.

[Velardi *et al.*, 2013] Paola Velardi, Stefano Faralli, and Roberto Navigli. Ontolearn reloaded: A graph-based algorithm for taxonomy induction. *Computational Linguistics*, 39(3):665–707, 2013.

[Weeds *et al.*, 2014] Julie Weeds, Daoud Clarke, Jeremy Reffin, David Weir, and Bill Keller. Learning to distinguish hypernyms and co-hyponyms. In *Proceedings of COLING 2014, the 25th International Conference on Computational Linguistics: Technical Papers*, pages 2249–2259. Dublin City University and Association for Computational Linguistics, 2014.

[Yahya *et al.*, 2013] Mohamed Yahya, Klaus Berberich, Shady Elbassuoni, and Gerhard Weikum. Robust question answering over the web of linked data. In *Proceedings of the 22nd ACM international conference on Information & Knowledge Management*, pages 1107–1116, 2013.

[Yu *et al.*, 2015] Zheng Yu, Haixun Wang, Xuemin Lin, and Min Wang. Learning term embeddings for hypernymy identification. In *Twenty-Fourth International Joint Conference on Artificial Intelligence*, 2015.

Anuj@FINSIM–Learning Semantic Representation of Financial Domain with Investopedia

Anuj Saini

Publicis Sapient, Los Angeles, CA, USA

anuj.saini@publicissapient.com

Abstract

Natural Language Processing and its applications are getting used in every domain, and it has become an important need to have domain specific knowledge representation in the form of ontologies, taxonomies or word embeddings like BERT. As most of these knowledge bases are generic and lack the specificity of a domain, it is very important to have semantic representation for domain separately. The FinSim 2020 shared task is colocated with the FinNLP workshop, and the challenge is to classify financial terms into their predefined classes or hypernyms. This paper explains a hybrid approach that uses various NLP, machine learning, and deep learning models to develop a financial terms classifier. Also the paper explains use of a financial domain encyclopedia called Investopedia to enrich terms for better context. The semantic representation of financial terms is a very important building block for NLP applications such as question answering, chatbot, trading applications etc.

Keywords

Financial Ontology, BERT, Investopedia, Machine Learning, Natural Language Processing, Support Vector Machine, Word Embeddings, Ontology

1 Introduction

Knowledge is semantic representation of data and can be defined in various forms such as ontologies with entity-relations or taxonomies with hypernyms/hyponyms relations or in the form of word embedding. Semantic knowledge representation is the core building block task of NLP systems and has been there since decades. A lot of work has been done on systems like OpenCyc, FreeBase, YAGO, DbPedia etc. However, most of these systems are generic and lack specialized detailed terms and entities such as medicine names for healthcare or financial lingo for financial domain. Another issue is that earlier work in the domain of semantic representation is mostly manual and took years of efforts. With technology and AI advancements along with high computational power available, a lot of work has been undergoing to develop various language models. Language models represent knowledge in the form of embedding or vectors which are context aware and can be used for various applications such as text similarity, machine translation or word prediction. Systems like BERT have stormed the NLP space and are beating most benchmarks across all NLP applications. XLNet, RoBERTa, ELMO etc. are some other different kind of word embeddings which are pretrained and can be easily applied for different NLP applications.

A lot of work has been done to develop financial domain specific knowledge base and embeddings. FIBO (Financial Industry Business Ontology) [Bennett, M. 2013] is an owl representation of entities and their relations. Similarity Fin-BERT [Araci, D. 2019] is BERT [Jacob Devlin, Ming-Wei Chang, Kenton Lee, and Kristina Toutanova (2018)] model trained on a huge financial corpus and provide pre-trained model for financial domain tasks.

The paper has been organized as follows. Section 2 gives the description of the training dataset provided by the FinSim organizing committee. Section 3 presents the proposed approach for Financial Terms Classification prediction. The experimental evaluation has been carried out in Section 4. Section 5 concludes our research work followed by acknowledgment and references given in Section 6 and Section 7 respectively.

2 Related Work

Similar tasks have been carried across different levels but most of them were generic in nature. SemEval-2015 [Georgeta Bordea, Paul Buitelaar, Stefano Faralli and Roberto Navigli (2015)] asked participants to find hypernym-hyponym relations between given terms. Similar work to extract knowledge from unstructured task were done at TAC, where the task was to develop and evaluate technologies for populating knowledge bases (KBs) from unstructured text.

Proceedings of the Second Workshop on Financial Technology and Natural Language Processing

3   Data Set Description

FINSIM is a supervised financial term classification task. The task has a total of 100 data points with 2 column data having term to be classified and its class. There are in total 8 classes (hypernyms) and training data was also imbalance wherein classes such as Bonds having 28% data and class Forward has only 5 data points. Overall, 100 data points is too little to train a model, so definitely we needed some more context to enrich data for better performance. Below is the distribution of classes and their respective counts from the training data as shown in table 1. For test data, there were 99 terms to be classified into the correct hypernym.

Data has only two columns: terms and their classes they belongs too. So there was not enough context for text to classify it into its right hypernym or class. There are terms which are self explanatory like Corporate Bond or Equity Future but on the other hand a lot of abbreviations have been used specially in test data like TIPS or ABS which are

Class	Count
Bonds	28
Swap	18
Option	12
Funds	11
Future	9
MMIs	9
Stocks	8
Forward	5

Table 1: Classes Count

totally impossible to classify without having enough context about these terms. That is where we tried to use external embeddings but eventually settled with Investopedia which is a rich dictionary of Financial terms. We enriched our data using Investopedia definitions and other Investopedia topics containing term to classify into it.

3   The Proposed Solution

The proposed approach includes enriching text with Investopedia as first step so that we have enough context for classification. Further, we carried out standard text preprocessing steps and then feature engineering, which includes a set of new features that we generated out of raw text and then trained model using various classification algorithms.

3.1   Investopedia

Investopedia is the world's leading source of financial content on the web which contains a huge financial dictionary for all financial jargons. We collected in total of 15347 fi-

nancial terms and their definition and detailed description out of Investopedia by simply scrapping site https://www.investopedia.com/. Then we created definition of all the terms for training and test data. This enrichment of texts really helped a lot especially for financial terms which had very little context or were complete slangs or abbreviations. Some examples of Investopedia enrichment are:

Example *TIPS: Treasury inflation-protected securities (TIPS), The actual financial benefit of an investment after accounting for inflation and taxes. The after-tax real rate of return is an accurate measure of investment earnings and usually differs significantly from an investment's nominal rate of return, ...*
Example *T-note:The purchase of treasury notes or bonds from dealers, by the Federal Reserve. The "coupon" refers to the coupons which are the main difference between T-notes and T-bills....*

So after the data enrichment process, we had a full definition of terms rather than just the terms for both training and test data.

3.2   Text Pre-Processing

For each data point, the preprocessing steps are as follows:
Text Encoding
We have encoded the definitions using standard UTF-8 encoding that handles scripting of foreign languages.

Tokenization
We applied text tokenization for data analysis and finding important words or tokens, also for removing punctuations and stop words we needed tokenization. We have tokenized the financial text into words using NLTK library.

Punctuation and numbers extraction
All numbers and punctuations are simply don't help in hypernym classification of text. So we used regexes to extract functions and digits.

Stop Words Filtering
We have used standard English stopwords to extract and mark them as English (en) language

WordNet
We have used English WordNet to detect synonyms for terms in general English. WordNet is an extensive lexical dictionary mostly being crafted manually and English WordNet has around 200K word and can be downloaded from the mentioned link in [5]. We used English WordNet form the NLTK python package.

POS Tagging
Part of Speech tagging is the process of tagging every token with its grammatical tag such as noun/adverbs/adjective etc.

As we are more focused on nouns here, it is important to label each word in order to identify nouns.

3.3 Feature Engineering

We tried a lot of various features and tested on different models. We list below all the features created and tested models on:

Character Count
Simply taking count of term in terms of characters.

Words Count
Number of words in the term to be classified.

Word Density
Computed as character Count/words count.

Title Words Count
Words starting with upper case letter.

Upper Case Words Count
Number of words where all characters are upper case letters.

Nouns Count
Number of nouns in the text.

Adjectives Count
Number of adjectives in the text.

Words Embedding
We also tried to use wiki-news-300d-1M.vec embeddings and generated token level embeddings.

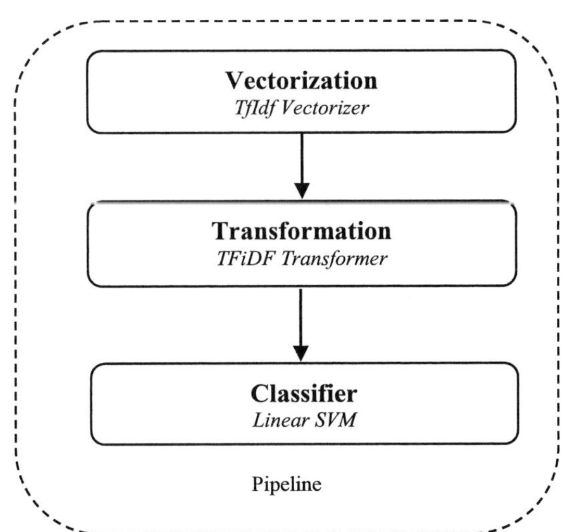

5 Model and Pipeline

We experimented a number of models along with text processing pipeline including CountVectorizer and TfIdfVectorizer. We created a NLP pipeline which pre-processes raw text and then step by step transforms text into vectors, run model, and generates results using a SVM classifier.

5.1 Vectorization

Vectorization is an important process of converting text into numbers. We tried a number of approaches here starting with CountVectorizers that simply count the occurrences of words in the text, CountVectorizers at character level with trigrams. Finally, we got best results using TfIdf Vectorizer with the following configurations:

Analyzer
Splitting text by set of characters or words. We used word level, as we had enough text to get tfidf scores at word level.

Ngram-range
This feature creates ngrams for the given text. We got good results with bigrams.

Max Features
Property to define how many total words to be used for the model to train on. With ngrams enabled and text enriched using Investopedia, we had a lot irrelevant tokens to consume. So we limit our model to use only top 5,000 tokens.

5.2 Transformation

The next step in our pipeline is to transform text into vectors defined in the previous step. We used TfidfTransformer to convert text into vectors.

5.3 Classification

The last step in our pipeline is to classify text into hypernyms. Again, here we attempted different models like RandomForest, XGBoost, Naïve Bayes etc. We got better results with Support Vector Machine (SVM) using LinearSVC with the following configuration:

Kernel
We tried various kernel and cleaner data and features, we got better results with linear kernel.

Penalty
Penalty specifies the norm used in the penalization. We used standard SVC penalty, which is 'l2' penalty.

5.4 Multi-label Classification

One of the ask in this task was to generate all labels in ranked order. Therefore, we have to train our model with probability=true parameter in LinearSVC model that results in probability for each class.
Example (Green Bond): [('Bonds', 0.5137775373484725), ('MMIs', 0.12466465491304607), ('Swap', 0.07597307049335765), ('Funds', 0.06947138280959159), ('Future', 0.06498779183269941), ('Option', 0.061816001759789255), ('Stocks',

0.052482381962057296), ('Forward',
0.03682717888098626)]

6 Results

As there were only 100 data points to develop and test models and even certain classes had too few occurrences, so we decided to use 28 cross validation cycles. Cross-Validation also known as CV is a better way to test data specially when we don't have enough data to train as well test on. Given formula to compute Cross Validation.

$$CV\ (\lambda) = 1/K \sum (K, k=1)\ Ek(\lambda)$$

Where K=28

Still the official results were not the results that we were expecting. The final task was to generate multi-label classification, but for benchmarking our results we restricted the model to validate data on single class only. Finally, after trying various models and vectorization we got our best model results mentioned below in table 2.

class	precision	recall	f1-score	support
Bonds	0.74	0.89	0.81	28
Forward	1	0.6	0.75	5
Funds	1	0.82	0.9	11
Future	1	0.89	0.94	9
MMIs	0.71	0.56	0.63	9
Option	0.86	1	0.92	12
Stocks	0.88	0.88	0.88	8
Swap	1	0.94	0.97	18

Table 2: CV Scores Summary

With overall accuracy of 87% and average precision of 89% is what we got best from our cross validation tests.

6   Future Work

Building fully automatic or semi-automatic taxonomies or ontologies is an important NLP task. This shared task is the perfect step in the direction of developing taxonomies in the financial domain. There are a lot of other experiments that can add more accuracy to the solution. The most important missing method is using BERT or FinBERT embeddings. As BERT is trained on a huge corpus so it can definitely bring a lot of context to the solution, it can help to find out relationships between hypernyms and the term. Secondly, organizers have provided FIBO ontology as part of resources, but we haven't used that and it could definitely have helped us to get more information related to each term. FIBO ontology has triples for entities and it can be useful to identify the full form of abbreviations or even direct hypernyms mentioned in the ontology.

Another important observation and definitely a need to be extended as part of this research is to add more training data to the corpus. It will help the community to train better and robust model with more experiments. This research can be further extended toward building an automatic ontology wherein we can extract triples, find out relationship (synonym, hypernym, hyponym etc.) between term and class, or classifying a term into its type like company, property or concept etc.

7   Conclusion

Natural Language Processing has a very big role to play especially in the financial domain. A lot of financial reports needs to be parsed and consumed which require a lot semantic text understanding. Having a semantic knowledge base is the most important building block for any text parsing system. Language models and word embeddings have their own limitations as they do not tell us much about the quality of the results, no explainability or for instance won't give us the type of relation. So our understanding is that a hybrid solution for this task will be a way forward. Moreover, most existing work is highly manual and stale at current state whereas the financial world is getting daily updated with new companies or new financial jargons.

We have tried to keep our solution very simple and standard with a simple pipeline and focused more on data analysis and data enrichment. We simply used common machine learning instead of making more complex models using deep learning or BERT embeddings simply because of lack of lot of training instances.

Acknowledgements
We would like to thank organizers [Ismail El Maarouf and Youness Mansar and Virginie Mouilleron and Dialekti Valsamou-Stanislawski 2020] for conducting this shared task and also building the training data. We also would like to thank Sapient Corporation for giving us an opportunity to work and explore the world of text analytics.

References

[Araci, D. 2019] Finbert: Financial sentiment analysis with pre-trained language models. Computing Research Repository, arXiv:1908.10063

[Georgeta Bordea, Paul Buitelaar, Stefano Faralli and Roberto Navigli (2015)] "SemEval-2015 Task 17: Taxonomy Extraction Evaluation (TExEval)". In *Proceedings of SemEval 2015*, co-located with NAACL HLT 2015, Denver, Col, USA.

[Georgeta Bordea, Els Lefever, and Paul Buitelaar (2016). "Semeval-2016 task 13] Taxonomy extraction evaluation (TExEval-2)". In *Proceedings of the 10th International Workshop on Semantic Evaluation*, San Diego, CA, USA.

[Jose Camacho-Collados, Claudio Delli Bovi, Luis Espinosa-Anke, Sergio Oramas, Tommaso Pasini, Enrico Santus, Vered Shwartz, Roberto Navigli, and Horacio Saggion (2018)] "SemEval-2018 Task 9: Hypernym Discovery". In *Proceedings of the 12th International Workshop on Semantic Evaluation (SemEval-2018)*, New Orleans, LA, United States. Association for Computational Linguistics.

[Jacob Devlin, Ming-Wei Chang, Kenton Lee, and Kristina Toutanova (2018)] "BERT: Pre-training of Deep Bidirectional Transformers for Language Understanding". https://arxiv.org/abs/1810.04805v2.

[Bennett, M. 2013] The financial industry business ontology: Best practice for big data. J Bank Regul 14, 255–268. https://doi.org/10.1057/jbr.2013.13

[Ismail El~Maarouf and Youness Mansar and Virginie Mouilleron and Dialekti Valsamou-Stanislawski 2020] "The FinSim 2020 Shared Task: Learning Semantic Representations for the Financial Domain",proceedings of IJCAI-PRICAI 2020"

ProsperAMnet at the FinSim Task: Detecting hypernyms of financial concepts via measuring the information stored in sparse word representations

Gábor Berend[1,2] , **Nobert Kis-Szabó**[1] , **Zsolt Szántó**[1]

[1]University of Szeged, Institute of Informatics
[2]MTA-SZTE Research Group on Artificial Intelligence
{berendg,ksznorbi,szantozs}@inf.u-szeged.hu

Abstract

In this paper we propose and carefully evaluate the application of an information theoretic approach for the detection of hypernyms for financial concepts. Our algorithm is based on the application of sparse word embeddings, meaning that – unlike in the case of traditional word embeddings – most of the coefficients in the embeddings are exactly zero. We apply an approach that quantify the extent to which the individual dimensions for such word representations convey the property that some word is the hyponym of a certain top-level concept according to an external ontology. Our experimental results demonstrate that substantial improvements can be gained by our approach compared to the direct utilization of the traditional dense word embeddings. Our team ranked second and fourth according to average rank score and mean accuracy that were the two evaluation criteria applied at the shared task.

1 Introduction

We introduce our contribution to the FinSim 2020 shared task [Maarouf *et al.*, 2020] where the task was to classify financial terms according to their ontological properties.

As sparse word embeddings have been reported to convey increased interpretability [Murphy *et al.*, 2012; Faruqui *et al.*, 2015; Subramanian *et al.*, 2018], we investigated the extent to which applying them can improve the extraction of financial taxonomic relations. To this end we carefully evaluate in this paper an algorithm in the task of extracting taxonomic relations for financial terms on the shared task dataset by exploiting an algorithm for extracting commonsense knowledge from sparse word representations proposed in [Balogh *et al.*, 2020]. Our results corroborate previous claims that the application of sparse word representations not only result in a more interpretable representation, but the systems built on top of them often outperform approaches that employ dense word embeddings [Faruqui *et al.*, 2015; Berend, 2017]. We release our source code and trained embeddings in order to foster reproducibility of our results[1].

---

[1]https://github.com/begab/prosperAM-finsim

2 Related work

Hypernym discovery has spurred substantial research attention with one of the 2018 SemEval shared task being focused on the detection of hypernyms in multiple languages and domains [Camacho-Collados *et al.*, 2018]. The top-performing system applied a combination of supervised learning and unsupervised pattern matching techniques [Bernier-Colborne and Barrière, 2018]. [Held and Habash, 2019] also argued for the applications of hybrid approaches involving Hearst patters [Hearst, 1992] for extracting hypernyms. Most recently, [Dash *et al.*, 2020] introduced Strict Partial Order Networks (SPON), a neural network architecture for detecting word pairs for which the `IsA` relation holds paying special attention to the fact of the relation being asymmetric.

[Berend *et al.*, 2018] employed sparse word representations and formal concept analysis for building a model that decides if a word is a hypernym of another by investigating the non-zero coefficients for a pair of input expressions. Even though our work also exploits sparse word representations, we rather build our framework on an information theory-inspired approach that we introduce in the followings.

3 System description

Our framework adapts recent algorithm in [Balogh *et al.*, 2020] which devises an information theory-inspired algorithm for quantifying the extent to which the individual dimensions of sparse word representations relate to certain commonsense properties of concepts. The basis of the algorithm is to measure the amount of information overlap between the properties of concepts and the nonzero coefficients of sparse word representations. [Balogh *et al.*, 2020] took ConceptNet [Speer and Havasi, 2012] as the basis for measuring the information overlap, however, the approach is generalizable to any commonsense knowledge.

We next summarize our approach in details. As a first step, we extract the raw text from the prospectuses that were provided by the organizers in pdf format using Tika. As a subsequent step, we trained standard static word embeddings using approaches fasttext [Bojanowski *et al.*, 2017] and Glove [Pennington *et al.*, 2014].

We relied on the default tokenization protocol and set all the hyperparameters of the algorithms for creating the embeddings to their default settings as well in order to avoid ex-

Proceedings of the Second Workshop on Financial Technology and Natural Language Processing

cessive hyperparamter tuning. In the end, we were left with a vocabulary of 17,105 unique word forms and 100 dimensional dense embeddings.

Our next step was to derive the sparse word representations from the dense embeddings that we created earlier. For this step, we relied on the algorithm proposed in [Berend, 2017], that is given matrix $X \in \mathbb{R}^{n \times m}$ ($n = 17,105, m = 100$) containing a collection of stacked dense embeddings of cardinality n, we strive to solve

$$\min_{\alpha \in \mathbb{R}^{n \times k}_{\geq 0}, D \in \mathbb{R}^{k \times m}} \frac{1}{2} \|X - \alpha D\|_F^2 + \lambda \|\alpha\|_1, \quad (1)$$

with the additional constraint that the vectors comprising D have a bounded norm. That is, we would like to express each dense word embedding as a sparse linear combination of the vectors included in D. The number of vectors included in $D \in \mathbb{R}^{k \times m}$ is controlled by the value of k. We conducted experiments for $k \in \{1000, 1500, 2000\}$.

The ℓ_1-based penalty term included in (1) causes most of the coefficients in α to be zero, and we tread the rows of this matrix as our sparse word representations. Larger values for the regularization coefficient λ results in higher levels of sparsity in the word representation that we obtain. We performed our experiments with $\lambda \in \{0.1, , 0.2, 0.3, 0.4, 0.5\}$. For solving (1), we used the dictionary learning algorithm introduced in [Mairal *et al.*, 2009].

Next, we constructed the matrix of representations for the terms in the training dataset. This resulted in a matrix of $T \in \mathbb{R}^{100 \times k}$, with 100 referring to the number of terms included in the training dataset. The embeddings for multi-token terms got determined by taking the centroid of the vectorial representation of the words that are included in a multi-token expression.

We subsequently constructed a binary matrix $B \in \{0, 1\}^{8 \times 100}$. In this matrix, every row corresponds to one of the eight labels, i.e., {Bonds, Forward, Funds, Future, MMIs, Option, Stocks, Swap} and an entry b_{ij} was set to 1 if training term j was labeled by label i in the training data and 0 otherwise.

By multiplying matrices B and T we obtained such a matrix $M \in \mathbb{R}^{8 \times k}$ which includes the sparse coefficients of the terms aggregated by the labels they belong to. We treated this matrix as an incidence matrix and calculated the normalized positive pointwise mutual information [Bouma, 2009]. For some label l_i and dimension d_j, we calculated this quantity (that we abbreviate as NPPMI) as

$$\text{NPPMI}(l_i, d_j) = \max\left(0; \ln \frac{P(l_i, d_j)}{P(l_i)P(d_j)} \middle/ -\ln P(l_i, d_j)\right)$$

In the above formula $P(l_i)$ refers to the probability of observing label i, $P(d_j)$ indicates the probability of dimension j having a non-zero value and $P(l_i, d_j)$ refers to the joint probability of the two events. We derived these probabilities by taking the row and column marginals of the ℓ_1-normalized version of the incidence matrix M. By performing NPPMI over every entry of M, we obtain matrix $A \in [0, 1]^{8,k}$, every entry of which determines the strength of association between label i and dimension j.

When facing a new term that is associated by vector $\mathbf{v} \in \mathbb{R}^k$, we take the product $\mathbf{s} = A\mathbf{v}$. An element s_i from $\mathbf{s}$ can be regarded as a score indicating the extent to which $\mathbf{v}$ refers to a vector that describes a term that belong to label i. Our final prediction hence is going to be label i^* for which $i^* = \arg\max_i s_i$.

4   Experiments

We first report our experiments that we obtained for our official submissions in the shared task. During this batch of experiments, we were working with 100 dimensional fasstext vectors created based on the training data provided by the shared task organizers, using the CBOW training approach with the default hyperparamter settings. We used the training set as the development set by measuring the performance of our algorithm over the 100 training instances in a leave-one-out fashion, i.e. averaged the evaluation metrics on every training term, while excluding the currently evaluated term from building our model.

For evaluating purposes we used the two official measures for the shared task, i.e. Mean Accuracy (MA) and Average Rank (AR). MA quantifies the percentage of terms for which a model regarded the true class label as the most likely one, whereas AR also takes into consideration the position of the correct label within the ranked list of class labels for an individual term. For the MA metric higher values mean better performance, whereas AR behaves in the opposite manner.

4.1   Centroid-based baseline

In order to see the added value of using sparse representations, we performed a comparison towards a baseline approach that was based on those dense embeddings. To ensure comparability, our baseline approach was based on the very same fasttext CBOW dense embeddings that we later created our sparse embeddings from.

Notice that the dense embeddings fit naturally into our framework, since utilizing the raw $m = 100$ dimensional dense embeddings can be viewed as performing (1) by choosing $k = m$, $\lambda = 0$ and $D \in \mathbb{R}^{k \times k}$ to be the identity matrix. Under these circumstances, the $\alpha = X$ is a trivial solution for (1), meaning that we are essentially using the original dense embeddings X. Applying our methodology involving the calculation of NPPMI based the raw dense embeddings, however, resulted in poor results.

In order to favor the application of dense embeddings, we made slight modifications in our framework when the inputs were dense emebddings. For the dense embeddings based baseline, we created a matrix $M \in \mathbb{R}^{8 \times 100}$, the rows of which contained unit normalized centroids for each class label that we obtained from averaging the term vectors that belong to each label. Upon making prediction for a dense embedding $\mathbf{v} \in \mathbb{R}^{100}$, we followed the same strategy as before, i.e. formed the product $\mathbf{v}M$ of the term vector and the matrix of unit normalized label centroids and took the argmax of the resulting vector. Table 1 includes the results of our baseline approach which was based on the centroids of the dense fasttext-CBOW embeddings.

Input	MA	AR
100d fasttext CBOW	78.0	1.35

Table 1: Baseline results for the label centroid-based approach using dense embeddings. MA and AR stands for mean accuracy and average ranking, respectively.

$\lambda = 0.1$	$\lambda = 0.2$	$\lambda = 0.3$	$\lambda = 0.4$	$\lambda = 0.5$
85.0	84.0	82.0	84.0	**86.0**

(a) Mean accuracy (MA)

$\lambda = 0.1$	$\lambda = 0.2$	$\lambda = 0.3$	$\lambda = 0.4$	$\lambda = 0.5$
1.33	1.34	1.33	1.33	**1.24**

(b) Average Rank (AR)

Table 2: Average Rank (AR) and Mean Accuracy (MA) metrics of models obtained for using different regularization coefficient λ when evaluated on the training data in a leave-one-out fashion using fasttext CBOW input embeddings and $k = 1000$.

4.2 Evaluation of our approach

Regarding the hyperparameters influencing our approach, we performed controlled experiments for analyzing the effects of changing the hyperparameter of both λ and k.

Controlling the regularization coefficient λ

We first performed controlled experiments to measure the effects of the regularization coefficient $\lambda \in \{0.1, 0.2, 0.3, 0.4, 0.5\}$ while fixing the value of k to be 1000 following [Balogh *et al.*, 2020]. These results are included in Table 2. We can see that the choice for the regularization coefficient did not severely influence our evaluation scores.

By comparing the results in Table 2 with those in Table 1, we can see that our approach performs at least as good as the baseline approach which is based on the centroid of dense fasttext-CBOW embeddings. The contents of Table 1 demonstrate that the results obtained by relying on the sparse CBOW word representations were the best for the highest level of sparsity, i.e. when using $\lambda = 0.5$.

Jointly controlling the regularization and the dimensions

We subsequently measured the effects of simultaneously modifying the regularization coefficient λ and k, i.e. the number of basis vectors to be included in D. Figure 1 includes the results of those experimental settings for $(\lambda, k) \in (0, 100) \cup \{0.1, 0.2, 0.3, 0.4, 0.5\} \times \{1000, 1500, 2000\}$, i.e. we experimented with 15 different combinations of λ and k besides relying on the original 100-dimensional dense embeddings.

Figure 1 displays the MA and AR metrics along the x and y axis, respectively. We can see a negative correlation, i.e. the higher MA values we obtained the lower AR scores we registered. Since lower AR scores mean better performance this is a desired property of our approach. We can further notice that our approach produced substantially better results compared

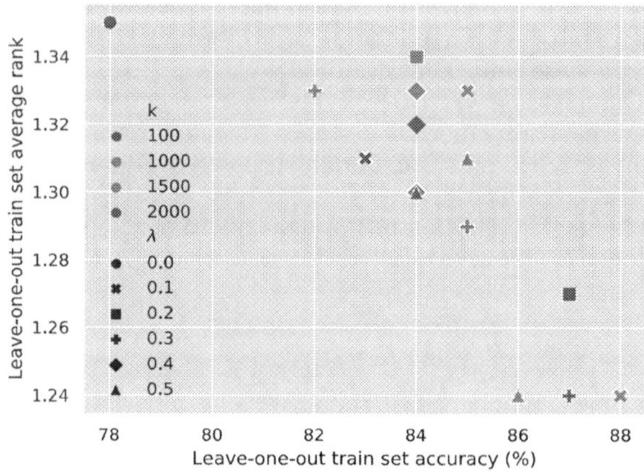

Figure 1: The joint effects of modifying the regularization coefficient λ and the number of basis vectors k when using 100-dimensional dense fasttext-CBOW embeddings as input. The performance of the centroid-based baseline is indicated by the blue dot in the upper-left corner of the scatter plot.

	Train (LOO)		Test	
Aggregation strategy	MA	AR	MA	AR
Ranking-based	**86.0**	**1.27**	77.7	1.34
Preceded by ℓ_2 normalization	85.0	1.30	74.7	1.37
Based on raw scores	85.0	1.30	73.7	1.38

Table 3: The effects of the different aggregation strategies when ensembling. The three aggregation strategies correspond to our three official submissions. Our official results are the ones labeled as Test.

to the dense embeddings-based baseline. This is true for any combination of hyperparameters we tested our algorithms for and both for the MA and AR evaluation criteria.

Taking an ensemble of models

In order to combine the independently constructed models that were obtained by different choices of hyperparameters, we derived our final predictions as a combination of the prediction of multiple models. We randomly chose 7 different models that were the result of different (k, λ) choices[2] and combined the predictions of these models.

We came up with three different ways of combining the predictions of the same independent models. The first approach only took into consideration the rankings that we obtained for each model but not the actual numerical scores of $\mathbf{s}^{(j)} = A^{(j)}\mathbf{v}$ with $\mathbf{s}^{(j)}$ denoting the association scores for the jth model towards each class label.

The remaining two models differed in that they also considered the numeric scores for $\mathbf{s}^{(j)}$ upon combining them. One of the approaches that considered the actual numeric scores performed ℓ_2-normalization of the individual $\mathbf{s}^{(j)}$ vectors prior to summing them up, whereas the other alternative just summed up the raw scores in the distinct $\mathbf{s}^{(j)}$ vectors for making the final prediction.

---

[2](1000, 0.4), (1000, 0.5), (1500, 0.3), (1500, 0.4), (2000, 0.1), (2000, 0.3), (2000, 0.5)

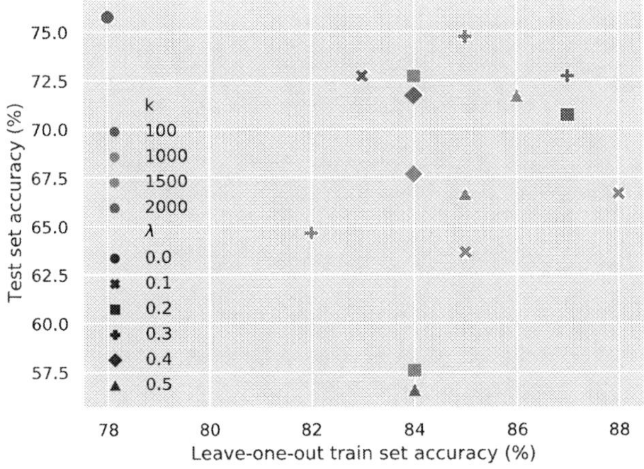 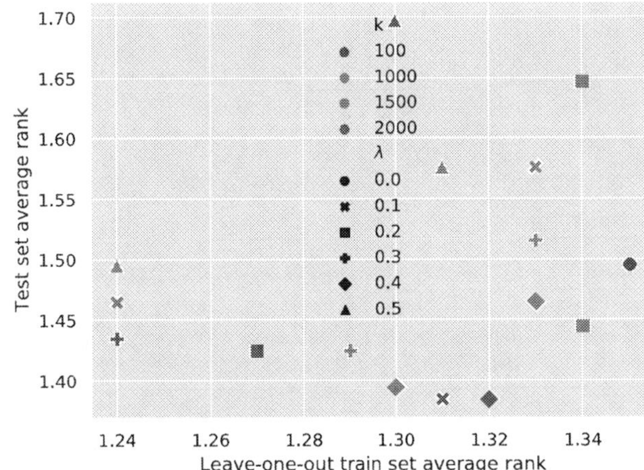

(a) Comparing the MA scores for the leave-one-out evaluation on the training data and the test set

(b) Comparing the AR scores for the leave-one-out evaluation on the training data and the test set

Figure 2: Systematic evaluation of selecting the various hyperparameters (k and λ) differently. The scatter plot includes the results of the MA and AR evaluations on the training set using leave-one-out evaluation and on the test set across the x any y axis, respectively. The $\lambda = 0$ ($k = 100$) case corresponds to the utilization of our dense embeddings-based baseline approach.

Table 3 includes the results of the ensemble models according to the three different ways of aggregating the $s^{(j)}$ vectors for both the training terms in a leave-one-out manner and the test set. The results for the test set constitute the results of our official submission.

Our official results over the test set coincidentally resemble our leave-one-out evaluation scores obtained over the training set when employing our baseline approach which relies on the centroids of dense term embeddings (cf. the blue point in the upper-left corner of Figure 1) and the best test set results in bold included in Table 3).

Experiments with different input embeddings

After the gold labels for the test set of the shared task were released, we conducted a detailed experiment measuring the extent of different hyperparameter choices had similar effects when applying them on the training instances (in a leave-one-out fashion) and the test set. Figure 2 includes our comparison for all the combinations of λ and k when using the same fasttext-CBOW embeddings as before.

By looking at Figure 2, we can see that the relative performance of the dense embeddings based baseline is dominantly better on the test set when evaluated using MA as opposed to its performance over the training set. Interestingly, our baseline would even deliver the best performance on the test set in terms of MA, however, it would still offer a mediocre performance in terms of AR over the test set (cf. the blue points along the y axis in Figure 2). It is important to emphasize that the test set performance of our official submissions relying on an ensemble of sparse embeddings-based models outperforms that of the baseline approach for both evaluation metrics, i.e. it achieves a 77.7% MA (as opposed to 75.7% for our baseline) and a 1.34 AR (as opposed to 1.49 for the baseline).

We next conducted similar experiments on alternatively trained dense embeddings. Besides the previously used fasttext-CBOW embeddings, we also trained fasttext-skipgram and Glove embeddings. Similar plots for the one in Figure 2 for these additional kinds of emebddings can be seen in Figure 3 for fasttext-skipgram (cf. Figure 3a and 3b) and Glove (cf. Figure 3c and 3d).

As illustrated in Figure 3, the dense fasttext-skipgram embedding baseline behaves complementary to what was seen for the fasttext-CBOW case, i.e. it yields the best AR performance, while not having outstanding capabilities in terms of MA. In summary, the best test set performance of the individual models based on fasttext-skipgram embeddings are 72.7% for MA (for $k = 2000, \lambda = 0.3$) and 1.45 for AR (for $k = 100, \lambda = 0$), none of which manages to surpass the performance of our ensemble model.

Looking at Figure 3, we can also conclude that Glove has the poorest performance on this task compared to any of the fasttext variants. Even the best MA scores delivered by Glove are around 80% and 60% when evaluating against the training and test set, respectively, whereas the fasttext variants are able to perform close to 90% and above 70% for the training and test sets, respectively.

5 Conclusions

In this paper we investigated the applicability of a general-purpose information theory-inspired algorithm for extracting ontological knowledge for the financial domain. Our experiments verified that by employing our algorithm allows us to predict ontological relations better as if we were relying on standard dense embeddings. Our source code for replicating our experiments is accessible from `https://github.com/begab/prosperAM-finsim`.

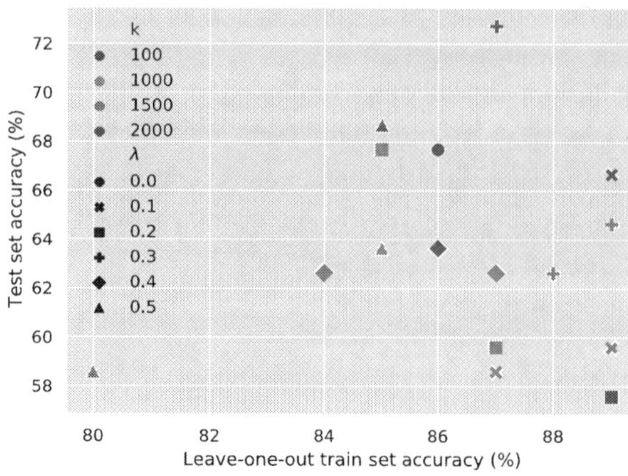

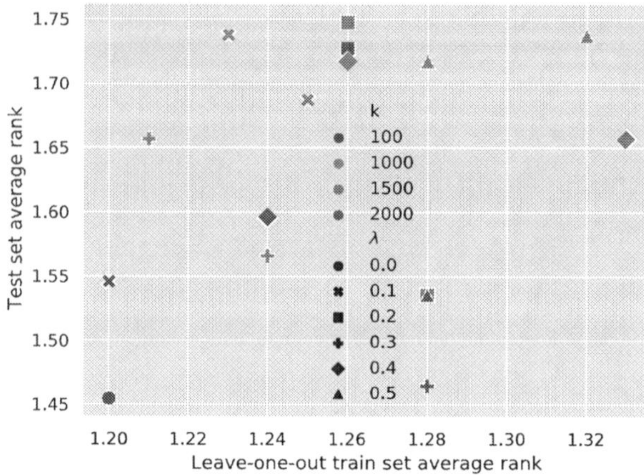

(a) Comparing the MA scores for the leave-one-out evaluation on the training data and the test set using fasttext-skipgram embeddings

(b) Comparing the AR scores for the leave-one-out evaluation on the training data and the test set using fasttext-skipgram embeddings

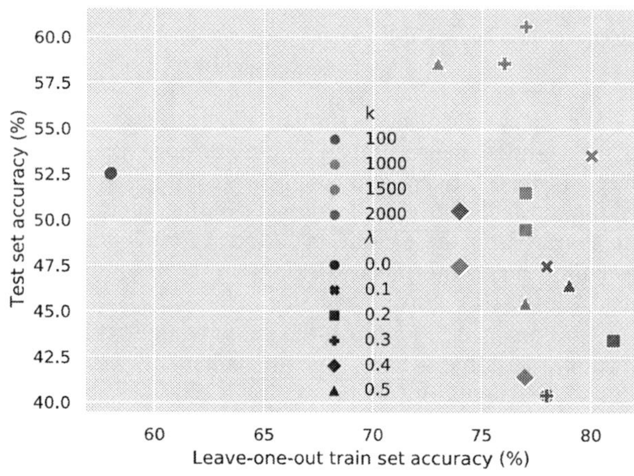

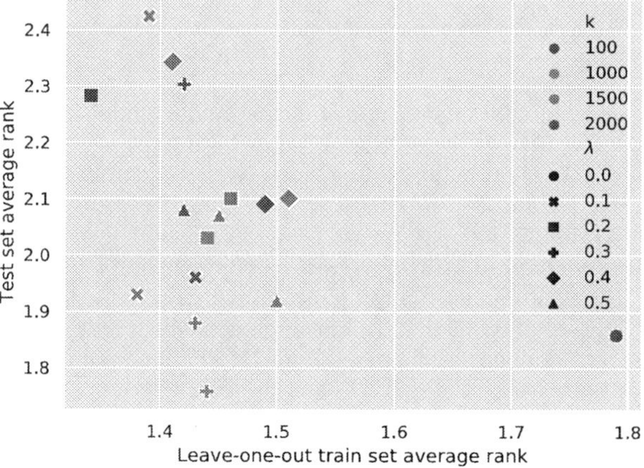

(c) Comparing the MA scores for the leave-one-out evaluation on the training data and the test set using Glove embeddings

(d) Comparing the AR scores for the leave-one-out evaluation on the training data and the test set using Glove embeddings

Figure 3: Systematic evaluation of selecting the various hyperparameters (k and λ) differently when employing fasttext-skipgram (3a, 3b) and Glove (3c, 3d). The scatter plot includes the results of the MA and AR evaluations on the training set using leave-one-out evaluation and on the test set across the x any y axis, respectively.

Acknowledgments

This research has been partly conducted in the project "Progressing Service Performance and Export Results of Advanced Manufacturers Networks", no CE1569 ProsperAM-net. The project has been supported by the European Fund for Regional Development in the framework of Interreg CENTRAL EUROPE 2019-2022. This research was also supported by the European Union and co-funded by the European Social Fund through the project "Integrated program for training new generation of scientists in the fields of computer science" (EFOP-3.6.3-VEKOP-16-2017-0002) and by the National Research, Development and Innovation Office of Hungary through the Artificial Intelligence National Excellence Program (2018-1.2.1-NKP-2018-00008).

References

[Balogh *et al.*, 2020] Vanda Balogh, Gábor Berend, Dimitrios I. Diochnos, and György Turán. Understanding the semantic content of sparse word embeddings using a commonsense knowledge base. In *The Thirty-Fourth AAAI Conference on Artificial Intelligence, AAAI 2020, The Thirty-Second Innovative Applications of Artificial Intelligence Conference, IAAI 2020, The Tenth AAAI Symposium on Educational Advances in Artificial Intelligence, EAAI 2020, New York, NY, USA, February 7-12, 2020*, pages 7399–7406, 2020.

[Berend *et al.*, 2018] Gábor Berend, Márton Makrai, and Péter Földiák. 300-sparsans at SemEval-2018 task 9: Hypernymy as interaction of sparse attributes. In *Proceedings of The 12th International Workshop on Semantic Evaluation*, pages 928–934, New Orleans, Louisiana, June 2018. Association for Computational Linguistics.

[Berend, 2017] Gábor Berend. Sparse coding of neural word embeddings for multilingual sequence labeling. *Transactions of the Association for Computational Linguistics*, 5:247–261, 2017.

[Bernier-Colborne and Barrière, 2018] Gabriel Bernier-Colborne and Caroline Barrière. CRIM at SemEval-2018 task 9: A hybrid approach to hypernym discovery. In *Proceedings of The 12th International Workshop on Semantic Evaluation*, pages 725–731, New Orleans, Louisiana, June 2018. Association for Computational Linguistics.

[Bojanowski *et al.*, 2017] Piotr Bojanowski, Edouard Grave, Armand Joulin, and Tomas Mikolov. Enriching word vectors with subword information. *Transactions of the Association for Computational Linguistics*, 5:135–146, 2017.

[Bouma, 2009] Gerlof Bouma. Normalized (pointwise) mutual information in collocation extraction. In *Proceedings of GSCL*, pages 31–40, 2009.

[Camacho-Collados *et al.*, 2018] Jose Camacho-Collados, Claudio Delli Bovi, Luis Espinosa-Anke, Sergio Oramas, Tommaso Pasini, Enrico Santus, Vered Shwartz, Roberto Navigli, and Horacio Saggion. SemEval-2018 task 9: Hypernym discovery. In *Proceedings of The 12th International Workshop on Semantic Evaluation*, pages 712–724, New Orleans, Louisiana, June 2018. Association for Computational Linguistics.

[Dash *et al.*, 2020] Sarthak Dash, Md. Faisal Mahbub Chowdhury, Alfio Gliozzo, Nandana Mihindukulasooriya, and Nicolas Rodolfo Fauceglia. Hypernym detection using strict partial order networks. In *The Thirty-Fourth AAAI Conference on Artificial Intelligence, AAAI 2020, The Thirty-Second Innovative Applications of Artificial Intelligence Conference, IAAI 2020, The Tenth AAAI Symposium on Educational Advances in Artificial Intelligence, EAAI 2020, New York, NY, USA, February 7-12, 2020*, pages 7626–7633, 2020.

[Faruqui *et al.*, 2015] Manaal Faruqui, Yulia Tsvetkov, Dani Yogatama, Chris Dyer, and Noah A. Smith. Sparse overcomplete word vector representations. In *Proceedings of the 53rd Annual Meeting of the Association for Computational Linguistics and the 7th International Joint Conference on Natural Language Processing (Volume 1: Long Papers)*, pages 1491–1500, July 2015.

[Hearst, 1992] Marti A. Hearst. Automatic acquisition of hyponyms from large text corpora. In *COLING 1992 Volume 2: The 15th International Conference on Computational Linguistics*, 1992.

[Held and Habash, 2019] William Held and Nizar Habash. The effectiveness of simple hybrid systems for hypernym discovery. In *Proceedings of the 57th Annual Meeting of the Association for Computational Linguistics*, pages 3362–3367, Florence, Italy, July 2019. Association for Computational Linguistics.

[Maarouf *et al.*, 2020] Ismail El Maarouf, Youness Mansar, Virginie Mouilleron, and Dialekti Valsamou-Stanislawski. The finsim 2020 shared task: Learning semantic representations for the financial domain. In *Proceedings of IJCAI-PRICAI 2020*, Kyoto, Japan (or virtual event), 2020.

[Mairal *et al.*, 2009] Julien Mairal, Francis Bach, Jean Ponce, and Guillermo Sapiro. Online dictionary learning for sparse coding. In *Proceedings of the 26th Annual International Conference on Machine Learning*, ICML '09, pages 689–696, 2009.

[Murphy *et al.*, 2012] Brian Murphy, Partha Talukdar, and Tom Mitchell. Learning effective and interpretable semantic models using non-negative sparse embedding. In *Proceedings of COLING 2012*, pages 1933–1950, December 2012.

[Pennington *et al.*, 2014] Jeffrey Pennington, Richard Socher, and Christopher Manning. Glove: Global vectors for word representation. In *Proceedings of the 2014 Conference on Empirical Methods in Natural Language Processing (EMNLP)*, pages 1532–1543, October 2014.

[Speer and Havasi, 2012] Robert Speer and Catherine Havasi. Representing general relational knowledge in conceptnet 5. In *Proceedings of the Eighth International Conference on Language Resources and Evaluation (LREC-2012)*. European Language Resources Association (ELRA), 2012.

[Subramanian *et al.*, 2018] Anant Subramanian, Danish Pruthi, Harsh Jhamtani, Taylor Berg-Kirkpatrick, and Eduard H. Hovy. SPINE: sparse interpretable neural embeddings. In *Proceedings of the Thirty-Second AAAI Conference on Artificial Intelligence, (AAAI-18), the 30th innovative Applications of Artificial Intelligence (IAAI-18), and the 8th AAAI Symposium on Educational Advances in Artificial Intelligence (EAAI-18)*, pages 4921–4928, 2018.

FINSIM20 at the FinSim Task: Making Sense of Text in Financial Domain

Vivek Anand[1*] , **Yash Agrawal**[1*] , **Aarti Pol**[2] and **Vasudeva Varma**[1]

[1]International Institute of Information Technology, Hyderabad
[2]VIT, Pune

{vivek.a, yash.agrawal}@research.iiit.ac.in, aarti.pol12@vit.edu, vv@iiit.ac.in

Abstract

Semantics play an important role when it comes to automated systems using text or language and it is different for different domains. In this paper, we tackle the FinSim 2020 shared task at IJCAI-PRICAI 2020. The task deals with designing a semantic model which can automatically classify short phrases/terms from financial domain into the most relevant hypernym (or top-level) concept in an external ontology. We perform several experiments using different kinds of word and phrase level embeddings to solve the problem in an unsupervised manner. We also explore the use of a supplementary financial domain data; either to learn better concept representation or generate more training samples. We discuss both the positive and negative results that we observed while applying these approaches.

1 Introduction

Semantics has been a tough area in NLP research. This also comes in the disguise of getting to know the taxonomy or hypernymy relations of terms. There have been tasks in NLP for this purpose [Bordea *et al.*, 2016; Camacho-Collados *et al.*, 2018]. These tasks get tougher when applied for a specific domain; for example, the word "stocks" can have several meaning in general sense but while in financial domain; the meaning can be narrowed down. Thus making the semantics a bit more clear.

The purpose of FinSim 2020 Shared Task is to automatically map financial phrases/terms to a more general financial concept. Alternatively, it means to map a hyponymy to its hypernymy. This kind of task in financial domain has been introduced for the first time.

The task provides us with a training data that maps some of the financial concepts to its hypernymy; for example, "Alternative Debenture" is mapped to "Bonds". The given set of hypernymy labels has cardinality of 8. This set includes Bonds, Forward, Funds, Future, MMIs, Option, Stocks and Swaps. The pre-mapped data (training data) contains very

low number of labelled examples so we explore unsupervised techniques.

We explore the use of pre-trained word embeddings [Pennington *et al.*, 2014]. These pre-trained word embeddings are trained on general corpus and not domain specific. We make use of the given training data to explore if the pre-trained word embeddings can be used for this financial domain task. We perform experiments with several kinds of unsupervised algorithms based on word embeddings using cosine similarity and variants of KNN algorithm as well as using some deep learning based methods.

Further the task also provides us with corpus of financial domain text. This text can be used to learn representations or patterns useful for the task. We explore the use of Hearst Patterns [Hearst, 1992; Seitner *et al.*, 2016] on this text to automatically mine hypernymy-hyponymy relations from the given text which is useful in extending the training dataset. We perform similar experiments on this extended dataset and report the results.

The remainder of paper is organized as follows. Section 2 describes the approaches we have tried for the task. Section 3 describes experimental setting and some details regarding the approaches. Section 4 describes the results achieved from several methods and out ranking in the task. We then conclude in Section 5.

2 Our Approach

2.1 Cosine Similarity Based

We explore the use of pre-trained word and sentence embeddings in this approach. For basleine, we consider GloVe [Pennington *et al.*, 2014] word embeddings and it's finetuned versioned on given financial documents. Since, GloVe embedding are word based, to get the embedding of financial concept; we take pre-trained word embedding of each word in the input financial concept and average it. For each of the input financial concept we try and map it to its hypernymy using the averaged word of both the input financial concept and the hypernymy label itself. We find the cosine similarity with each of the average embedding of hypernymy labels to get a ranked list of labels for a given financial concept.

We also experiment with mapping financial concept to averaged embedding of the description of hypernymy as per The Financial Industry Business Ontology (FIBO). Due to the av-

---

*Authors contributed equally.

Proceedings of the Second Workshop on Financial Technology and Natural Language Processing

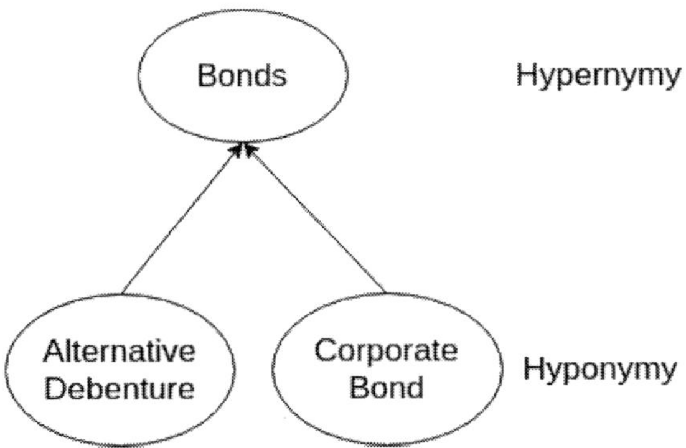

Figure 1: Example of financial concept labeling

eraging, description based approach performed poorly compared to just using embedding of hypernymy. For sentence embeddings, we use Universal Sentence Encoder (USE) [Cer et al., 2018] pre-trained embeddings. USE gives 512 dimensional embedding of the given input phrase. A t-SNE representation of these embedding is for each financial concept is shown in Figure 3. Again, we find the cosine similarity of given financial concept with each of the hypernymy labels to get a ranked list of labels for that concept. In case of USE, description of labels performs better than GloVe embeddings but is still worse than using hypernymy labels only.

2.2 Deep Learning Based

We have very few labeltavled examples to train a supervised model and the class distribution isn't consistent. For example, label "bonds" and "swap" have close to half training samples and other half is distributed among six labels. In order to handle class imbalance, we use weighted cross-entropy loss function. We experiment with CNN for text [Kim, 2014], LSTM [Hochreiter and Schmidhuber, 1997] and a transformer based RoBERTa model [Liu et al., 2019]. We find that these supervised model are able to learn the task to a reasonably good extent and all gives almost similar results. However, even with a very large number of parameters, RoBERTa model gives only comparable scores to both CNN and LSTM based models. This might be due to the fact that RoBERTa model need larger number of labelled samples for the fine-tuning.

2.3 Naive KNN Based

In this approach, the main idea is to map the given input financial concept with one of the financial concept in the training set. We use average pre-trained embedding to get representation of the given financial concept. We get the cosine similarity score with average pre-trained embedding of all the financial concepts present in the training set. We only consider the top k most similar financial concepts to the input financial concept. We finally consider the label of these k financial concepts and output the most frequent label.

This intuition behind this approach is that the input financial concept will be most similar to all the other financial concepts which come under the same category. Alternatively, it can be said as find the most similar sibling and concluding they have same parent.

2.4 Extended KNN based

This approach is similar to the Naive KNN based approach but we introduce the external financial domain documents in this case. We consider all the documents and run Hearst Patterns [Hearst, 1992; Seitner et al., 2016] on it. We get a database of automatically extracted hyponymy-hypernymy relations in financial domain form this. We make use of these extracted relations to infer relations for concepts during test time. We hypothesize that the input financial concept whose hypernymy is to be predicted is present in the automatically extracted database. However the exact term match would be crude way to do so. So we use word embedding based similarity to get a perfect match. even if there is an exact match, word embedding based similarity would give the highest score in that case.

For a given test financial concept, we take its average pre-trained embedding. We also consider average pre-trained embedding of all the hyponymys present in automatically extracted database. We compare both these embeddings using cosine similarity. We find the most representative hyponymy from automatically extracted database. This can be thought of as KNN with $k = 1$. We then take this representative hyponymy and compare its hypernymy with our set of labels. This is again done by taking average pre-trained embeddings and taking cosine similarity. This gives us the most similar label from the set.

2.5 Graph Based

We again make use of the automatically extracted hyponymy-hypernymy relations from external financial domain text. This database can contain different type of entities which may not be the exact match with concepts of our interest. There can be several hops in relations before we finally reach the parent hypernymy. For example "Equity Linked Bond" is a "Variable Coupon Bond" which in turn is a "Bond". Therefore we have to traverse the relations completely in order to get the broader picture. For this effect we turn to a graph based approach. We build a graph with entities as nodes and relations as edges. These entities come form the automatically extracted hypernymy-hyponymy database done using Hearst Patterns [Hearst, 1992; Seitner et al., 2016]. For each relations we add an undirected edge.

We leverage the connections in the graph to predict the hypernymy of the financial concept. For the input financial concept we find a representative node using cosine similarity among the average pre-trained embeddings. Once we get the representative node we consider the connected component of the graph containing that representative node. The intuition is that the hypernymy label should be present in one of the nodes in this connected component. This is because of the whole taxonomic structure and relations among entities. So we only consider the connected component containing the representative node and find the hypernymy label node in it.

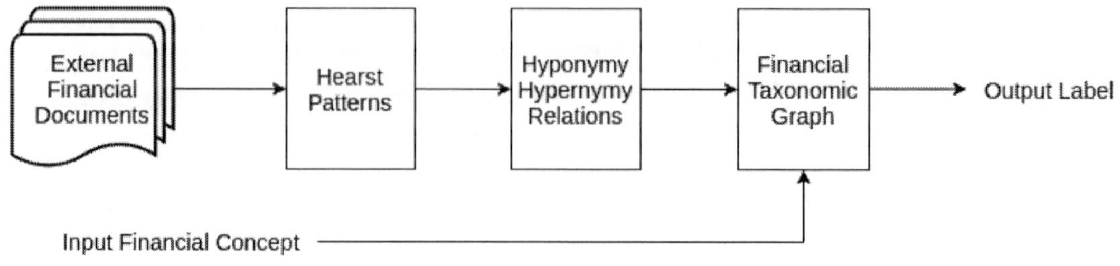

Figure 2: Overview of Graph Based Approach

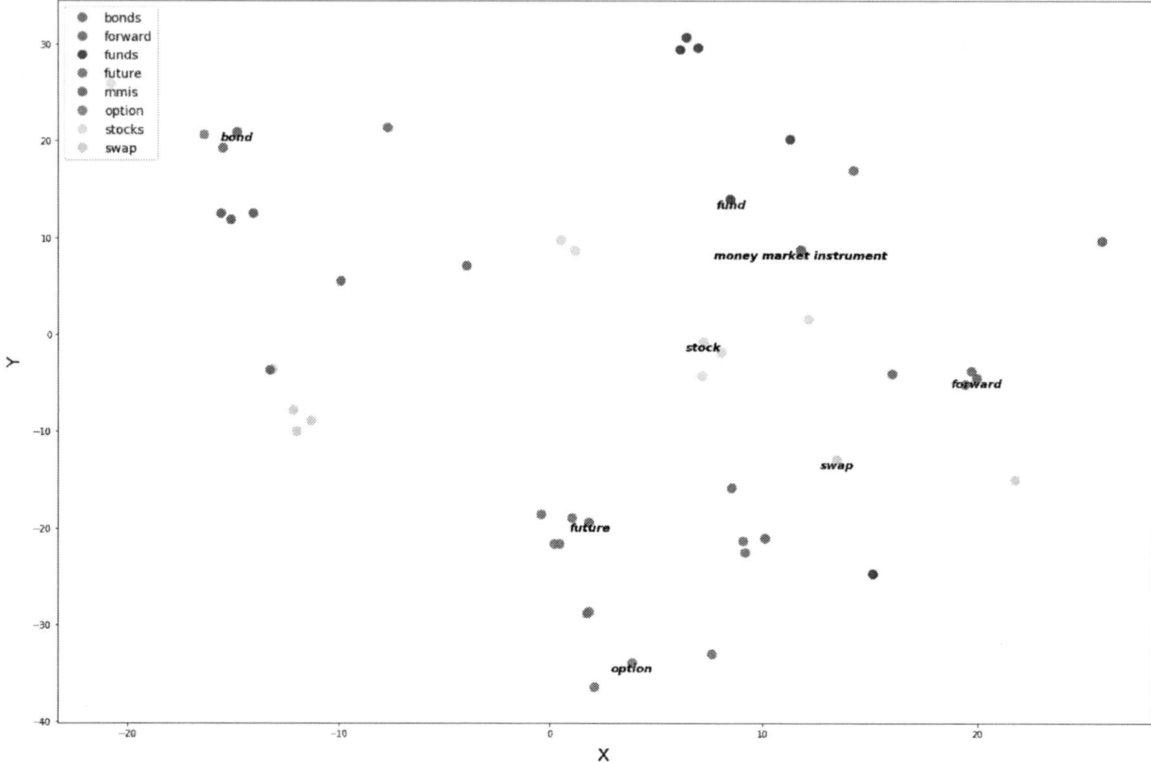

Figure 3: Illustration of financial concept USE embeddings using t-SNE

For each possible label we compute similarity scores again using average pre-trained embedding. We consider the maximum similarity score that we get when comparing each node with the label and assign it to that particular label. This way we will have scores for each of the label. Label with the maximum score is given as the prediction. Figure 2 gives the overview of the overall graph based approach.

3 Experiment

For pre-trained embeddings, we use 100 dimensional GloVe word embeddings and 512 dimensional USE sentence embeddings. We trained all deep learing architechure using Adam optimizer [Kingma and Ba, 2014] with 0.001 learning rate. For Naive KNN based we use the $K = 10$ as it gave best results for this method. We use hearstPatterns python library for the implementation of hearst patterns. It was used the extended mode to mine additional patterns. NetworkX python library was used for implementation of graph based algorithms.

4 Results and Discussion

Table 1 summarizes the results for various methods described above. USE embedding based cosine similarity gave the best results in both metrics - mean rank and accuracy. Deep learning based architectures also gave similar good scores while graph based methods didn't perform well.

Method	Mean Rank	Accuracy
GloVe	1.84	0.63
GloVe (fine-tuned)	1.79	0.67
GloVe (FIBO Description)	2.07	0.43
USE	**1.43**	**0.79**
USE (FIBO Description)	2.08	0.46
CNN	1.44	0.77
LSTM	1.44	0.78
RoBERTa	1.45	0.78
Naive KNN Based	1.75	0.61
Extended KNN based	3.80	0.08
Graph Based	2.68	0.19

Table 1: Results Table. Glove and USE embedding methods are Cosine Similarity based.

5 Conclusion

This paper mainly discusses how we tackle the FinSim 2020 shared task. The task is to automatically map financial concepts with its hypernymy. For this purpose we we explore the different ways in which we can learn the semantics in financial document for automatically predicting the hypernymy relations of financial concepts. We explore how pre-trained word and sentence embeddings can be used for this task. We experiment with both traditional and current deep learning architectures. We further explore how external financial documents can be useful. Our best method accomplishes good results for the task and puts us in one of the top positions among other participants of the task.

References

[Bordea *et al.*, 2016] Georgeta Bordea, Els Lefever, and Paul Buitelaar. Semeval-2016 task 13: Taxonomy extraction evaluation (texeval-2). In *Proceedings of the 10th International Workshop on Semantic Evaluation*. Association for Computational Linguistics, 2016.

[Camacho-Collados *et al.*, 2018] Jose Camacho-Collados, Claudio Delli Bovi, Luis Espinosa-Anke, Sergio Oramas, Tommaso Pasini, Enrico Santus, Vered Shwartz, Roberto Navigli, and Horacio Saggion. Semeval-2018 task 9: Hypernym discovery. In *Proceedings of the 12th International Workshop on Semantic Evaluation (SemEval-2018); 2018 Jun 5-6; New Orleans, LA. Stroudsburg (PA): ACL; 2018. p. 712–24.* ACL (Association for Computational Linguistics), 2018.

[Cer *et al.*, 2018] Daniel Cer, Yinfei Yang, Sheng yi Kong, Nan Hua, Nicole Limtiaco, Rhomni St. John, Noah Constant, Mario Guajardo-Cespedes, Steve Yuan, Chris Tar, Yun-Hsuan Sung, Brian Strope, and Ray Kurzweil. Universal sentence encoder, 2018.

[Hearst, 1992] Marti A Hearst. Automatic acquisition of hyponyms from large text corpora. In *Proceedings of the 14th conference on Computational linguistics-Volume 2*, pages 539–545. Association for Computational Linguistics, 1992.

[Hochreiter and Schmidhuber, 1997] Sepp Hochreiter and Jürgen Schmidhuber. Long short-term memory. *Neural Comput.*, 9(8):1735–1780, November 1997.

[Kim, 2014] Yoon Kim. Convolutional neural networks for sentence classification. In *Proceedings of the 2014 Conference on Empirical Methods in Natural Language Processing (EMNLP)*, pages 1746–1751, Doha, Qatar, October 2014. Association for Computational Linguistics.

[Kingma and Ba, 2014] Diederik P Kingma and Jimmy Ba. Adam: A method for stochastic optimization. *arXiv preprint arXiv:1412.6980*, 2014.

[Liu *et al.*, 2019] Yinhan Liu, Myle Ott, Naman Goyal, Jingfei Du, Mandar Joshi, Danqi Chen, Omer Levy, Mike Lewis, Luke Zettlemoyer, and Veselin Stoyanov. Roberta: A robustly optimized bert pretraining approach. *arXiv preprint arXiv:1907.11692*, 2019.

[Pennington *et al.*, 2014] Jeffrey Pennington, Richard Socher, and Christopher D. Manning. Glove: Global vectors for word representation. In *Empirical Methods in Natural Language Processing (EMNLP)*, pages 1532–1543, 2014.

[Seitner *et al.*, 2016] Julian Seitner, Christian Bizer, Kai Eckert, Stefano Faralli, Robert Meusel, Heiko Paulheim, and Simone Paolo Ponzetto. A large database of hypernymy relations extracted from the web. In *Proceedings of the Tenth International Conference on Language Resources and Evaluation (LREC'16)*, pages 360–367, 2016.

Association for Computational Linguistics
209 N. Eighth Street
Stroudsburg, Pennsylvania 18360

ISBN 978-1-7138-2827-3